TALES OF THE WORKING GIRL
WAGE-EARNING WOMEN
IN AMERICAN LITERATURE,
1890–1925

Twayne's

LITERATURE

&

SOCIETY

SERIES

Leo Marx, General Editor
Massachusetts Institute of Technology

TALES OF THE WORKING GIRL

WAGE-EARNING WOMEN IN AMERICAN LITERATURE, 1890–1925

Laura Hapke

Twayne Publishers • New York

MAXWELL MACMILLAN CANADA • TORONTO

MAXWELL MACMILLAN INTERNATIONAL • NEW YORK   OXFORD   SINGAPORE   SYDNEY

Twayne's Literature & Society Series No. 2

Tales of the Working Girl: Wage-Earning Women in American Literature, 1890–1925

Laura Hapke

Copyright © 1992 by Twayne Publishers

Twayne Publishers
Macmillan Publishing Company
866 Third Avenue
New York, New York 10022

Maxwell Macmillan Canada, Inc.
1200 Eglinton Avenue East
Suite 200
Don Mills, Ontario M3C 3N1

Macmillan Publishing Company is part of the Maxwell Communication Group
of Companies.

Library of Congress Cataloging-in-Publication Data

Hapke, Laura.
    Tales of the working girl : wage-earning women in American
literature, 1890–1925 / Laura Hapke.
      p.   cm. — (Twayne's literature & society series ; no. 2)
    Includes bibliographical references and index.
    ISBN 0-8057-8855-7 (alk. paper)—ISBN 0-8057-8860-3 (pbk.: alk. paper)
    1. American fiction—20th century—History and criticism.
    2. American fiction—19th century—History and criticism.   3. Women
and literature—United States—History.   4. Working class women in
literature.   5. Work in literature.   I. Title.   II. Series.
PS374.W6H36   1992
813'.5209352042—dc20   92-10568   CIP

10 9 8 7 6 5 4 3 2 1 (hc)

10 9 8 7 6 5 4 3 2 1 (pb)

Printed in the United States of America

To the memory of my father,
Daniel Harris

CONTENTS

ILLUSTRATIONS

Facing Chapter 1: The woman-fueled Pilgrim Steam Laundry, South Brooklyn, New York, c. 1910

Facing Chapter 2: An ever-dancing "Dutch Kitty" from Julian Ralph's *People We Pass* (1896)

Facing Chapter 3: Bessie and Marie Van Vorst as workers from their book *The Woman Who Toils* (1903)

Facing Chapter 4: Dulcie in her furnished room, from O. Henry's "An Unfinished Story," published in *McClure's* (August 1905)

Facing Chapter 5: "A Meeting of the Girl Strikers" by W. T. Banda, published in *McClure's* (November 1910) just before the end of the Shirtwaist Strike

Facing Chapter 6: *Hairdresser's Window*, a John Sloan homage to the working-class woman as celebrity

Facing Chapter 7: In front of—and behind—the machinery at the Eberhard Faber Pencil Factory, Greenpoint, Brooklyn, New York, c. 1900

FOREWORD

Each volume in the Literature and Society Series examines the interplay between a body of writing and an historical event. By "event" we mean a circumscribable episode, located in a specific time and place; it may be an election, a royal reign, a presidency, a war, a revolution, a voyage of discovery, a trial, an engineering project, a scientific innovation, a social movement, an invention, a law, or an epidemic. But it must have given rise to a substantial corpus of interpretive writing.

The idea of elucidating the relations between writing and its historical context is not new. In the past, however, those relations too often have been treated as merely ancillary, static, or unidirectional. Historians have drawn on literary works chiefly in order to illustrate, corroborate, or enliven an essentially socioeconomic or political narrative; or, by the same token, literary scholars have introduced a summary of extraliterary events chiefly in order to provide an historical setting—a kind of theatrical "backdrop"—for their discussions of a body of writing.

In this series, however, the aim is to demonstrate how knowledge of events and an understanding of what has been written about them enhance each other. Each is more meaningful in the presence of, than apart from, the other. Just as history can only be created by acts of interpretation, so any written work invariably bears the marks of the historical circumstances in which it was composed. The controlling principle of the Literature and Society Series is the reciprocal relation between our conception of events and the writing they may be said to have provoked.

Leo Marx

PREFACE

Storytelling is never an innocent occupation.
                    Lucy Hughes-Hallett, *Cleopatra: Histories, Dreams,*
                                                    and Distortions

The last decade of the nineteenth century witnessed a massive feminine entry into an industrial workplace whose need for cheap labor had increased steadily since the Civil War. For the next 35 years, until their relative acceptance after World War I, "working girls," rarely dignified by the term "working women," were the subjects of a heated cultural debate. Liberal reformers decried the "slavery" of the sweatshop, factory, department store, and domestic service jobs held by most female workers, the majority of whom were unskilled immigrants or their daughters. Traditionalists, searching for culprits, not victims, held that all work outside the domestic sphere was unwomanly. For well over three decades, defenders argued with detractors who impugned the woman wage earner's fitness for wife- and motherhood, her "unsavory" companions, late hours, and sinful ways, and, with the American entry into World War I and the new opportunities it created, her desire for "men's jobs" instead of or after marriage.

By joining this debate, fiction helped shape it. Authors as diverse as Jacob Riis, the famed photojournalist of the New York tenements; the literary voice of the East Side ghetto, the *Jewish Daily Forward* editor Abraham Cahan; the rebellious naturalist Stephen Crane; the giant of urban realism

Theodore Dreiser; the popular storyteller O. Henry; the labor romancer Marie
Van Vorst; the strike novelist Arthur Bullard; and the "sweatshop Cinderella,"
Anzia Yezierska, all wove the working girl controversy into their narratives.
How they and their contemporaries dealt with the new mass phenomenon—
documenting, indicting, glorifying, and transforming their heroines and anti-
heroines—is the subject of this book.

As early as the 1940s and 1950s, Walter F. Taylor, in *The Economic
Novel in America* (1942), and Walter B. Rideout, in *The Radical Novel in the
United States, 1900–1954* (1956), initiated the modern discussion of labor
fiction, one carried on largely without reference to the woman worker to
this day.[1] Benedict Giamo's *On the Bowery: Confronting Homelessness in
American Society* (1989), despite its title a study of turn-of-the-century tenement fiction, similarly omits mention of the sweatshop innocents, ladylike
laborers, garment-trade firebrands, and ambitious shop girls who, among
other types, people fiction about the late-nineteenth- and early-twentieth-
century working woman.[2] Only sections of works like Fay M. Blake's *The
Strike in the American Novel* (1972) or introductions to specialized antholo-
gies on American labor press fiction—discussions restricted to the female
militant—treat working women in American fiction. Strangely, save for the
occasional chapter section or article, feminist scholars ignore the subject.[3]

This study reevaluates well-known and neglected texts on the white
laboring woman, books successful or fairly so, produced in the late-Victorian,
Progressive, World War I, and immediate postwar eras.[4] Black women certainly figured in the female work force and routinely suffered discrimination;
as late as 1920, 80 percent still toiled in the unpromising work of maids,
cooks, and washerwomen.[5] Because they were excluded from most factory,
clerical, and sales jobs and numbered a small percentage of the total population in northern urban areas, where most fiction of the working woman was
set, they are regrettably absent from the texts scrutinized here. So are agrarian
wage earners, who rarely occur in mainstream fiction and who were not
distinguished from other women in agricultural pursuits as paid labor until
as late as the 1910 census.[6] Their literary embodiments, as well as those of
farm wives or daughters, or independent farmers, properly belong to another
study. My focus, then, is the female work experience as imagined in urban
mainstream literature: tenement tales, labor romances, and novels and stories
of cross-class conflict, of social protest, and of the "white-collar girl," all
known to a wide middle-class audience.

At issue is the imagining of the breadwinning heroine—the slum flower,
victimized innocent, lady in disguise, resilient "fallen" (or near-fallen)
woman, labor helpmeet, and aspirant to, or failure at, upward mobility. Of
paramount interest is how literature defied, or failed to defy, the strictures of
the genteel marketplace to treat the "lower depths" subject of the laboring
woman. Equally significant are the artistic goals—literary opportunism, the
documentary or reform impulse, the attempt to create high art about a suppos-

edly low subject—that inspired writers as different as Crane and O. Henry, Bullard and Van Vorst, Dreiser and Yezierska. What conventions and strategies did they employ to achieve their goals? And what was the evolution of the working girl as the slum melodrama of the 1890s was replaced by the strike fiction of the 1910s and the economic ascension novel of the 1920s?

Questions of narrative strategy lead back to cultural concerns. Works such as James W. Sullivan's *Tenement Tales of New York* (1896), Mary Wilkins Freeman's *The Portion of Labor* (1901), Arthur Bullard's *Comrade Yetta* (1913), and Anzia Yezierska's *Bread Givers* (1925) were, despite the ambivalence of their creators, defenses of the woman worker in a culture that continued the debate on her morality until the First World War, and in some quarters, after it. Indeed, to many Americans the female worker posed a challenge to the Victorian ideology of woman's separate sphere. By entering the capitalist workplace, she was rebelling against woman's "natural" role, exposing herself to sexual peril and carnal knowledge. Just as disturbing, she could become so debilitated by the rigors of the workplace—work for which, medical "experts" argued, she was unfit—that she harmed her reproductive organs or, equally crucial, lost her interest in motherhood. Whether prone to immorality, disease, or subversive ideas about her independent future, she was more threat than victim.

As important as the long-lived controversy about the propriety of women in the workplace were women's own responses to it, or in the fashionable phrase, their work culture. Substandard conditions and increasing struggles with employers characterized women's labor history from the late nineteenth century to the onset of the war, when, in the absence of male industrial workers, the working woman became a more valuable commodity. To what extent did the creators of the fictional working woman accurately reflect her often squalid conditions, depressing surroundings, and assorted job-related trials? Did writers acknowledge her endurance? The bonds of her workplace friendships? Her participation in the labor movement? Did they romanticize or sensationalize her working and after-hours life? Last but not least, did female writers respond differently to these concerns than males?

By placing the answers to these questions in the context of the all too durable belief in "true womanhood," we can better understand why for over 30 years literary defenders and detractors alike, in service to their culture, spun tales to rescue the working girl—until "woman worker" was no longer perceived as a contradiction in terms.

ACKNOWLEDGMENTS

I extend my thanks to Pace University, which generously supported this project through sabbatical, summer, and Scholarly Research Committee grants. My gratitude is extended as well to the library staff, particularly Elizabeth Birnbaum, for dedicated help with many elusive sources.

Grateful acknowledgment is made to the Ella Gallup Sumner and Mary Catlin Sumner Collection of the Wadsworth Atheneum in Hartford for permission to reprint the John Sloan painting on the cover and opposite chapter 6; to the Brooklyn Historical Society for permission to reproduce the period photographs facing chapters 1 and 7; to the Astor, Lenox, and Tilden Foundations of the New York Public Library for use of the turn-of-the-century illustrations facing chapters 2, 4, and 5; and to A. & C. Black Publishers for use of the Van Vorst illustrations prefacing chapter 3.

The woman-fueled Pilgrim Steam Laundry, South Brooklyn, New York, c. 1910
Brooklyn Historical Society

1

Enter the Working Girls: The Debate on Women's Labor

Work is for men.

"Marry the Women" (1901)

[For] the woman who elects to earn an honest living . . . [n]o more heroic battle has ever been fought than this daily one, waged silently and uncomplainingly in our midst by these workers.

"The Working-Women of To-Day" (1891)

BY THE END OF THE NINETEENTH CENTURY, ARMIES OF WOMEN— termed working girls as much for their low social status as their youth—were entering the work world in force. As early as the Civil War there had been an increased demand for women's work outside the home, and by war's end women were filling the job void caused by the loss of a half-million soldiers.[1] Burgeoning urban centers and rapid industrialization in the two and a half decades after the war strengthened the need for—if not the respectability attached to—women's wage earning. But only in the last 10 years of the century did a combination of circumstances produce a dramatic female influx into the workplace. Almost 4 million—close to 20 percent of all American women, a sizeable increase over the number of 10 years before—were by 1890 what the Census Bureau classed as "gainfully employed."

The year 1890 was, significantly, the first year in which the Department of Labor collected data on wage-earning women and the Census Bureau published comparative statistics on male and female factory work.[2] Certainly by the last decade of the century, new technology characterized by machinery that was easier to use and by methods for "breaking up processes previously performed by skilled men" allowed unskilled women to enter the labor market in record numbers.[3] From the sweatshops of New York's Lower East Side and the paper-box factories of Brooklyn to the packinghouses of Chicago, the laundries of Buffalo, and the textile mills of Atlanta and the industrializing South, technology reduced the skill required for most jobs and enabled women to do the repetitive tasks they were "deemed capable of performing."[4]

From 1890 until the mid-1920s, when restrictive immigration laws were passed, great waves of women, courted by promises that "for girls there is work in America," streamed into the United States.[5] These young immigrants—and soon their first-generation daughters—accounted for three-quarters of the cheap urban labor pool otherwise populated by women born in the United States. Recent foreigner, immigrant daughter, or native-born, all of these working women—for the most part single, white, and under 25—received wages far below those of their male coworkers. Though they looked to marriage as a deliverance from the workplace, many could expect to toil for years at the exhausting, ill-paid work to which they were typically consigned. The least desirable labor, that of domestic servant, which before the 1890s employed the bulk of female workers, continued to furnish work for one-third of white laboring women and for most black women, who, largely denied factory work, could find little employment other than as domestics or laundresses.[6]

Women with a rudimentary education who wished to avoid the servitude connected with domestic and factory labor took on department store work, which, in 1890, was attracting over seven times the number of women it had a decade earlier.[7] The counter was considered more genteel than the workroom, but long hours, low wages, and little provision for sitting and resting made sales work almost as taxing. For women who had more schooling there were nursing and teaching jobs, yet conditions and pay rendered them as much wage earners as professionals. Viewed by society as extensions of the domestic sphere, the hospital and the schoolroom provided little upward mobility. Women could also enter the expanding clerical field, and by 1890, when public high schools first instituted commercial courses, the percentage of women office workers jumped from 3 to 17 percent. But even in this world they were relegated to low-level jobs. Like their blue-collar counterparts, white-collar girls were on the bottom rung of the ladder, their pay half that of men.[8]

By the end of the nineteenth century, then, woman's factory, shop, and domestic service work was synonymous with economic hardship, monotony, and subservience. Even her duties as teacher, nurse, or office worker were extensions of the traditional maternal or wifely roles. Yet so massive an entry into the work force suggested that women were not merely carrying their traditional roles into the world outside the home; if anything, the feminization of the workplace "had become symbolic of the movement of women away from traditional domestic pursuits."[9] But unmarried working women of the lower classes seldom had the luxury of domesticity, and their growing numbers generated public attention. Clearly, wage-earning women were a threat to cherished notions of womanly behavior. There was widespread—and rather fearful—curiosity about the controversial new phenomenon.

Nowhere was this interest more apparent than in fiction. There had been a limited literary contribution to the debate about the "womanliness" of work well before the 1890s. From the Civil War onward, novels by John Hay and Charles Bellamy featured mercenary underclass women whom work only corrupted further. Cautionary fiction of the 1870s and 1880s, longer on compassion for the working girl but similarly short on pragmatism about her need to earn a living, warned parents to keep their virtuous daughters away from the urban employer or rake. A minority view among writers of fiction was held by the feminists Rebecca Harding Davis in the Civil War and Elizabeth Stuart Phelps in the postbellum era: they made tragic heroines of the textile workers. Creating eloquent fictions about the shadowed lives and stunted opportunities of their pathetic heroines, Davis and Phelps pointed to the economic bondage of women's work and—as shocking to the Hays and Bellamys—called on the privileged women of the upper classes to extend the hand of friendship to their oppressed sisters.

But it was only with the coming of the 1890s that a heightened bourgeois interest in women at work produced what one student of the literary marketplace termed "a fiction that would entertainingly . . . explain social change."[10] Against the background of what would today be termed an information explosion—which was spurred by the quality magazines *Atlantic Monthly* and *Scribner's, New York Tribune* exposés, women's magazine columns, and photojournalistic essays like Jacob Riis's "The Working Girls of New York" in *How the Other Half Lives* (1890)—writers swiftly capitalized on middlebrow interest in the feminine "other half." In the 1890s the "discovery of poverty" generated a range of widely read fiction about the unsavory conditions of tenement, street, dance hall, and workplace.[11] These were all locales in which the working girl figured prominently, and perceived as being at moral risk, she began to emerge as a heroine.

What helped foster her emergence as a popular character was a new mass market born of improved book production and distribution and increased literacy. Straitlaced devotees of fiction about what William Dean Howells called the "smiling aspects of American life" deplored "this great animal, this American public," so eager for books "it will devour anything."[12] But as critical battles raged about the propriety of introducing Americans to the subject of "low life," feminine or otherwise, writers refashioned the sensational melodrama of earlier "wicked city" or "virtue betrayed" fiction.[13] Infusing that formulaic subgenre with a quasi-sociology of the female workplace, the working girl's literary imaginers soon included the genteel practitioners of the Lower East Side seduction tale, who catered to middle-class preferences for the eleventh-hour rescue and the romanticized poor, and Stephen Crane, the bad boy of turn-of-the-century American fiction, who did not. Whether their orientation was sentimental or social Darwinist, romantic or naturalistic, such writers produced a body of work that explained the embattled urban working girl to an audience with no relation to her other than a condescending one.

From the 1890s onward, staid publishing houses with a wide middle-class readership brought out numerous tenement tales with sweatshop and box-factory workers, shop girls and cloak models, genteel daughters of failed businessmen reduced to department store work, even former dance hall girls who manage saloons and female stevedores who take men's names. For many arbiters of "serious" literature, distaste for these "lower depths" subjects was paralleled by a preference for the "angel of the hearth." The working woman remained a tabooed subject to the same critics who deemed prostitution an unfit literary concern. Yet it should be remembered that as early as the 1880s Henry James had tried his hand at a shop-girl character in *The Princess Casamassima* (1886), and by the 1890s grande dame Edith Wharton had produced a short story about a drug-addicted workingman husband and the respectable wife he reduces to destitution, about the hardships of impoverished but well-born working women. Considered uncharacteristic of her work, it did not find its way into print until well over a decade after *The House of Mirth* (1905), in which Wharton "punishes" aristocratic Lily Bart for questioning the mercenary society marriage by having her fall into the working class. And well past the 1890s most writers who dealt with working women's lives were wary enough of censorship to load their narratives with didacticism about her fate should she defy conventional morality—in which case, they stressed, her "wages" would be those proverbial for female sinners.

Notwithstanding the concern to present a virtuous working girl or castigate her moral fall, as the new century dawned popular writers began to offer a heroine who spent more time speaking out against harsh employers than fending off (or succumbing to) their advances. Her real-life counterparts began, however haltingly, to participate in the labor movement—though under 10 percent were union members as late as 1920 (Woloch, 241)—becoming what the noted labor organizer Agnes Nestor called "that absolutely new feminine type, the genuine spontaneous workingwoman leader of workingwomen."[14]

Popular novelists responded by offering heroines who encouraged males and females alike to rebel. As with the heroines of even "radical" press fiction, however, the militance of these heroines rarely led to any outcome other than a conventional marital ending, their political fires quenched by marriage and motherhood. Yet literature on the female striker offered a disturbing new image and paved the way for works appearing during and after World War I, when social and literary interest focused on the white- rather than the blue-collar woman and on the conflict between vocation and marriage. What is clear is that as early as 1890 and as late as the 1920s, to write about the working girl was to capitalize on popular interest in—and disapproval of— the woman outside the domestic sphere in pursuit of the American dream.

In the hands of a Dreiser or, more fleetingly, a Wharton, the working girl's successes and sufferings took on a universal meaning. But whether of enduring value or fallen into obscurity, tales of the working girl—from the sentimental tenement tale of the 1890s to the sociological strike novel of the 1910s, from the romantic 1900s novel of ladylike workers to the World War I–era bildungsroman of feminine vocation, from Julian Ralph's stereotyped vignettes of fallen shop girls to Edith Wharton's near-tragic portrait of the aristocratic Lily's debasement—provided a powerful forum for the debate about woman's work. This is not to reduce this fiction to the role of litmus test for cultural prejudices, but to acknowledge that fiction and history are interwoven, whether in the earliest slum story, which, in defending sexual morality, attempted to control it, or in the autonomy novels of the 1920s, which supported woman's bid for more than an assembly worker's life. It is to understand that behind the numerous tenement stories of the Maggies and Kittys who "fall" or are rescued at the eleventh hour is their creators' desire to regulate their threatening sexuality.

So pervasive was this narrative strategy that even by the Progressive era (1907–17), the socialist writer James Oppenheim silenced his labor agitator "Joan of the Mills" by having her recognize that men, not women, are born to rouse their class to action. And even the political fires of Arthur Bullard's Comrade Yetta—modeled in part on the leader of the 1909 New York City Shirtwaist Strike, Clara Lemlich—are subdued by marriage and motherhood. Conversely, the fictional alter egos of the 1920s author Anzia Yezierska who battle Old World patriarchs, nativist Americans, and a host of others opposed to the working woman's desire to "make myself for a person" provide formidable voices in her defense.[15]

Nor was ambivalence absent from many of the texts. From the local-color realist temporarily forsaking stories of home-loving New England spinsters to paint a portrait of a shoe-factory girl who leads workers to strike but in the end recoils from what she has done, to the middle-class woman posing as an investigator to write novels about factory life, to an artist like O. Henry with his finger on the public pulse, many of those who claimed to defend the character of the working girl tried to either make her over into a bourgeois or, as in the previous century, marry her off and cancel her worker's identity. After World War I, when the white-collar girl became the subject, there was a far greater range of plots. Yezierksa and Edna Ferber's superheroines combine careers with (or prefer them to) marriage; some of Sinclair Lewis's career seekers flee work, then marriage, then flee work again, but others triumph; and a host of forgotten heroines in the mold of Booth Tarkington's Alice Adams pine through novels in which they decide to take jobs because they cannot win the affections of a "good provider."

Mainstream working girl fiction, produced largely by and for middle-class consumption, gave voice to the late-nineteenth- and early-twentieth-century controversy about women and work, whether presenting the protagonist's struggle to make ends meet as pathetic or heroic, whether excoriating or defending her removal from the domestic sphere, denying or trumpeting her right to a living wage through solidarity with a striking labor sisterhood, or deploring or applauding her newly won upward mobility. Reflecting the gender, class, and political orientation of their creators, these works comprised a diverse cultural response to woman's movement away from the "separate" sphere in which she had dwelled. And if none of this fiction advocated economic equality with men, neither did the fiction for working-class audiences, whether the Laura Jean Libbey romances read by working girls or the radical fiction published in the labor press.

These novels and short stories served the working girl by breathing life into the voluminous statistics that government and social service agencies, reformers, and journalists were gathering on women's work conditions, budgets, health, family life, companions, leisure activities, and, above all, morality. Furthermore, in a way no other social document could, this fiction illuminated a debate about working women's femininity and fitness for motherhood that, in many ways, continues today. The chapters that follow discuss how that controversy was central to the fiction. But it would be well to flesh out the debate itself, in both the years leading to the rise of the working girl and those when she rose to cultural legitimacy.

By the beginning of the 1890s opponents of women's work had a host of arguments in place. Despite the fact that a sex-segregated workplace had routinely denied women access to most men's jobs, these critics, including those in the labor movement itself, contended that employing women, who were willing to work for any wage, depressed the labor market and led to "the enforced idleness of men."[16] A corollary belief was that women accepted low wages "to supplement the wages of their fathers or husbands."[17] Although many female wage earners were members of patriarchal families, such an argument ignored the almost half a million "women adrift" who, by the turn of the century, had traveled alone to urban centers to live in boardinghouses and furnished rooms. One-fifth of them lacked the home and family ties of the working girl who turned over her pay envelope to her family. Furthermore, although needy women had eked out an existence from the early days of the Republic, those who espoused the male-head-of-household theory ignored the ever-expanding group of the self-supporting feminine poor—the impoverished woman, the widow, the deserted mother.

By the end of the century, as more women streamed into the workplace, the traditionalists defended the ideology of the hearth ever more vigorously. One ideologue vented his scorn on those who were under the "epidemic delusion that home is no place for a girl." Relying on his home-loving readership's agreement, he found it "selfish [and] suicidal" for women to go out and work.[18] Nor was this view restricted to prosperous defenders of the status quo. Stormed one late-nineteenth-century spokesman for the male worker, women breadwinners were "the error of the age."[19] As the new century dawned, an anonymous advocate of labor reminded the readership of his pro-union newspaper, "Work is for men."[20]

After the First World War, when women's "taking up men's jobs" was a national necessity rather than the sin it had been earlier dubbed, the foes of work as unfeminine took a different tack. Women who sought men's wages or careers came up against what one 1922 observer, not the first or last to use the term, called "masculine antagonism."[21] As late as 1925 crusaders for industrial legislation, such as Mary Anderson, deplored those who "still believed women should not be permitted to enter industrial occupations."[22]

Nevertheless, the great debate had cooled. A few diehards shifted the argument against women in the factory to the business world, contending that women were unable to withstand the pressures and temptations of the office. But even that argument gave way to the view that, like teaching and nursing, office work was an extension of women's home functions and thus was an acceptable stop before marriage. By 1920, when the clerical sector employed one-fourth of all women wage earners, opponents had made some concessions. Women could work for a time, though not so long as to turn their attention from matrimony by "endangering" their life interests "pertaining to marriage, motherhood, and housekeeping."[23]

At the core of all of these statements—whether the turn-of-the-century diatribes about the morally poisoned factory or the tamer 1920s pronouncements on the dampening effect of ambition on woman's marital-maternal urges—was a Victorian vision. By the middle of the nineteenth century, a thriving middle class, anxious to declare its status, respond to a competitive society, and preserve the sanctity of the home, had eagerly espoused the ideology of a separate sphere for Victorian womanhood. Woman's "piety, purity, submissiveness, and domesticity"—the historian Barbara Welter's oft-quoted summary of feminine virtues—qualified her for moral guardianship of the home, but she was too fragile to survive contact with a corrupted world, exemplified by the unprotected workroom.[24] In the guise of a compliment to her as the "guardian of all the humane values absent in the squalid world of economic and business transactions,"[25] this sanctification of woman as mother and wife masked a fear of her unregulated sexuality. For the ideal Victorian lady must be protected from "unsupervised association with men . . . from any source of knowledge about or interest in sex."[26]

The antithesis of the lady, the working-class woman, crystallized fears about woman's vulnerability and her susceptibility to corruption. As if un-aware of the necessity propelling poorer women to abandon domesticity as a vocation, a proliferation of essays in the 1890s contended that woman's purity and fitness for motherhood could only be maintained by isolation from the "violent . . . struggle for life," for she was womanly "only in so far as her emotional experiences are sweet, tender, and peaceful" (Ferrers, 309). Such experiences were far removed from the female work life of a crowded, noisy, badly lit, and unventilated Lower East Side coat factory or from the Broome Street dance hall to which many immigrants' daughters escaped after an exhausting day. Blaming rather than pitying or trying to understand those whose 60-hour workweeks thrust them headlong into the "life struggle," traditionalists frequently adopted an accusatory tone when characterizing the working woman, as if she were in the vanguard of a war on genteel womanhood and middle-class women were in danger of joining the revolutionary side. One incensed critic of feminine work warned of the woman breadwinner's "foolish and criminal warfare on home life" (Finck, 834). To another she violated "a natural law that woman should neither labor nor struggle for her existence" (Ferrers, 308). Well past the 1890s the otherwise liberal *Everybody's* magazine linked her to warlike activity, and a 1908 series termed the continued influx of female workers the woman's "invasion" (Hard, passim). So potent was this imagery that even by the mid-1920s, when the debate on women's right to work had largely shifted to her right to a career, the *New York Times* entitled a 12 August 1923 feature article, "Woman Workers Invade Nearly All Occupations" (126).

The most strident "separate-sphere" thinkers argued that working women were abdicating their duties as future mothers. By exposing themselves to the hazards and fatigue of the unsanitary workplace, these future wives were "unsexing" themselves by endangering their unborn children and "denying their maternal functions."[27] The 1890s saw a heightened interest in the premEternal health of the female worker. In its enlightened form in the Progressive and early war years, this interest led to campaigns for protective legislation, improved sanitary conditions, a minimum wage, and equal pay for equal work and, in 1920, to the founding of the U.S. Woman's Bureau to improve the welfare of wage-earning women. Yet to "true womanhood" apologists, concern for the health problems brought about by unclean workplaces and enervating work was an excuse to resurrect decades of pseudoscientific arguments about woman's frail constitution and limited intellectual capacity.

Important Victorian medical theorists, such as Edward Clarke, employed this argument to limit women's access to higher education and the professional jobs; Dr. Azel Ames, whose ideas were still influential at the turn of the century, applied it to industrial jobs as well. An industrial physician, Ames warned women that "labor requiring great celerity of manipulation coupled with intense concentration and activity of mental forces" could produce sterility or other reproductive problems.[28] He also saw health risks in all of the unskilled tasks that characterized many women's long workday. His reports on the damaged health of factory workers anticipated the Progressive-era investigations conducted into deaths among women cotton-mill operatives and the 1920s inquiries of the industrial physician Alice Henry into the reproductive problems of and the effects of lead poisoning on women factory hands. More foe than friend of working girls, Ames himself combined medical assessments with tirades about the "moral poison" of factory life (56). He charged that women could neither be trusted to work near men nor resist any of the lures to pleasure and finery that earning their own livings could produce. His more positive legacy was that, by the late 1890s, almost all of the states had begun to debate—and in the next century, many would put in place—legislation to regulate the hours women could work, although to many reformers such legislation did not protect women's health so much as disguise the wage inequities that drove them to work so many hours.

By the early twentieth century the theory of feminine physical inability to work outside the home had been discredited by feminist arguments about the strength needed for childbearing and by social scientific studies that directed public attention to improving conditions rather than removing "the mothers of the race" from work. In 1908 one advocate of recent advances in that direction wrote: "[T]he presence of women in industry [is] . . . one of the most effective levers ever found for lifting the weight of excessive toil from the neck of the human race" (Hard, 885). Whether or not women were perceived as the barometers of excessive work demands, their performance in heavy wartime tasks demonstrated that once mechanical devices had been installed to permit them to lift and handle, they "were turning out considerably more work than men on the same job."[29]

Yet widespread prejudice against wage-earning work as a female moral peril was slower to die. The argument that wage-earning work was not respectable had been gathering force since well before the Civil War, when New England farmers would permit their daughters to work in the Lowell textile mills only if the mill owners provided paternalistic moral guardianship at the mill and mandatory Sunday worship outside of it, not to mention the maternalistic "housemothers" who enforced a myriad of curfew and visitors' rules.[30] However well "moral policing" worked for the earliest generation of female factory workers—who were already well acquainted with a paternalistic moral authority—the native-born women soon departed from Lowell, to be replaced there and throughout the country by immigrant laborers less amenable to it.

This suspicion of female laborers, whether immigrant or not, was in full flower in the nineteenth century's last decade. By rejecting the protection of the home they were exposing themselves to advances from coworkers and employers; though their chastity was deemed superior to men's, their inferior powers of judgment would thus place them at constant risk. The worst fate to befall girlish innocence was, of course, its corruption; the "virtue betrayed" theme permeates the prose literature and the fiction of detractors and defenders alike. Opponents of working women more often pointed to the incipient immorality of the working classes than did those who wished to reform the inequities of the workplace. Many deplored the "lack of confidential family intimacy" supposedly characteristic of many poor families. In such environments, even before she went out to work, a girl could not be "carefully guarded, tenderly trained."[31]

To such detractors, the inevitable exposure to work experience threatened to coarsen and corrupt the working girl, whether she was brought up poorly or well. (In a nativist era, the latter was more likely if she was native-born.) The woman worker could not or would not combat the "bad companions" of both genders so often mentioned in interviews with prostitutes who had once labored in shops or factories. An allied conviction held by unfriendly commentators, such as Harold Frederic, was that the monotony and harshness of the work regimen engendered in the working woman an unsavory combination of greed and hedonism. Frederic was the newsman-author of *The Lawton Girl*, an 1890 novel about a seamstress who falls into prostitution and tries to redeem herself by warning factory girls not to take her path. Significantly, she is killed off before she makes much progress among them. Remarked Frederic in an essay written around the time of the novel, "[t]he tendencies of industry are always to multiply the numbers of working women, and the thirst for finery and excitement among these women tends to counteract their natural and indoctrinated . . . tendency to chastity."[32] The uncertainty about whether woman was innately pure did not die with the century. The historian Robert Smuts quotes a well-known 1908 legal case in which protective legislation to limit the workday used as its rationale the idea that "the prevailing ten-hour workday was likely to leave a woman exhausted, her higher instincts dulled, craving only excitement and sensual pleasure" (118–19).

Prejudice against the woman worker as one with "lascivious and immoral tendencies"[33] that were easily ignited by the ennui of the job or the temptations of the "dance garden" burgeoned during the Progressive era, a time more traditionally associated with heightened fears that young women coming to the city to find work were trapped into white slavery. But those hostile to both working women and the entrapment theory pointed out that many women who fell short of professional prostitution still acted sensually, whether from "innate depravity" or the desire for a good time and pretty clothing (Peiss, 110). Dubbed "charity girls," they were frequent subjects of condemnatory pieces such as Hutchins Hapgood's 1910 essay on the leisure activities of women workers who "go to the dance-halls . . . [where] they are easily approached." He continued disgustedly, "[w]ith the men they 'pick up' they will . . . have . . . their fling."[34] Voicing a common sentiment, he further contended that working women were really "adventuresses," aping refinement but seeming cheap. He took particular care to explode what he termed the myth that women in sales work, which many working-class women preferred to factory labor, dwelled in a more moral environment. Department store jobs only made girls greedy for the things they sold to the affluent, and worse, they were prone to making assignations with customers. Hapgood went against the Progressive-era grain in his lack of tolerance for the temptations that working women encountered on the job, what Elizabeth Butler's pioneer study *Women and the Trades* (1909), published just a few years before, termed the "moral jeopardy of shopgirls."[35] Yet more compassionate reformers than Hapgood could not conquer a prejudice against the moral looseness of the working girl who, after a nerve-jarring, 10-hour day in the shop, could not still her "craving for excitement."[36]

It was often class bias as much as opposition to women's work that fueled the many denigrating statements about what the labor historian Alice Kessler-Harris aptly terms the working girl's "personal moral laxity" (98). Dorothy Richardson, born in relative affluence, was orphaned and had to support herself for a time in unsavory positions ranging from sweatshop worker to artificial-flower maker to laundress. Not once in her 1905 narrative, does she place the women she encountered—and who befriended her—on her own moral level. Acknowledging the hardness of their lives, she nevertheless brands them her mental and moral inferiors. She would have concurred with the many irate observers who had never had her "insider's look" but who still found anathema those women like the "hoydenish laundry girls" of large urban hotels who were as easy with their virtue as they were sloppy in manners.[37] Too, by Richardson's time, there were complaints about the sartorial vulgarity of the working girl, with her gaudy imitation of "lady's" finery in the form of large plumed hats and showy jewelry, or the peroxided hair and provocative clothes with which, to hostile onlookers, she seemed to court resemblance to a streetwalker.[38] Her more incensed critics reminded the public of Dr. William Sanger's famous midcentury study (twice reprinted by 1906) of prostitutes' former occupations: three-quarters of the 2,000 prostitutes interviewed were working women, and the remainder had been content to live off their parents or friends before entering the trade.[39] Critics echoed Sanger's view that when women mingled with men in the workplace, "modesty and reserve" were bound to weaken (Sanger, 534).

Opponents of the working girl, then, implicitly condemned her for being poor and unprotected and having to go to work in the first place. Yet with no sense of contradiction, they minimized, dismissed, or ignored her economic motive in favor of the "pin-money" theory, cast doubt on her morality and her potential for motherhood, and advocated her return to domesticity. When they did come to grips with the toll the workplace took on her, they focused on the danger to her unborn children rather than to herself. Above all, they fixated on her imagined immorality, not her real poverty.

Yet she was not lacking in defenders, who were largely drawn from those who attacked traditionalists' belief in the "moral" as opposed to the "objective" causes of poverty (Bremner, 159–60). To her befrienders, the overworked woman who toiled at dead-end jobs did not deserve the low wages and unwholesome conditions any more than she did the misunderstanding of those who, as one 1893 reformer remarked satirically, felt "there was no real poverty in the Republic."[40] As part of a widespread campaign to awaken American society to moral responsibility for the welfare of the poor, newly formed charitable organizations, settlement houses, and a wide range of reformers, from the labor researchers of the Russell Sage Foundation to muckraking journalists, made the working woman a subject of particular concern. The idealists of the social settlement movement wished to provide her with social and educational opportunities; the philanthropic founders of the Women's Trade Union League (WTUL) tried to school her in joining or forming unions to better her working conditions; the head of the Consumers' League of New York pressured her employers by urging women of the leisure classes to refuse to buy products made by her sweated labor and to not shop at stores that overburdened their saleswomen.[41] Even the government statisticians wanted to discover whether she could live on earnings her employers contended were perfectly adequate. Exploding the pin-money theory, they consistently reminded the public of her contributions as daughter or mother to the support of her family or of her status as a wage earner on her own. They typically advocated protective legislation to ensure her fitness for future motherhood. But they emphasized that marriage and, presumably, motherhood were far from automatic for women who were, as a contributor to *Woman's Work in America* (1891) put it, "obliged to work if they would live."[42]

Most important, they rescued her character from the charges leveled by those like the author of "Employments Unsuitable for Women" (1904), a misleading title since he was opposed to all feminine employment outside the home. To him, the girl who worked had "rubbed off the peach bloom of innocence by exposure to a rough world" (Finck, 834). In its veiled, genteel way, this kind of thinking allied working women with the immorality of prostitution, a charge that would cause a split even among her defenders. Yet those who rallied to her defense did not employ the rhetoric of damaged virtue with its dominant metaphor of "lost bloom." Criticizing the ideology such rhetoric fostered, one representative author argued that it was the "first and most important business of a nation to protect its women, not by any puling sentimentality of queenship, chivalry or angelhood, but by making it possible for them to earn an honest living."[43] Employing the investigative mode increasingly common among those who wished to improve the woman worker's lot, from the survey-oriented 1890s onward, one muckraking reporter quoted a shoe worker: "The stitching room will take the bloom out of any girl's cheek."[44]

The 1880s and 1890s saw not only the beginning of large-scale investigations of women's work but the forging of the heroic working girl. Establishing the terms of inquiry for future commissions, the Massachusetts labor statistician Carroll Wright reported in 1884 on the health, work conditions, incomes, home life, and, last but not least, "moral condition" of 20,000 Boston women in manufacturing, sales, clerical, and restaurant work. Wright somberly concluded, as would those who followed him, that the working girls of Boston were ill paid, overworked, and undernourished, and he expressed his admiration for the courage with which they endured lives of such privation. By 1887, 22 states had established fact-finding bureaus and gathered similar data on female labor. The federal government compiled an 1889 survey of 17,000 women employed in over a score of cities, complete with statistics on "every phase of the working-woman's life, from the trade itself, with its possibilities and abuses, to the personal characteristics of the woman who had chosen it."[45] The report went to pains to point out that the "virtuous character of our working women is all the more attractive when the cost of their virtue is recognized." For with their poor pay, if they continued virtuous, "they were the more entitled to our applause, and certainly one must recognize the heroic struggle they make to sustain life."[46]

The New York State Assembly followed suit in 1895—a year, incidentally, that marked the heyday of the tenement tale—by appointing its own committee to investigate female labor. Like the forthcoming U.S. Industrial Commission of 1900 and the many state and federal investigations of the labor of factory and department store women that would follow in the next two decades, it offered a picture of women struggling in conditions that spoke far better of them than of employers, whose abuses ranged from paying $3.25 a week, the average wage for women in industries in 1905 (board and lodging typically cost $2.25), to requiring overtime work but refusing to pay accordingly.

In the second decade of the twentieth century, Progressives—so labeled because of their dedication to correcting social ills by controlling the kind of business greed that fought the minimum wage, protective legislation for women and child workers, and the investigation and upgrading of slum buildings—widened the scope of the inquiry into women's wages. Edith Abbott of Chicago's Hull House was one of a number who placed women's ill-paid work in its historical context. To dispel the theory that women were stealing men's jobs, she included in her 1910 study, *Women in Industry*, statistics from the previous decades proving that "women were receiving less pay than men for equally efficient work."[47] The same year, the attempt to provide exhaustive studies of women's work resulted in such massive publications as a 19-volume study of women and child wage earners. Convinced that numbers would help foster public awareness of and respect for the plight of working women, researchers tried to include as wide a sample as possible. By 1915, in the most extensive investigation of female labor ever undertaken in any state, the New York State Factory Investigating Commission produced 13 volumes, or 15,000 pages, much of which, as the labor historian Philip Foner notes, revealed to the public the exploitation of women workers: their long hours, low pay, and arbitrary treatment and the unhealthful conditions under which they worked (459).

By the mid-1920s, when women made up almost one-quarter of the labor force, newspaper and magazine muckraking about the female workplace had largely abated. Governmental recognition of the above problems had resulted in the establishment of the U.S. Women's Bureau, which affirmed the still-controversial principle of equal pay for equal work. Though by the mid-1920s the bureau was still battling proponents of the pin-money theory, it did much to improve the public perception of women's need for better wages and shorter hours. Historians are divided about the ameliorative effect of the 1920 suffrage amendment on working women's lives; by and large, what one 1929 observer termed woman's status as "the cheap or marginal worker"[48] was little altered in the manufacturing trades, although there were advances in nonfactory work. But whether the focus is on woman's status or on the very real gains women had made in climbing to white-collar and even professional work, widespread condemnation of the single woman as worker, and the corollary tendency to blame the sweatshop victim for her plight, had certainly abated by the mid-1920s. From the 1890s onward, what helped bring about a recognition of woman's right to earn an adequate living was her defenders' depiction of her as a labor martyr. Many fine women's histories have recently chronicled the deplorable conditions of women in the unskilled trades from the turn of the century until postwar agitation for employer accountability. A few telling examples, culled from celebrated period sources, should suffice here. In *Women Wage-Earners* (1893), Helen Campbell gave a shocking overview of women's exploitation in the industries in which they predominated at the lower levels: textile mills, canneries, and factories for food preparation or the making of matches. She described the conditions in all of them of extreme overcrowding, dangers to breathing, skin, or limbs, and virtually no facilities for washing or eating meals. Dangers to dignity accompanied those to health: insults, rules forbidding talking at work, and harsh fines for lateness.

One strike history written in 1910 reported that in the New York City garment industry—a huge employer of immigrant women—operators not only had to put up with such debasing conditions but were required to pay for the electricity to run their machines, had to rent their own chairs, and were fined for the very needles they broke, injustices that the massive 1909 Shirtwaist Strike (20,000 women participated), however successful in forcing other economic concessions from employers, did little to remedy.[49] Conditions in steam laundry work, another industry in which women typically held the jobs on the lowest rung of the ladder, were eloquently described in the early 1900s by Dorothy Richardson, who toiled in a New York City laundry, and a few years later by Elizabeth Butler, who studied Pittsburgh's laundry women. These writers offer a composite portrait of agonizing heat, few rest periods, and drainage so poor that the women had to stand in water all day.[50] As if speaking for all women in the labor trades, not to mention domestic work, the incognito investigator Bessie Van Vorst cried of her work in a bottling factory: "Oh! . . . the never-ending supply of work to be begun and finished, begun and finished!"[51] Another dedicated investigator ridiculed the idea that such work provided a refuge from industrial excesses; in the two weeks, or 175 hours that she worked in a department store, Annie MacLean could not sit down, take a sick day, or get overtime pay. Her wages, she calculated, amounted to 6¢ an hour.[52]

Such studies helped counter the belief that the working woman was immoral, and they even improved her situation to a certain extent. From 1912, the second year of the important New York State Factory Investigating Commission's report, to 1917, many states enacted laws legislating women's wages or working hours. Although conditions in many industries continued to be cause for alarm, a mandatory minimum wage for women workers was upheld in a number of states before the war and in many more afterward. (Ironically, though women would continue to make economic gains, the wage battle would be fought anew in the mid-1920s when protective legislation was deemed unconstitutional.)

Until the 1920s, when the single—though not the married—woman worker was no longer perceived as a social or moral oddity, her defenders were acutely aware that neither volumes of data nor a depiction of her heroinism could refute the charge that, as a class, working girls were easily corrupted. It was widely believed that women often either chose prostitution as the "easy way out" or, though technically virtuous, doled out sexual favors for a variety of reasons ranging from employer harassment to the desire for gifts of clothing or a gaudy evening of "treating" from the men they encountered in bars and dance halls or on the job.

In *Prisoners of Poverty* (1887), written in the 1880s and influential enough to be reprinted in the next decade, Helen Campbell, who observed social work efforts among New York City prostitutes in the 1880s and 1890s, rejected the more misogynistic reasons for a woman's fall. Contending that economic pressures, not an easily tempted nature, forced poor women to sell themselves, she offered the argument that the woman who fell ideally desired virtue. Campbell also started the trend of drawing more impressionistic portraits of women workers, fallen or otherwise, by presenting not statistics but vignettes of valiant sweatshop "prisoners" who spoke to her about their lives. Rose Haggerty, born in a Cherry Street tenement and raised to drudge in a neighborhood sweatshop, was the subject of her most famous tale. By the time Rose was a young woman, both her parents were dead and her wages were still so meager that she was able to support her five siblings in only one way. Selling herself "might be dishonor," admitted Campbell, "but it was certainly food and warmth for the children."[53] The tenement writer Edgar Fawcett, whose novel *The Evil That Men Do* (1889) is about an impoverished seamstress who falls into prostitution when she is abandoned by an affluent man who had promised marriage, defended the fallen woman in the reform journal *Arena*. Fawcett warned the affluent of the city that the shop, factory, and servant girls desperate for decent wages and a friendly hand had no wish to lose their virtue. But if they were to be rescued not from themselves but from destitution, "two hundred thousand wretched New York working-women need . . . help."[54]

The Progressive era witnessed an unprecedented assault on the woman-corrupting workplace, tenement, and saloon, and on commercialized prostitution, particularly in the form of what was thought to be a sinister, international white-slave trade. Among many antivice reformers, the powerful campaign for what was dubbed the nation's "social purity" transformed the working girl who went wrong into a victim. To those who linked moral corruption to economic factors, "the connection between low wages and the appalling destruction of the women of the working class" was clear.[55] As in the previous era, defenders of the working-girl-turned-prostitute cited her need to support herself or her family rather than her moral failings or desire for finery or excitement, although those reasons, when cited as secondary causes for her downfall, were rationalized as overwhelming temptations to the underclass woman. The numerous vice commissions that were influential until the coming of World War I—when the nation's attention shifted to more global concerns (and to incarcerating the prostitute who threatened the soldier's health)—listened to working women's testimony. Department store and factory workers, as well as seasoned streetwalkers, all said they could not live on the wages of virtue. An early commission, formed in 1900, set the tone for future ones by recommending an improvement in the "material conditions of young wage-earning women."[56] Ten years later the era's preeminent committee on the "social evil," the Chicago Vice Commission, concurred: "Is it any wonder that a girl who receives only six dollars per week for working with her hands sells her body for twenty-five?"[57] The social worker Annie Allen urged that the girl who left wage work for the street be viewed in this exculpatory fashion: "She has not chosen, she has merely fallen."[58]

There were, however, those who were unsympathetic to the prostitute or, convinced of her victimization, still defended the working girl precisely because she had not chosen that morally tainted profession. In the 1890s that position was articulated by Clare de Graffenreid of the Department of Labor: "Our [female] breadwinners are . . . as chaste as [the women of] our middle and leisure classes. . . . The vast majority choose want rather than dishonor."[59] This insistence on the working girl's essential morality surfaced even in radical quarters. In *Diary of a Shirtwaist Striker* (1910), her semidocumentary account of the great New York City Shirtwaist Strike of 1909, the socialist labor activist Theresa Malkiel felt compelled to defend the vociferously militant strikers as "good girls," girls who were "good as gold" (103). To make the contrast between a life of "shame" and one of honest labor more telling, Progressive-era reformers cited surveys such as one of 200 underpaid but "respectable working girls" not one of whom, it was proudly asserted, was "vicious or immoral" (Chicago Vice Commission, 269).

Beneath the surface of these representative defenses, however, flowed an undercurrent of ambivalence. Sometimes it took the form of categorizing working women into either "virtuous" breadwinners or "rough" bar and dance hall frequenters, as if acknowledging the bad girl completely cut her off from the one who was not. The device of projecting fears of working women's immorality onto a corrupted subgroup was adopted by the same Labor Department essayist who earlier in her piece denied that working women chose "dishonor" (de Graffenreid, 76). Theresa Malkiel did not divide working women into moral categories, but she demonstrated her doubts by making contradictory statements. In one sentence she extolls garment workers' virtue; in another she envisions them as streetwalkers driven to sin by poor wages. Fears of the immoral nature of working women also surfaced in the countless antivice reports of the 1910s. Often a brief lament that some female workers lacked moral courage was the way Progressive writers accounted for the working woman who said she was "born bad."[60]

Clearly, defenders of working women did not concur on her susceptibility to sin. Antivice crusaders convinced that the prostitute was a pawn of sinister "interests" downplayed the distinction between the virtuous wage earner and the corrupted prostitute. To them, wage slavery threatened to turn the noblest working girl bad; they sentimentalized the prostitute as a child victim lured away from soul-destroying wage work and a wretched tenement home. Others more concerned with preserving the image of the virtuous worker argued that she may have begun her life in the same slum and her labors in the same sweatshop, but—like most working-class women, they hastened to add—she lived in a different moral universe than did the fallen one. For all who were not hostile to the woman at work, as Alice Kessler-Harris has remarked, "morality constituted the central feature" of their investigations of her plight (101), whether or not they saw a minority of working girls as "bad." Mary Gay Humphreys, an early defender of working women's right to strike, pointed out that, even among the most dedicated reformers, "it is the moral aspect that is urged out of all proportion." Preoccupied with moral purity herself, Humphreys added: "[T]he fact that a girl spends nine hours a day in a factory is an argument in her favor against Satan and all his works."[61]

Thus, although the period between 1890 and 1925 saw an enormous amount of "scientific" reporting on the exploited woman wage earner by compilers of federal and municipal surveys, reformers, women's trade union journalists (by the early 1900s), and other socially conscious observers, these writers also demonstrated a fixation on chastity. They could not separate a woman's morality from her work identity, whether they were conscious of it or not, and as a result, they sent the cultural message that proof of her worth lay in a woman's virtue, not in her productivity or talents on the job. Only with the revolution in manners and morals that liberated American middle-class womanhood after the First World War did the cautionary tone of even her most ardent defenders diminish. Although working-class sexuality was still viewed with far more suspicion than was bourgeois "liberation," the postwar working girl was considered her own moral guardian.[62]

Until well after the war, however, there was a concerted effort to sanitize the working girl, either by presenting her as a paragon of middle-class values or by regulating her morality "for her own good" in campaigns to close the dance halls or keep her out of the saloons she frequented. A glance at the literature disseminated by "working girls' clubs," formed to foster self-esteem among women wage earners and impart "culture" and homemaking skills, illuminates reformers' preoccupation with transforming lower-class girls into middle-class ladies. The 1892 study guide *Thoughts of Busy Girls* was purportedly written by club members themselves, girls from "silk and carpet mills, twine, vest and tobacco factories, from sewing rooms, flower and feather work . . . [from] behind the counters of New York's great stores . . . clerks,

stenographers . . . tailoresses . . . [even girls] fresh from the schoolroom."[63]
The claim that the working girl's own voice is presented seems dubious,
however, for nowhere in the volume, with its chapters on good manners,
women as moral reformers, family life, and "purity and modesty: two words
of value," is there any attention to what recent social historians have called
the common concerns of working girls: leisure activities and meeting young
men. Nor, for that matter, is there any recognition that dissatisfaction with
the factory regimen was a legitimate subject of conversation. The guide,
indeed, frowns on much of what must have constituted working women's
culture: an interest in clothes and places to display them, ennui with the
workday regimen, a desire to break free of family restrictions. In addition, the
reader finds in *Thoughts* not the language of the counter girl but that of the
ideal Victorian woman. Slogans like "freedom from moral defilement is purity"
(9) and "purity . . . once lost . . . can never be recovered" (11) seem far more
the lessons of these girls' instructors than the authentic voice of those whom
the book's subtitle acknowledges "have little time for study." *The Life Stories
of Undistinguished Americans*, a 1906 collection whose title reveals its condescending view of the working masses, includes a German servant's mono-
logue in which she reveals that she was so shocked at a male friend's attempt
to kiss her that she "gave a scream one could hear a mile and boxed his
ears."[64]

No doubt some young women were raised to bring to their workshop
lives the kind of puritanism preached in the above documents. Yet recent
women's historians have pointed to the female workroom as a place where
women spoke often of sexual feelings (Peiss, 50–51, 178–84). Certainly
reliable period observers who were not engaged in fostering the myth of the
saintly working girl were compelled to acknowledge that women who lived
and worked in a tenement or factory town milieu were not "fastidious" about
refusing a "caress."[65] New studies of working women's amusements suggest
that urban female workers embraced the new forms of commercialized recreation—dance halls, amusement parks, theaters—in which they "articulated
gender in terms of sexual expressiveness and social interaction with men"
(Peiss, 6), ideas absent from the above documents.

Other reformers equally dedicated to the image of the moral working girl
did admit that the lure of the dance hall surpassed that of the working girls'
club or settlement house social. But they were quick to add the disclaimer
that "the indictment is not against the girls, but what is offered them."[66]
Convinced that the dance hall corrupted the working woman by thrusting
her into indiscriminate contact with unsavory men and filling her head with
unwholesome ideas about provocative clothes and dance steps, reformers had
agitated for closing such places since the 1880s and 1890s.[67] Progressives
redoubled those efforts, contending that dances such as the bunny hug or
the kangaroo dip "encouraged close body contact"; they even formed the
Committee on Amusement—on which no working girls sat—to "oversee
[their] special needs" (Perry, 733). The argument that working girls, whose

fascination with dance halls helped "multiply their numbers by 50 percent from 1895 to 1910" (Peiss, 93), needed a "wholesome" vice- and alcohol-free atmosphere was part of the widespread "social purity" campaign to strengthen the moral fiber of the nation's cities. But in the case of the working girl, the attempt was, predictably, to curb if not deny her sexuality.

When the working woman wrote the article herself, she was likely to sound like the reformers who wished to speak for her. The working-class author of one early piece quoted with satisfaction those who argued that the "sewing woman of New York" took it as a sacred trust to "guard her honor" (qtd. Baxandall, 215). It was no accident that the German servant offered as a representative, if "undistinguished," American mouthed similarly reassuring views on her conduct with beaus. Her remarks were the antithesis of the sexually laden comments that the Chicago Vice Commission, in its interviews with working girls turned prostitutes, deemed "unprintable" (193). The interviewer who did quote a few "tough" factory girls took care to encircle those quotations with elaborate editorial comments on their rowdy home life and limited access to education. And even then the girls' comments were restricted to those on their search for or dissatisfactions with work. When the subject was moral rebellion, the author inserted euphemisms into the narrative, as if sexual behavior were merely a quest for "good times and fun" (True, 51).

In the 1910s and 1920s there was a vogue for the working woman's narrative of her life as a waitress, a servant, a shop girl in a large department store, a garment-trade worker, a packer of olives in a small town or of pickles in a metropolis. The titles of these works—"The Diary of an Amateur Waitress," "Pilgrim's Progress in a Packing House"—tell another story. The narratives were in the grammatical English of the college-bred woman who had investigated such lives or, occasionally, the onetime worker now entrenched in the middle class. One of the few to record the slangy speech of those who labored in the manufacturing trades was Dorothy Richardson, who was forced by necessity to join their ranks until she escaped to more suitable work in the business world. Yet Richardson quotes to ridicule rather than to document. Invariably prefacing quotations from her loutish coworkers with satiric comments, she reinforces the image of the uncivilized woman whose graceless battle cry is "I wuz here fust!" (61) and who retorts to the foreman, "My God! ain't we hustling . . . God Almighty! . . . my legs is 'most breaking" (105).

Richardson's condescension sours the flavor of working-class speech, that "explosion of [female] sociability" that, as the historian Leslie Tentler has remarked, characterized the work culture of those who took every occasion to speak when the boss's back was turned.[68] Richardson thus gave voice to the Rosies, Celies, and Phoebes for the same reason that more sympathetic observers censored such voices—detractors and defenders alike felt that when the working woman opened her mouth she damned herself as unladylike. How could she be a heroine if she spoke for herself?

Her defenders' efforts to sanitize her voice was part of a larger impulse to protect the working woman from charges that she had nothing of the true woman in her and much of the harlot. But the fact that a massive government survey posed as a central question, "Is the trend of modern industry dangerous to the character of woman?" (Kessler-Harris, 101), suggests that, however scientific the attempt to assess conditions, the overriding concern was for woman's morality and fitness for motherhood. During the years in which the working girl controversy raged, her attackers and opponents were closer in viewpoint than they realized. Both paid homage to an ideal woman; inherently chaste, dedicated to serving others, and prizing the domestic and the maternal over the worldly, her qualities were universally deemed inconsistent with wage-earning work.

By the mid-1920s the same journals that three decades before had published articles castigating the morals of the woman worker were featuring pieces espousing equal pay for equal work.[69] The self-supporting woman was finally "viewed as normal" (Weiner, 79), and even sensation-peddling Hollywood films were pointing out the dullness of the work regimen rather than its moral dangers. The gains won by women in more skilled work were summarized in the pronouncement that "young women with jobs didn't have to marry the first man who asked them" (Burton, ix). The preoccupation with womanliness did not, of course, disappear, and old fears took on new forms. The controversy about the propriety of woman's work shifted to the married worker and the "aggressive" or "overly ambitious" professional woman. The issue of autonomy rather than mere survival informed a new debate, still in progress today. Traditionalists of the 1920s felt that work "distorted" rather than corrupted woman's personality, filling her with dangerous new expectations of independence (Groves, 341). Those on the other side, less worried than the previous generation about poor work conditions, argued that work could "emancipate" her (Burton, 126). Americans still looked at wage-earning women through the screen of gender, but the movement away from such a vision was in its first phase.

The fiction studied in the following pages gives eloquent voice to the working girl's struggle to break through the boundaries between male and female worlds. As in all fiction, pleasure and edification come from the author's ability to dramatize the characters' desires, beliefs, and conflicts, to bring alive their participation in the private and public happenings of the day. Still, given the controversial nature of the working girl, these works could not help but mirror the culture's fixation of more than three decades on her morality. During that time, the working woman herself had changed in response to social and economic forces and stirred up more controversy by becoming, as the twentieth century arrived, vocal in her own defense and achieving, at least before she married, acceptance as a working person. Authors of mainstream fiction charted these changes. Most of their texts, forgotten now, reflected the dominant attitudes toward working womanhood. Some of the more famous texts introduced characters of lasting significance, re-shaping cultural and literary convention to the ends of art.

In the 1890s, whether in Julian Ralph's now-obscure "Dutch Kitty's White Slippers," or the era's most accomplished tenement tale, Stephen Crane's *Maggie: A Girl of the Streets* (1893), the theme was rescue from prostitution. In the works of O. Henry and Marie Van Vorst in the early 1900s, as in the work of more lasting talents, such as Theodore Dreiser and even Mary Wilkins Freeman, the theme was escape from economic oppression. In the century's second decade, the once widely read James Oppenheim and Arthur Bullard dramatized salvation by union women (later union wives) and their male comrades-in-arms. After the war, a materialistic individualism set in; books by Anzia Yezierska—and to some degree, those by Sinclair Lewis and Edna Ferber—let the ambitious worker speak for herself.

Female as well as male imaginers witnessed the working girl's movement from dependence to autonomy. The early tenement writers of the 1890s were members, variously, of a male journalistic and bohemian subculture or of a brotherhood of establishment authors. In the next century Dreiser and his once more-famous contemporary O. Henry championed the working girl's right to exist, as did their successors the strike novelists, who gave the idea a political dimension. As strike-decade (1910–1920) authors continued the male inquiry into female work, more women investigators doubling as novelists gained prominence when they urged womanly intervention in the problems of the female laborer. These women's fictions—most in the "lady bountiful" mode with conventional endings that pulled the worker back from unladylike militance—made tentative steps toward a cross-class sisterhood. Moral regulation, however, was still the watchword. In the post–World War I era the working woman became a true heroine (and sometimes a novelist as well) in works that rejected the biases of earlier writers and permitted a more authentic voice to emerge. These novels and stories, with surprisingly little difference between male and female authors, proclaimed her upward mobility or bitterly lamented her inability to attain it.

Given the slow death of cultural prejudice against their real-life counterparts, fictive working girls, from the slum flowers of the 1890s to the ambitious immigrants of the 1920s, were, to borrow from Dreiser's *Sister Carrie* (1900), "half-equipped little knights." In dramatizing their difficult battle with Victorianism, literature, sometimes in spite of itself, told a compelling story of social change.

An ever-dancing "Dutch Kitty" from Julian Ralph's *People We Pass* (1896)
New York Public Library, Astor, Lenox, and Tilden Foundations

2

Regulating Chastity:
Masculine Tenement Fiction

The harum-scarum . . . cloakmaker came to the end that was expected.

Out of Mulberry Street (1898)

"Oh!" [the shop girl] shouted . . . "I [don't] want no more dancing . . .
and I can't take care of meself, neither."

People We Pass (1896)

IN *HOW THE OTHER HALF LIVES* (1890), THE IMPASSIONED NARRATIVE
that helped shape the coming decade's discussion of the poor in American
cities, Jacob Riis paid particular attention to the young working woman of
the tenements. Using the rhetoric that her defenders so often employed, he
praised her as a heroine in the "battle with life."[1] To Riis as to many, the
economic struggle of those one *Other Half* chapter called "The Working Girls
of New York" symbolized that of all wage-earning women. But their struggle
was, if anything, more dramatic, for these women toiled in the place that
drew more female industrial workers than any other.[2]

By Riis's time, 350,000 women lived and worked in the nation's largest city and the world's greatest immigrant center.[3] New York was the hub of the garment trade, and 70 percent of clothing workers were women.[4] Women could also find employment in the countless low-level shop and service jobs the city offered. With the same flair for the dramatic that characterized his fiction, Riis transformed these facts into photographs and word pictures of sweatshop women "sewing and starving in an Elizabeth Street attic" (187) and counter girls who returned home defeated by the taxing workday.

His short stories, popular enough in their time, thus provided fictional versions of the lives he documented in *Other Half*. A number of them, including those on the working girl, appeared in the leading magazines of the time and were later collected in the aptly titled *Out of Mulberry Street* (1898). Like his nonfiction, the tales delve into the lives of the urban poor. As do the famous photographs, in which a hostile or disoriented underclass looks owlishly into his camera, his fiction provides "vicarious expeditions into mysterious quarters," from tenement cellar to police lockup.[5] Riis took the respectable reader on a literary tour of hidden locales like Rag-picker's Row and Cat Alley. He spun tales of derelicts and murderers, delinquent children and brutal parents. But he also unearthed the lives of laborers, lives led valiantly or eccentrically, in bitterness or in hope. Often using the working girl to represent the "deserving poor," he describes his cloak-maker Rosie Baruch climbing the stairs of her shabby tenement at day's end and pie-factory girl Kate Cassidy in a Dynamite Alley quarrel with her boyfriend.

Nor was Riis the only one to chronicle Lower East Side existence, whether in terms of the derelict, the "tough," or the working girl. Newspaper colleagues with less of his reform impulse capitalized on the new thirst for information on the poor. Riis and his fellow journalists responded with tales characterized by a romantic, sentimental, or naturalistic interest in a cast of city characters ranging from the street gamin to the widowed washerwoman, the hod carrier to the sweatshop seamstress, the saloon-keeper to the prostitute. Inspired by the people they met on their forays in search of "local color," writers of tenement vignettes met genteel protests that the poor were not fit literary subjects by prudently skirting sexual subjects or being carefully didactic about the moral failings of the impoverished. Still, tenement authors provided a literary sociology of slum life in studies of communities inhabiting densely populated blocks like the infamous Mulberry Bend or the five-story double tenement on Forsyth Street one author appropriately dubbed "The Barracks."[6]

The tenement tale was popular until it was superseded by the labor romances and social protest and white-slavery novels of the 1900s (whose muckraking attention to the woman at work is the subject of later chapters in this book). Although critics recognize the importance of this body of fiction in the American literary treatment of poverty, they discuss it, strangely enough, as if it cast the proletariat as male. Modern students of tenement fiction routinely omit the numerous sketches on the womanly work experience produced by Riis and his contemporaries. Even Crane's novella *Maggie: A Girl of the Streets* (1893), the focus of much critical attention, is viewed as if Maggie had never been a seamstress and had always worked at the prostitute's trade.[7] One of the ablest commentators on slum fiction inaccurately perceives the world of the tale as one in which men are "hard-working" but women are not workers at all, only "inviolate or cruelly betrayed," or overwhelmed by a vaguely defined "corrupting environment" that somehow excludes the workplace.[8] Other examiners render the tenement tale's working woman equally invisible. Robert Bremner, for one, scrupulously classifies the working man: unsung hero, pitiable underdog, member of the dangerous classes. But he implies that tenement women were denizens of the slum, not the workroom.[9]

Although the tenement story did depict the working woman, it did not produce rounded portraits of female breadwinners. Rather, the story gave fictional translation to widespread fears about the dangers of work to woman's purity and health. By their titles alone, tales like James W. Sullivan's "Minnie Kelsey's Wedding" (1895), Julian Ralph's "Dutch Kitty's White Slippers" (1896), and Riis's "Spooning in Dynamite Alley" (1898) imply the prejudices they claimed to attack. Attempting to regulate the sexuality of the woman worker, her male imaginers created situations that removed her from the workplace entirely. Although many authors were acting on a documentary impulse, dramatizing the New York working girl became less a study of her labor than a cautionary tale of the menace work posed to her character.

Before analyzing these depictions of the female laborer, it would be well to understand how earlier writers grappled with the subject. Such a survey locates 1890s fiction in a literary-historical context to illuminate the tenement writers who approached the working girl with such compassion—and such doubt.

Well before Stephen Crane's ill-fated Maggie fled the collar and cuff factory for an amoral Bowery bartender, James W. Sullivan's Minnie toiled at her clothing factory job and Edward Townsend's Carminella achieved a stage success denied the female toilers left behind in Mulberry Bend, working girl heroines dotted American fiction. Even prior to the Civil War they appeared in novels that described their expanding role in the textile trades. The representative title character of Ariel Cummings's *The Factory Girl* (1847) is a contented loom worker-boarder in the mill town of Lowell who is dutifully contributing to her farm family and saving for marriage on her return to rural life. In subliterary exposés of urban vice, such as T. S. Arthur's *The Seamstress: A Tale of the Times* (1843), she is less fortunate. A wretched piece-maker in a city garret, Arthur's seamstress is the quintessential victim of greedy contractors and a heartless metropolis. One employer sneers, "Girls that make . . . shirts and trowsers [sic] haven't much cause to stand on their dignity—Ha! ha!"[10]

In neither the Lowell nor the "wicked city" tale (both justly fallen into literary obscurity) is the working woman more than a cardboard figure. Hawthorne and Melville provided antebellum exceptions to such superficiality, although these writers' interest was more symbolic than documentary. Certainly in *The Blithedale Romance* (1852) Hawthorne's cursory description of Priscilla's former existence as a Boston purse-maker suggests a reluctance to probe the deprivations of that life. A similar inattention to individuating the female worker mars the portrait of female exploitation in early capitalist New England in "The Paradise of Bachelors and the Tartarus of Maids" (1855), Melville's chilling portrait of paper-mill girls.[11] In reiterating that machines have ground existence out of these women, Melville both examines and deflects attention from them as people. Furthermore, his genius for brilliantly symbolic fictions of "the metallic necessity, the unbudging fatality" (227) of life makes the focus not woman's particular but mankind's universal tragedy.

Only in the 1860s and 1870s did a small group of writers, all of them women, begin a serious literary exploration of the lives of female wage earners. Alarmed that women were often paid half as much as men, that work conditions typically ranged from the demeaning to the horrendous, that society assumed women were supported by male breadwinners and thus did not need a living wage, Rebecca Harding Davis, Elizabeth Stuart Phelps, Louisa May Alcott, and Harriet Beecher Stowe produced a composite portrait of manufacturing workers, seamstresses, domestic servants, and even teachers and governesses who were trapped by a harsh industrial order. In Davis's "Life in the Iron Mills" (1861), a secondary character, the deformed cotton-mill worker Deborah Wolfe, living with her large working family in two cellar rooms and breathing the foul air of the town and the factory, is a prisoner of abysmal conditions and, as the tale unfolds, of her own desperation. In another Davis piece, the cotton-mill bookkeeper who is the title character of *Margret Howth* (1862) daily witnesses the toll such work takes on female and male workers alike. A secondary character whom Margret befriends, the Dickensian cripple Lois, scarred by a mill accident, is a poignant example of the hazards of the workplace.

Phelps's post–Civil War *The Silent Partner* (1871) contrasts the lives of Sip Garth, "a miserable little factory-girl with a dirty face" left an orphan by the premature deaths of her overworked mother and alcoholic mill-hand father, and Miss Perley Kelso, the owner of the factory.[12] The latter is converted to sympathy for her workers by observing Sip's life of fighting "cotton cough" at work and caring for her deaf sister Catty, born of a mother whose health was ruined at the Kelso works. Alcott's protagonist in *Work* (1873), Christie Devon, rightly has a horror of factory work, but she leaves middle-class safety to sample the indignity of serving—and later, workshop sewing for—an overseer who fires any woman suspected of "light" conduct. And the noted antislavery writer Harriet Beecher Stowe, like Alcott a defender of working women tempted to "fall," included a subplot in *We and Our Neighbors* (1875) that warns affluent women not to mistreat their servant girls but to hold out the hand of friendship.

As concerned as these well-known authors were with defending the worth and dramatizing the trials of the lower-class woman, their fiction was divided between sympathizing with working women and praising the "lady bountifuls"—often the true heroines of their works—who sought a knowledge of the female underclass. Feminist critics have praised the cross-class solidarity such quests imply, and on one level this fiction does embody a radical feminism. Perley Kelso, for example, refuses marriage and its subordinate status to become a benevolent employer and a friend (though hardly a benefactor) to the impoverished Sip Garth. Alcott's Christie Devon, at the novel's end a rich widow, seeks to aid women by planning a feminist community for all social classes. In neither the Phelps nor the Alcott novel, though, does the impetus for reform come from the working girl herself.

When she is permitted to speak, she is the same voice of self-sacrifice as her middle-class counterpart, the Victorian domestic angel. And her rewards are often identical. For her patience and altruism, Davis's Margret Howth—who in fact was born into gentility—ascends to marriage with a manufacturer. Phelps's once-fiery Sip remains in the working class but preaches Christian resignation. Furthermore, the gentrified working girl and the labor saint whom Davis and the others depicted had little immediate effect on American fiction, which slighted the lower-class woman in favor of the "angel of the house." Female labor romancers of the 1900s would eventually rework the Davis, Phelps, and Alcott characters, transforming them into heroines both ladylike and militant. But before the 1900s—the tenement tale excepted—when the working girl was not killed off for desiring more than a dull rural beau and a hardscrabble life, she was either a cheap coquette or too unimportant to chastise, as in the early muckraking fiction of the Gilded Age or in the more conservative treatments of class struggle by John Hay and Charles Bellamy.

No author of his day was better able to breathe life into this stereotyped character than Henry James, and in *The Princess Casamassima* (1886) he elevates the working girl-adventuress to art. Where Bellamy in *The Breton Mills* (1879), Hay in *The Breadwinners* (1883), and Edmund Fuller in *The Complaining Millions of Men* (1893) dismiss the working girl as vapid and easily corrupted, James illuminates her survival ethic and drive to prosper. Having escaped her dreary slum family to live and work in central London, to satisfy "her theory of herself," the cloak-shop model Millicent Henning labors mightily at self-advancement.[13] A planner of boundless energy, she relishes the admiration her appearance in the shop provokes, seizes on offers for dinners and theater evenings, and studies the airs and costumes of rich women for future use. Repudiating her East End past, she taunts a tattered acquaintance: "Did you want me to stick fast in [that] low place for the rest of my days?" (66), as much a reference to her former lack of status as to her old neighborhood. James is too much the realist to furnish Millicent with a wealthy marriage or, given her nature, to punish her with poverty, wedded or not. With a shrewdness rare in her nineteenth-century imaginers, he simply lets this working woman be herself.

But like his masculine predecessors, he cannot do so without sneering at her "vulgarity" (66) and the perceived crassness of her aspirations. Even poor Hyacinth Robinson, the confused anarchist and social climber at the center of the novel, sees that flashiness pales by comparison with refinement. For a time he is taken with her sensual beauty—the standard period compliment to the lower-class woman—until he is roused to appreciate the superior loveliness of an aristocratic lady. As the plot hinges on Hyacinth's jumbled consciousness, Millicent's inability to compete with those from a higher class is predictable enough. But as he is obsessed with his imagined noble lineage, it seems gratuitous to push Hyacinth, and the reader along with him, to distrust Millicent's heady sexuality and musk perfume, to scorn her "show-room laugh" (65), to despise her vision of virtue as money in the bank, and—from the most snobbish of American authors—to smirk at her fascination with "the swells."

The New York tenement writers offer women who are neither Christian proselytizers nor workers ascended to the middle class, as in Davis and Phelps, nor the vulgar social climbers of Hay and Fuller. Certainly tenement fiction lacks the fervent sympathy of the Civil War feminists, as well as James's combination of imaginative power and fidelity to observed life. Yet, unlike the creators of Sip Garths, the new tenement writers recognized that the working girl's aspirations would not be pacified by religious conversion or realized by marriage to an unattainable upper-class man. Nor in these Bowery tales of Crane and his lesser contemporaries is she a secondary character too unimportant in a world ruled by the elite to merit her own novel.

Instead, writers of the tenement-tale school placed the working woman in a recognizable urban milieu and in a workplace whose hardships they made an attempt at least to delineate. Furthermore, by concentrating on a working heroine and refraining from Jamesian asides on the crudeness of the type, they defied genteel literary prejudice. Cultural prejudice posed more of a problem. Despite a surface compassion for blue-collar women and a nominal attention to their work conditions, these men responded to their culture's fears about the untamed sexuality of the woman worker. Rather than translate social scientific truth into documentary art, as the Progressive-era novel claimed to do, they regulated the chastity of the working woman. To that effort and the narrative devices that embodied it, we now turn.

The tales of James W. Sullivan and Julian Ralph unfold within tenement settings that testify to their journalistic skill at observing the city's social and economic contrasts. Sullivan gathered material for *Tenement Tales of New York* (1896) through writing a *New York Times* column in the 1880s, "Experiences of the Town."[14] During that period he became a friend of the founder-president of the American Federation of Labor (AFL), Samuel Gompers. Through that connection, and because of his interest in socialist theory, Sullivan familiarized himself with the unsavory conditions—reflected in the stories of the poor tailor Ivan Gigorovitch and the factory toiler Minnie Kelsey—of New York factories and sweatshops.

Julian Ralph was neither the believer in socialism and Henry George nor the friend of labor that Sullivan was. But as he noted in his preface to *People We Pass: Stories of Life among the Masses of New York City* (1896), he was a 20-year veteran of the *New York Sun* (a paper on which Riis worked as well); his reporting job furnished ample material "about the routine of work-a-day life" (*People*, vi). Such subject matter inspired his stories of German and Irish shop girls, stories that first caught attention in *Harper's* and were popular enough to be collected in book form.

Sullivan and Ralph demonstrated sensitivity in transforming the female workers of their metropolitan observations into the heroines of their fiction. They made no attempt to romanticize the nature of the working woman's tasks or the drabness of her surroundings. Although he neither names the product she works on nor does more than sketch her duties, Sullivan is moved to call the title character of "Minnie Kelsey's Wedding" a "prisoner in a treadmill" (49) that has stifled her initiative and ambition. One passage is reminiscent of Clare de Graffenreid's fact-filled 1893 essay, "The Condition of Wage-Earning Women": "[Minnie] sits, or worse, stands hour after hour, her eyes fixed on her work, her hands following motions which time makes automatic. . . . To her there is no raw material, no completed product. Nothing . . . at her left hand [but] a pile of work in the nineteenth stage, which she is to pass to her right, manipulated by her into the twentieth. . . . Penned up as she is in a hot, stifling room ten hours a day . . . [she feels] the heavy discordant buzz of the machinery grind . . . into her very brain" (49–50).

Another Sullivan story, "Cohen's Figure" (1895), alludes to the dehumanization of unceasing, mechanized toil. Jewish sewing-machine operators are bent over their machines as if frantically engaged in an "interminable bicycle race . . . at top speed" (81)—a result of their being paid by the piece. These are women who, unlike the still-attractive Minnie, will not be fortunate enough to find rescue by a neighborhood beau. They must remain workers, breathing the odors of "bad air . . . wet cloth. . . human bodies" (81).

Though immigrant women preferred store work to the grime of the factory and the sweatshop, the counter-girl protagonist of Ralph's "Dutch Kitty's White Slippers" fares little better in a store than do Sullivan's female toilers. Her lot is "eleven hours each day in the chinaware department of an uptown shop" (132), and to save for some clothing, no midday meal and a long walk back to her Lower East Side home. The only daily relief from shop servitude for the diminutive dressmaker's assistant Elsa Muller, the heroine

of another Ralph tale ("Love in the Barracks" [1896]), is to study the fine
ladies she waits on all day. Speaking to the other shop girls, she imitates her
rich customers' "soft low tones . . . and good grammar, as far as that can be
picked up in disconnected fragments" (56), although she is careful not to put
on airs when she returns home to the four-roomed back flat she shares with
eight family members and lodgers.

Rather than explore these women at work, either by analyzing the mores
of the workplace or their employers' treatment, Sullivan and Ralph, like many
other tenement writers, shift to what they perceive as the real issue for the
woman worker. Their stories thrust her into dangerous situations, most often
through associations with "bad girls" met at work whose male relatives or
friends are would-be seducers. Sullivan's Minnie Kelsey, "the prettiest girl in
the factory" (59), has caught the attention of Tom King, a racy local type who
has a new girl every season and whose source of income is clearly not hard
work. To ensure Minnie's attendance at a dance where he means to snare
her, King has sent her a gown anonymously and has his female emissaries—
former girlfriends who are her workmates—lure the untutored girl to the
event. Overshadowing the monotonous work that propels Minnie to crave an
excitement she knows may be illicit—she fears King but has his picture
in her little trunk—are the familiar conventions of midcentury melodrama.
Minnie, though an 18-year-old who has been working and contributing to
her family's support for a year, is now cast as a waif untutored in urban ways.

Undoing any life experience that workplace associations might have
provided her, Sullivan now emphasizes that Minnie is an orphan who came
to the city on the death of her mother. He certainly refuses to examine her
friendships with the more hardened women she meets at work. As Kathy
Peiss points out in her study of turn-of-the-century working women, there
was often "frank discussion of sexuality among laboring women."[15] To acknowledge that his virginal heroine had even heard such discussions would
have required Sullivan to cast doubt on Minnie's innocence. He therefore
redirects the plot to focus on her misfortune in her ugly, loveless home: she
has found no affection in the miserable fifth-floor apartment she shares with
an ineffectual aunt and a brutal, drunken uncle. Thus she readily agrees
when the artful King, seeking her out at the dance and getting her alone with
him, says, "[Y]ou can't have a worse life anywhere than with your folks" (65).

The stage is set for the seduction scenario that was a staple of nineteenth-
century popular fiction. Minnie's hastily sketched-in role as a worker drops
away, replaced by her plight as a virgin in the arms of a metropolitan rake. But
as a *Bookman* reviewer who praised Sullivan's other slum stories commented
gratefully, the tale has a happy ending, though he failed to mention that it is
one that goes against the logic of the story.[16] At the dance Minnie does not
take the wine the veteran lothario King offers, but he does succeed in luring
her into a dark street. Protesting that she is a good girl, she flees him, only
to be all but assaulted on her way home by her disapproving uncle, who

sees her wearing "guilty finery" (63). Despair at this implied accusation of prostitution propels Minnie to the river rather than to thoughts of moving out. At that suicidal moment, King, transformed by Minnie's purity—presumably not what he is used to in working girls—rushes to her rescue. He even proposes on the spot; Minnie need never return to her fifth-floor hovel, nor—almost as an afterthought—to the prisonlike factory.

Minnie and Kitty, their virtue intact, leave work without having any of the tainting experiences that Dr. Azel Ames and his successors argued were the working girl's likely fate. In another Sullivan story, and in one by Ralph as well, she is not as fortunate. "Cohen's Figure" by Sullivan, the story of a cloak model, Ernestine Beaulefoy, reveals much about the exaggerated association of work with carnal knowledge, an association that, though not explored in the earlier story, inspired its improbably protectionist conclusion. Ernestine's doom is that she has no male guardian. Fallen on hard times with the death of her father, she takes work in the lascivious Cohen's sweatshop, depicted by Sullivan as more brothel than business establishment. That lightly clothed men and women work next to one another in the overheated space prompts him to comment on the "repugnant mingling of the sexes" (81). The cloak models who work in the same room exhibit the same immorality as the female operators; they are "cheap" women, "talking and laughing with the men, unconscious of immodesty" (83).

Into this den of iniquity walks a "sweet and cultivated young woman" (74) who, in more affluent days, slapped any man who offered her an insult. But to work is to be sullied, and the very fact of her purity spurs her employer to move his hands lustfully up and down her body in the guise of fitting the garment she is modeling. In the course of this harassment, he signifies his awareness that she is his "figure." Her body is his, and he contemptuously blows smoke in her face to announce it.

What happens to the once-spotless Ernestine may well have been a fact of life for some or even many nineteenth-century working women dependent on the good graces of male supervisors or coworkers. What is not authentic is the assumption that to experience sexual harassment was tantamount to becoming a prostitute. Sullivan clearly thought so, for he propels Ernestine, who becomes suicidal because of her sullied purity, out of a window and to her death. She had chosen, he notes approvingly, "between death and degradation" (88).

It is telling that when, in *Tenement Tales*, Sullivan views the masculine work experience, it is a different matter entirely. In "Not Yet: The Day Dreams of Ivan Grigorovitch," the tailor Ivan is so robbed of judgment by his dislocating work environment that, too distracted to notice where he is, he is killed in a street accident. Yet Sullivan stresses that Ivan's mental disorientation is not madness but the response of an alienated worker to the tortures of the capitalist workplace. Sullivan had also begun to paint Minnie Kelsey's alienation, but he did not permit her to reflect on it, much less to have a vision of a better work world. Ivan, in contrast, is a utopian, dreaming of a better day for all workers. He filters out his shop companions—the avaricious boss and the brutalized employees who boast of putting their 11-year-olds to work—by fantasizing about a beautiful tomorrow. Feminine dreams of rescue are pathetic or narrowly self-interested; those of male workers, notes a critic who analyzes this tale but not Sullivan's stories of women, are noble. Presumably because men are the real toilers, only through Ivan can Sullivan "express . . . his interest in the condition of poverty and in the constructs of environment and socialist intervention" (Giamo, 63).

Julian Ralph's working men are more typical of those who people the tenement story; they have none of Ivan's tragic fervor. They are little more thoughtful than the sisters and fiancées whose chastity they guard and the more sexually available working girls of the neighborhood whose chastity they challenge. In most Ralph stories, the men function to threaten—or, less often, to protect—those like the flighty heroine of "Dutch Kitty's White Slippers." Kitty is also saved from the tragic necessity of Ernestine Beaulefoy, or the unwise escape from work that Minnie Kelsey's untrustworthy coworkers force on her at the behest of Tom King. But Ralph adds a dimension to the theme of the corrupting workplace and the woman worker as an imperiled or fallen innocent. In so doing, he shifts the focus from female labor to marital rescue—and reveals his own prurience regarding the working woman.

Ralph's German-American title character "Dutch" Kitty responds to her 11-hour stint as a shop girl with far more assertiveness than does the passive Minnie Kelsey. Though longing for the pleasure of dancing after an imprisoning day in the factory, Sullivan's Minnie is wary of the perils a neighborhood dance might offer. Against her better judgment, she goes, but only after being unfairly lured by the gift of a dress and the manipulations of untrustworthy coworkers. Like Sullivan, Ralph exhorts working girls to shun the dance floor. Kitty of the pretty face and trim ankles has put on her dancing slippers so many times that, as Ralph notes significantly, her shoes, like her reputation, are becoming tarnished. Sketching in rather than discussing the "nothing else but hard work" (137) that characterizes her day, Ralph sees her frantic dancing as an inevitable response to it. In a brief bow to social scientific observation, he explains that Kitty is "hard-working" (136) and "has no other fun" (137). But when he observes that Kitty has "danced as much as any working-girl in New York" (138–39), he is criticizing rather than chronicling. Like the period reformers who crusaded against the dance hall—"drawing," as the historian Kathy Peiss notes, "a lurid connection between working girls' recreation and vice" (98)—Ralph sees trouble ahead for a young woman who prefers the pleasures of dancing with strangers to staying home with her family or, in this cautionary tale, her beau, Lewy Tusch. "Drop der dance— see?" (142), he implores before beginning a marriage proposal, which she interrupts with a defiant no, reminding him she is a working girl. "I'm earning me own living," she proclaims (as Ralph confuses Irish- and German-American dialect), "and I'm big enough to take care of meself" (141).

Kitty's rejection of her would-be protector clarifies the negative effect of feminine working-class breadwinning. Kitty challenges convention by refusing the marriage that would take her away from wage work and unescorted recreation alike. In her defiant response, she mirrors her real-life working sisters who frequented the over 100 Manhattan dance halls—the majority on the Lower East Side—accepting "treats" (Peiss, 93), sometimes in exchange for sexual favors. Thus Kitty expresses her sense of herself as both a wage earner, if not a very affluent one, and, as if such a status gives her further male prerogatives, a sexual free agent.

Not only does Kitty's insistence on herself as a working woman and pleasure seeker disturb Ralph, but, although he cannot acknowledge it, so does his attraction to the working-class woman. In one passage he transforms her from the flirtatious girl with a passion for dancing whom he initially described into an erotic object. Betraying his fantasy about her sexual availability, his prose runs over her face and body much as Sullivan's alter ego, the lustful Cohen, let his hands roam over Ernestine's figure. Ralph exclaims over Kitty's "red-lipped, kissable mouth," passes to her "sturdy little brown neck," her "shapely bust and waist," and then, as if too frightened to continue the exploration, to "all the rest" (134). Even so abbreviated a tour of her body alarms the Victorian gentleman in him, and he retreats, first by projecting his own sexual desires onto Kitty, and then by punitively nipping her sexual rebellion in the bud.

Ralph makes it clear that, unless she is stopped by a guardian male who will place her in a kind of moral custody, Kitty is well on her way to sexual danger. Soon after the description of her sexual appeal and the scene in which she defies Lewy, she sets out with the racy Rosy Stelling for Crimmins Park, the kind of "typical uptown pleasure ground" (146) that was the bane of antivice crusaders. To leave the reader in no doubt of its dangers, its name is a play on the word *criminal*. To add to Kitty's perils, Lewy dubs Rosy a girl who is not "straight" (144), an allusion to her amateur (or professional) status as a prostitute. The unprotected Kitty may soon enter the life of the sexual criminal herself.

In the park a familiar nineteenth-century fallen woman scenario begins to unfold. Rosy introduces Kitty to a well-dressed cad with a soft voice, perfect clothes, and a suspicious desire to ply her with champagne. Kitty's self-reliance turns to putty as Ralph calls this would-be scoundrel a "revelation to the poor working-girl" (151), reinforcing the association between being a worker and being a woman of easy virtue.

But the world of the tenement tale is one in which the working girl, if she is fortunate, can save herself by fleeing sexuality and then abandoning both work and the leisure activities of which her life has consisted. Like Minnie Kelsey, Ralph's Dutch Kitty runs from the promiscuity of the dance garden into the sheltering arms of the Dobbin-like Lewy. Fear has been her punishment; her penance begins with renouncing her wage earner's independence. Flinging her slippers away, she vows that she will dance no more. "You was right," an abject Kitty cries. Reversing her earlier claim, she adds, "[A]nd I can't take care of meself, neither. I ain't got no more conceit left in me" (153).

If, despite Kitty's budding immorality, Ralph saves her, he punishes Elsa Muller, the romance-obsessed shop assistant of "Love in the Big Barracks." As the story opens he establishes the familiar period connection between woman's work and flighty conduct. In one sentence he introduces Elsa as a worker in a Fifth Avenue clothing shop and in the next as a girl with a "head full of romantic notions" about her tenement inamorata, Yank (53). The workplace proves no friend to Elsa, for it is there, among talk of love affairs and infidelity, that she hears of a book of spells to cast on the elusive man. Her purchase of the book, Ralph emphasizes, further separates her from the ranks of "honest young girls" (66). It also seals her doom. In an effort to climb into Yank's apartment to sprinkle a love potion on his food, she slips off the fire escape and soon dies of the injury.

The fall, of course, is a metaphor: this wayward girl must pay for kissing men in public parks and entering their rooms to entice them back to her. Kitty curbed her dangerous impulses, or rather, had them curbed for her; Elsa is tainted by them. Viewed another way, Elsa must die because she plays out the fantasies inspired by Kitty of the kissable mouth. In a scrutiny of mid-nineteenth-century American "wicked city" literature, David Reynolds finds a surprising number of texts with willing women, who both release male fantasies and reflect an increased interest in the sexuality of women.[17] Although in his attempt to give more balanced descriptions of urban poverty and immorality Ralph differs from an urban Gothicist like George Lippard, he too projects his guilty interest in women of the working class onto them and dooms (or rescues) them with good conscience.

In Sullivan and Ralph, the workplace is the chief threat to female innocence, but it cannot permanently taint a woman if she is saved from it early or, in exceptional cases, atones through suffering. For Riis, no such redemption seems possible. His praise for the "sad and toil-worn lives of New York's workingwoman" notwithstanding, in his nonfiction he is ambivalent about the working girl, alternately extolling her for not "going astray" and advocating "death to dishonor" (Other Half, 183). His 1898 story collection Out of Mulberry Street reflects far less understanding. Because all of Riis's sketches grew out of his coverage of fires, accidental deaths, and other tenement house or pavement disasters, both men and women in his stories perish in what he calls the "maelstrom" of the slum environment. But of the worker heroines—or rather, antiheroines—of his two principal tales, one, the Jewish cloak-maker of "The Cat Took the Kosher Meat," is a "hoydenish," and the other, the pie-factory girl of "Spooning in Dynamite Alley," a manipulative flirt.[18] In the first story, the mere fact that Rose Baruch has become Americanized—that is, has her own job at 17—makes her wish to be independent. Riis acknowledges her long hours and low wages but deplores her "animal spirits," her "noisy feet on the stairs" late at night, and her "harum-scarum ways" (122). Rosie is heading for a fall, and soon her impulsive nature sabotages her. Angered that a stray cat has walked off with the meat for dinner, she tries to retrieve the food by climbing down an air shaft. As willful in disregarding her neighbors' warning as she is about the moral danger of staying out when "nice girls" are home, Rose learns caution, too late, giving herself a deadly injury. She falls, and as if mourning her dual folly, her "voice rose in pain and in bitter lamentation from the bottom of the shaft" (125).

Woman's avidness for life and experience, learned both at and as an escape from work, is no more positive in Riis's "Spooning in Dynamite Alley." This time the promiscuity is more apparent and the woman inspires rather than bears the brunt of slum violence. Kate Cassidy, proud to be a girl who greases pies in a Sullivan Street bakery, is no less proud of her ability to play off the smitten but married Tom Hart against her "steady," George Finnegan. The enraged Hart catches her kissing Finnegan in the alley; a bloody fight ensues, the end of which finds Hart in the hospital and Finnegan in hiding. To Riis, Kate is a tenement Pandora. She, not Hart's roving eye, is the "cause of it all" (227). Worse, there is no air-shaft plummet to curb her tendencies toward "spooning"; all she can think of is a forthcoming workers' picnic and, presumably, new opportunities to create havoc.

Many of Riis's lower-class *Mulberry Street* women, whether workers, termagant wives such as the aptly named Carmen in "The Christening in Bottle Alley," or the crazed streetwalker of "A Chip from the Maelstrom," are Liliths. Although Riis believes that woman workers imbibe dangerous ideas, resulting in self-destruction or the destruction of others, his point is not simply that work has baleful effects on women. Rather, it is that instead of bringing her a measure of emancipation from the place known as Mulberry Bend, woman's work is as demoralizing as marriage to a criminal or selling oneself. Like the other tenement writers, Riis echoes the words of those who felt women's work "undermine[s] principles and jeopardize[s] character."[19]

Some tenement writers of the 1890s explored the connection between wage work and prostitution. Riis's rebellious contemporary Stephen Crane wrote a seamstress-turned-into-prostitute novel, *Maggie: A Girl of the Streets*, which, in its unexpurgated edition, was turned down for publication by Appleton and Company, the same firm that published Riis's less controversial work.[20] Though he was more careful to limit allusions to prostitution, the genteel critic Brander Matthews also produced a story with a wayward heroine, "Before the Break of Day" (1894). Given the pervasive perception that the working woman was more sexual than the woman of the middle classes, Crane and Matthews merely made explicit what had been implicit in the works of the writers discussed above. But their works reveal how deeply writers willing to dramatize the promiscuity of working women blamed the victim rather than, as they claimed, the environmental factors that propelled poor women into the workplace, and then into prostitution to escape it.

By the mid-1890s Stephen Crane was the celebrated author of *The Red Badge of Courage* (1895), whose reputation finally persuaded Appleton to reprint a rather bowdlerized *Maggie* the next year. Both the Civil War novel and the slum tale contain bewildered protagonists in a world at war, but in the latter novel the battle begins at birth. Well before Maggie Johnson feels "strangled" (25) by her life as a worker in a Lower East Side factory, she must struggle to survive in the hostile universe of Rum Alley.

Critical discussions of *Maggie* have ignored the fact that, as Crane himself characterizes her early in the novel, his hard-pressed title character is a "girl who . . . worked in a shirt factory" (28). For one thing, her vicious family and squalid home environment contribute to the turmoil in her life long before she is of working age. More important, Crane presents a vision of the slum that transcends "the immediate prison of home and factory."[21] With a satirical tone, Crane illustrates the real problem of the "other half:" their self-deceiving-theatricality. From the dissolute neighbors jeering Maggie about her sexual "fall" to her family's cursing her and casting her out, the characters' delusive ideas of their own importance and their absurdly inappropriate moral judgments preclude sympathy for their unenviable situation. In a related way, Maggie's foolish romanticism, through which she sees the repulsive Pete as a "knight" (20), produces annoyance at her self-deluding behavior and its pathetic consequences.

Despite an original vision of the problems of the working poor, Crane joins his contemporaries in fixing blame on the working girl. Like Minnie Kelsey and all the fictive factory girls who court sexual peril, Maggie is eager to escape industrial bondage. To contrast with her frenzied home—her mother destroys the furniture, drinks, and screams obscenities that ring through the tenement halls—even the monotonous grind of the factory might have been pictured as a relative refuge. Conversely, Crane might have pointed to Maggie's low wages as a cause for her quick descent into prostitution. But he views the workplace in formulaic terms only; a truncated description of Maggie "shrivelling in the hot, stuffy" factory (25) presents her as a potential seduction victim just waiting for a companion to lead her astray.

Like his fellow tenement writers, Crane skips over his heroine's work identity. True to harlot's progress convention, he has Maggie place her faith in a scoundrel. In Crane's vision, the seduced worker, her virtue gone and her spirit crushed, takes up streetwalking and soon succumbs to a river death, too despondent to consider a sensible alternative. Certainly the logic of the story requires that, as the rose of the slums, Maggie be sacrificed to her foul environment while the predators who surround and scapegoat her survive. Viewed as a study of working-class womanhood, however, the novel is dishonest about Maggie's imagined suicide. Carol Hurd Green comments that Crane "condemned Maggie to death with the same regretful stringency" as "the genteel reformers of the purity crusade" (235).

Maggie's fate belies what Crane knew of women whom he elsewhere moralistically characterized as "unchaste."[22] Not only was he well acquainted with sexual survivors, women who moved in and out of the barroom demi-monde, but his Methodist mother had taken in a pregnant, unwed girl, a social type viewed by some in her New Jersey community as akin to a prostitute, until the girl could achieve reentry into another community. None of these real-life "fallen" women judged their own sexual activity, hired or otherwise, with Maggie's self-destructive harshness. In this survivalist mentality they resembled the thousands of former working women, prostitutes for longer than Maggie's brief time, who were interviewed in a government survey published a few years before. One-quarter of them were drawn from "a perfect cross section of women's occupations."[23] Although including a financially successful minor character, the seasoned prostitute Nell, Crane denies the possibility that the wages of Maggie's sin might replace those of the factory. Nor does he recognize that a woman could survive, as was common enough, as a worker who supplements her wages with payment or gifts in return for sex. Like Sullivan, Ralph, and Riis, Crane controls woman's chastity by taking her life in the process.

In contrast to the newsmen discussed above, Brander Matthews—wealthy, well connected, a belletrist and Columbia University English professor—was gentility itself. But his slum tale has obvious parallels with Crane's work. The box-factory heroine of "Before the Break of Day" is also called Maggie; she too is beaten by drunken parents, left to a shrewish mother on her father's death, tossed out by that inebriated moralizer when she stays out with a flashy local type, propelled to quit work and live with him, and pushed to prostitution when the man soon throws her over.

Matthews's contribution to the tale of the tenement working girl, however, was to combine two usually antithetical plots, the sexual fall and the atonement through marital rescue. In so doing he effected what was rare in his day—a compromise between forgiving and killing off. As "Before the Break of Day" begins, the heroine, Maggie O'Donnell, is tainted by her friend-ship with other women in the paper-box factory, who introduce her to the thieving Jim McDermott. He initiates her further into sin, keeping her out all night and, in a move to recruit her into prostitution, taking her to the dance hall, where "she went . . . when she was left alone in the world."[24] Soon her activity there places her well "on the way [to the] Morgue" (92), a standard reference to the perceived self-destructiveness of dance hall prostitution. This Maggie, though, is fortunate. Unlike her namesake, who is jilted by Crane's worthless bartender Pete, Matthews's Maggie meets Terry, who believes in her worth. He marries her, opens a saloon (a male preserve with no dance hall), and sets her to honest housekeeping in the rooms above it. Alone in the bar one night, Maggie sees her past return when McDermott tries to rob it. She telephones for the law and successfully defends the bar—at the cost of a bullet wound. Though the blood that soaks her white night-gown is proof of her repentance, it is also a necessary metaphor for her past impurity.

Crane and Matthews display the familiar punitive attitude toward the working girl. Though they acknowledge her victimization by a numbing job, a poor environment, and a set of bad companions, they blame and punish her. Crane kills her off; Matthews exacts a near-death repentance, putting her through a wounding experience in which her suffering is the price of her redemption. In Sullivan and Ralph, the Ernestines and Elsa Mullers, though technically virtuous, come to a bad end, too. Other sketches by these two writers are more benevolent toward the woman worker, but even these tales cast her rescue from work as placement in the moral custody of marriage to a paternalistic neighborhood man. The Tom Kings and Lewy Tusches expect their women to forget workroom associations and behave themselves—to drop the dancing.

Not every practitioner of the tenement story who cast the working girl as a heroine censored her for risking the feminine work experience. Edward W. Townsend, famed as the creator of the Bowery dialect hero Chimmie Fadden and, like most of the other tenement-tale writers, a New York newsman, was one of the few who, at least on the surface, had faith in the purity of the working woman. But his heroine in *A Daughter of the Tenements* (1895) is far removed from the average type he claimed to portray.[25] His novel departs from the tenement tale's emphasis on feminine chastity only because his Carminella is not really a working woman at all. By creating a world in which women at work are sweatshop slaves (68) or slum princesses in transit to wealth and fame, he legitimizes his own refusal to provide more than a tourist's view of the female toilers in the sweater's den. His local colorist's attention to other details—the noisy, crowd-filled streets, the feuding vendors, the exploited child workers—veils the fact that he employs the same Cinderella plotting favored by Laura Jean Libbey in flimsy romances like *Only a Mechanic's Daughter*, published the year before. At the core he is not only extricating woman from the work situation, as do the Ralphs and the Sullivans, but as in the fantasy world of the Libbey romance, repudiating the workers among whom she once dwelled.

One of the few to deviate from the moral control implied by the rescue theme was the storyteller of the Jewish ghetto, Abraham Cahan. By 1897 he was the editor of the *Jewish Daily Forward* (the secular voice of the Yiddish-speaking community), a position he was to hold for over 50 years. The introspective product of "enforced daily contact with [the] slums," he had arrived from Lithuania, fed on dreams of American opportunity, in 1882.[26] He organized sweatshop workers, taught them night-school English, spoke and wrote on socialism in English and Yiddish, and absorbed literary influences as diverse as Shakespeare, Hawthorne, and Dostoyevski. Uniquely qualified to explicate the laboring, Jewish Lower East Side to American readers, he did so in *Yekl: A Tale of the New York Ghetto* (1896), which Appleton and Company published the same year as it reissued a now-expurgated *Maggie: A Girl of the Streets.* Two years later the prestigious Boston firm of Houghton Mifflin brought out Cahan's *The Imported Bridegroom and Other Stories* (1898).

William Dean Howells, the editor of the *Atlantic Monthly* and a luke-warm promoter of realism about slum women—he liked Crane's literary boldness but did not advance the uncensored *Maggie* when it appeared—applauded Cahan's dialect tales of the sweatshop and street. Like Crane's novella of the Lower East Side poor, Cahan's work departed from sentimental period treatments. To Howells, Cahan's comprehension of the conflicts be-tween immigrant ambitions and American ways, the very image of "work-worn, ambitious, blundering, grotesque lives . . . [of] often noble aspiration," marked him as a "new star of realism."[27] Howells mentioned Cahan's female characters, however, with an evasiveness that concealed their unorthodox nature. For instance, a lovesick married woman interested in a younger man is not one with adultery on her mind, but a woman "whose heart goes out" to him (qtd. Richards, vi). Not only did Howells transform feminine motive so that the Jewish housewife could remain praiseworthy—not surprising in one who called Maggie's life a Greek tragedy but never alluded to her as a prostitute—but he refused to acknowledge the nondomestic women in Ca-han's repertoire. Like the less friendly reviewers who found Cahan's charac-ters crude and grasping, Howells saw only men as workers.

The reality, as Cahan well knew, was that Jewish women made up over half of those in the garment trade. He offers a gallery of these hardy women, who often live alone in Chrystie or Division street hall bedrooms, supporting themselves and, occasionally, a female parent. For Cahan's protagonists, unlike Sullivan's Ernestine or Matthews's Maggie O'Donnell, paternal ab-sence strengthens their resolve to survive and prosper. They are no slum flowers, wilted by a look or defeated by a pinch from a masculine coworker. Untrammeled by a lengthy day followed by a lively evening at the "dance academy," they trade jibes or flirtatious banter with immigrant men as newly arrived from Eastern Europe as themselves. In "A Sweatshop Romance" (1898), Beile, a "finisher girl" (a reference to the poorly paid piecework given women in the industry), retorts in reply to a male worker's remark that she stop singing, "Don't you like it? Stuff up your ears, then" (189). After-hours, the Polish shirtmaker Mamie Fein meets men with the no-nonsense "Vill you treat?" (20). Nor are these young women so divided from the men with whom they spar. Whatever the culturally expected separation of spheres upon marriage, while in the work world women help each other and men. As Cahan's literary sociology reveals, they are anxious to shed the greenhorn image quickly and at work discuss the customs of the new country and practice the difficult new language.

Jews were the largest immigrant group from the 1880s through the First World War; by 1914, one-third of all Jews had left Eastern Europe for the "Golden Land."[28] Jewish women as well as Jewish men brought over a knowl-edge of industrial work, particularly work connected to cloth production. Women from other immigrant groups worked at the garment trades in America; Italians, for example, constituted the second largest female group. But in Italy work for women was agricultural and their role confined to that of marital helpmeet. Jewish women, on the other hand, worked in textiles, tobacco, flower making, and millinery before they came to America, work they continued in the United States.

Cahan chronicled the way they negotiated their new freedom to interact with men and the concomitant desire for self-expression fostered by America. His diamond-hard Mamie Fein is a dramatic example of the garment-center immigrant who feels that she has "the right to a personality" (Ewen, 106), a right predicated on the feeling that she can support herself if need be. She is thus a far cry from the enfeebled type pictured in Elizabeth Butler's *Women and the Trades* (1909), Edgar Fawcett's "The Woes of the New York Working-Girl" (1891), and the other works discussed in chapter 1. In *World of Our Fathers* (1976), Irving Howe provides a gloomier assessment of Jewish shop girls and, by implication, those from other ethnic groups who had autonomy thrust upon them. "Lonely, vulnerable, exhausted, these girls were the lost souls of the immigrant Jewish world, rescued, if they were 'lucky,' by marriage or solaced by political involvement."[29] As Howe's title suggests, he sees women through the prism of normative maleness, and his comment implies that the Jewish working girl rightly felt defeated if unmarried. Cahan seems oblivious to female political involvement, whether as solace or not, but to read his accounts of single women is to receive a different impression from that provided by Howe's study. It is true that Mamie Fein plots to lure the cloak-maker Jake away from the depressingly Old World wife he regrets marrying; that in "A Sweatshop Romance" Beile is content only when she replaces the beau who has thrown her over with a coworker who is willing to defend her at the cost of his own job; that in "A Ghetto Wedding" (1898) Goldy labors hours at her sewing job and makes "heroic economies" (226) to save for her bridal dinner. But that is what these women do, not what they are.

Cahan's women do not wait to be acted upon. Patriarchal Jewish culture dictates that they be subordinate to men, but their strong personalities and managerial abilities suggest otherwise. Mamie, described as the one with more "initiative" (81) than Jake, engineers his defection from a wife whose "spotless purity" (45), tellingly, proves no match for Mamie's worldliness, sensuality, and plans for making money. Jake's "greenhorn" wife herself loses no time in weeping but, with the substantial divorce settlement she pries out of him, opens a new business with a new husband. Writes Cahan of another character of undampened resolve, Beile was "mortally offended" by the "commanding tone" (189) of the boss's wife. She shows her mettle and quits, a decision applauded in the denouement when a coworker joins his admiration for what she has done to his marriage proposal.

Furthermore, although Cahan deemphasizes the purity issue that obsessed so many practitioners of the tenement tale, he does reassert another charge about the effect of work on women—that it makes them into men. Indeed, he both documents and criticizes the role reversal to which the strong-minded Jewish woman worker was prone. He thus gives voice to the same fears of "unsexed" working women as do period opponents like Grant Allen. To an extent, of course, Cahan allays these anxieties by providing conventional marital finales. He cannot, of course, suppress his own anxieties about the masculine woman he has created. But he can justify her by the necessities of the immigrant experience.

In creating the title character of his novel *Tom Grogan* (1895), Francis Hopkinson Smith responds to the same fears.[30] Though not strictly a tenement tale, the novel contains scenes in which the protagonist, who runs a Staten Island hauling concern almost single-handedly, visits workers' wives, her life away from the housewives of the teeming Lower East Side being a further testament to her autonomy. And autonomous she certainly is, an Amazon who drives the horse-drawn wagons in what she claims is her husband's absence—actually his death, though the novel is initially mysterious about this. In any case, she manages Grogan's cargo-hauling concern with manlike capability.

As a female breadwinner with two children to raise, Tom is the antithesis of the ultrawomanly widow reading her Bible and eking out an existence until her children are grown, a stock character in countless midcentury tearjerkers by the hugely popular Mrs. E. D. E. N. Southworth. Surprisingly, Smith, a onetime engineer and political conservative known for his profitable conventional novels, loads descriptions of Tom with apparent praise for her masculinity. He continually lauds her "great physical strength" (7) and her ability to "work like a man" (36). Smith's own alter ego, a male narrator who employs Tom's hauling concern, marvels that she is stronger than the workers she employs. He is further awed that she commands respect everywhere but with the slackers of the union, who, unlike antiunion Tom, work hand in glove with thieving businessmen.

In the course of so adulatory a narrative, Tom's heroics include paternalistically keeping a workman from trifling with her daughter and foiling a corrupt union delegate in his plans to both steal her city contract and do away with her. Still, this ultimately is praise that damns. For like the most zealous opponents of working girls—or for that matter, her tenement-writer "defenders"—Smith associates hard work with men, or with women who are thereby unsexed by it. Thus the favorable reviewer who commented that Tom is "everything the American workingman ought to be" certainly had no thought that, in her will to endure, Tom is everything that the American working woman should be, too.[31]

Significantly, the 1890s' most dramatic literary defense of woman's right to engage in manual labor placed her beyond charges of immorality or unfeminine aggressiveness only by placing her beyond femininity as well. The thriller with a female swashbuckler in a working-class milieu was not without precedent. Mrs. Southworth had created such a protagonist in the vastly popular *Hidden Hand* (1853), still in print in the 1890s. Her heroine for a time outdoes Tom: cross-dressing Cap le Noir, cheated out of her inheritance, lives for a time in New York's Dickensian Rag Alley, throws would-be rapists down trapdoors, and, in romance style, recovers her lost fortune by story's end. But even the fiery Cap is tamed, incredibly settling down to high-Victorian wifehood. Tom, in contrast, finds no pot of gold and continues at her Herculean labor. Economic necessity, often used in plots of married women workers, legitimizes her remaining outside womanhood. But her creator knows he has given birth to a grotesque, and to make sure that she offers no role model for women workers, he has her daughter wed a conventional husband and embrace the female normality denied the mannish mother. Ironically, the only popular writer to keep a woman at work did not create a woman at all.

Tenement writers were virtually alone among the writers of the 1890s in defending the working girl, yet they were convinced that she could not withstand assaults on her virtue. Like the era's nonfiction writers, both her opponents and defenders, they viewed the working woman in sexual terms. They lacked a sense of the importance or value of work for the poor, largely unskilled woman. They paid lip service to the idea that she had to support herself or help her family, but they had difficulty focusing on her in a work role or discussing work-related themes. Instead, they presented the workplace as a corrupting urban influence leading to loss of chastity and translated her economic plight into a sexual one.

Despite the many exploited immigrant or first-generation seamstresses in the tenement tales, there is no echo of the militant response of some of their real-life sisters in the trade. No silent sufferers, these Jewish women contributed to the founding of the New York Cloak Union, the first real trade union for cloak-makers, and to the important strike of 1894 in the streets of the Lower East Side, terrain familiar to journalists like Sullivan and Riis. Indeed, Joseph Barondess, the New York Cloak Union leader, was once hauled into the same Elizabeth Street police station where Riis had covered the crime scene for the *Sun* and taken some of his most telling photographs of the criminal class in custody.[32] Nor were strike leaders exclusively male. The seducible shop girls of New York sweatshop fiction could have profited from contact with the newly emergent feminine labor militants. Their numbers included firebrands like Leonora O'Reilly, the Irish organizer of New York City's women shirtwaist workers, Mary Kenney, who helped organize a women's local of the United Garment Workers, and Dora Sullivan, who worked with New York State collar and cuff workers more responsive than Crane's Maggie (Foner, 254, 224). Representing the many Jewish garment-trade women organizers ignored by Cahan was Rose Schneiderman. Even as early as 1904, this 19-year-old was leading women cap-makers in a successful strike, and she was referring to women when she wrote, "[W]e must stand together to resist."[33] Clearly, political involvement did more than provide this self-supporting Russian woman with solace.

By the new century, a small percentage of women had joined labor unions or supported the kind of labor Joan of Arcs just described. But marriage as rescue continued to be prized by many if not most of the New York working girls relegated to the lower depths of employment. Although in interviews former working women who had turned to prostitution cited "bad influences," including those at work, such a response has to be decoded. For one thing, it was self-serving—it was what interviewers wanted to hear. No doubt, workplace encounters and associates did inspire some to enter the world of commercialized sex. Yet to view women in terms of their sexual lives, as did Sullivan, Crane, and their contemporaries, or as "mannish" is to overlook woman's work culture, "the patterns of daily work into which any newcomer would be initiated . . . the unwritten rules, the ways of doing the job, and how [she] thought about . . . her work."[34] Reading the tenement tale, one gets no sense of how physically demanding any given job actually was, or of how much, simply by doing her job for 10 or more hours a day, a woman was as productive as a man. Nor can the reader determine if a Minnie Kelsey gains job confidence, is given new tasks or increased wages after her initial weeks in the factory, or feels a sense of her ability to find other work, to join a working girls' club or settlement house class to improve her skills, or to become the working-class equivalent of the "new woman"—more interested in work advancement than marriage and family.

In writing about a controversial woman worker, the laundress, in late-nineteenth-century French culture, Eunice Lipton notes that the "very nature of her work exposed her to public scrutiny and sensuous delectation, both of which were translated in middle-class cultural norms into sexual accessibility."[35] To judge by the popularity of the tenement tale, urban culture, though puritanical about the images mainstream literature could present, expressed a similar obsession with working-class female sexuality. The tales marry off the working heroine as the reward for her purity. But the repeated insistence on her as a slum flower, untainted by the impurity of work and home life, was belied by an unwillingness to allow her to survive as a worker. Unlike Tom Grogan's creator, tenement writers did not rob the working girl of sexuality. But they did split her into paragon or harlot, or, like Cahan, made a distinction between her work life before and her real life after marriage. Their distrust of all working women was the real issue. The protection they offered her was from herself.

MRS. JOHN VAN VORST AS "ESTHER KELLY"
Wearing the costume of the pickle factory

MISS MARIE VAN VORST AS "BELL BALLARD"
At work in a shoe factory

Bessie and Marie Van Vorst as workers from their
book *The Woman Who Toils* (1903)
A. & C. Black Publishers

3

Ladies in Disguise:
Feminine Cross-Class Fiction

Work girls aren't looked after the way you [ladies] are, and they don't
always know how to look after themselves.

The House of Mirth (1905)

"And think how much you're doing to help [us]," said Katie, "you and
the other ladies. . . . Why, [we] used to talk all the time of silliness
. . . and now it's all books and pictures an' poetry."

A Listener in Babel (1903)

THE FICTION OF THE 1890S BY STEPHEN CRANE, JACOB RIIS, AND THEIR
colleagues dramatized the working girl's response to the extractive sweatshops, congested tenements, and cheap dance halls that defined her world.
These men's sympathetic attention to the deadening rhythms of her work
and home life, though eclipsed by their obsessive emphasis on her sexuality,
heralded a new literary seriousness about the working heroine. Yet it was not
until the early 1900s, a time that witnessed the rise of the female "undercover"
labor investigator and the entry of women into the settlement house and

social welfare movements, that public attention shifted to fiction by female imaginers of the wage-earning woman.

From the long-neglected Marie Van Vorst to the rediscovered Mary Wilkins Freeman to an author of enduring eminence, Edith Wharton, female writers cleverly integrated their knowledge of the social chasm between privileged and laboring women into texts that placed the two in contact. The successors of the Dutch Kittys and Minnie Kelseys of the previous decade are befriended by lady philanthropists in Mary Wilkins Freeman's *The Portion of Labor* (1901) and Marie Van Vorst's *Amanda of the Mill* (1904).[1] Education-minded laundry girls find the rewards of culture in meetings with proselytizing settlement workers in Vida Scudder's autobiographical *A Listener in Babel* (1903).[2] In her best-selling *The House of Mirth* (1905), even Wharton, not often credited with an interest in the working girl, much less cross-class sisterhood, explores both issues through the eyes of the socially fallen Lily Bart, who in better days gave impulsively to a working girls' club and who learns of the worker's lot firsthand through her sad time in the millinery trade.[3]

Such woman-authored texts come under the umbrella of the economic novel but exist in a range of subgenres. The most common is the cross-class labor romance, which, in fiction like *The Portion of Labor*, Van Vorst's *Philip Longstreth* (1902), and *The Fruit of the Tree*, a forgotten 1907 novel by Wharton, subordinate a critique of women's labor to a conventional love plot of a beautiful, innately refined worker (in *Fruit of the Tree* she is a "poor, unattached" nurse "with her own way to make") and her paternalistic employer.[4] Other forms include the novel of female philanthropy, a response to works like Paul Leicester Ford's immensely popular *The Honorable Peter Stirling* (1894), in which the patrician hero forsakes privilege for involvement with the poor. In the "lady bountiful" novels by Scudder, Margaret Sherwood, and, to a certain extent, the economic reformer Charlotte Perkins Gilman, it is the heiress or the well-bred do-gooder who takes center stage.[5] Even the novel of manners, dedicated to the wealthy Four Hundred rather than the impoverished "submerged tenth," is excellently represented by *The House of Mirth*, which, in juxtaposing working-class Nettie Crane with leisure-class Lily Bart, examines both distinctions and similarities between hired workers and decorative ladies who are uneasily dependent on their affluent relations.

Though these differences in form reveal diverse approaches to imagining working women, they share a crucial similarity. Novels by prominent women writers of the 1900s studied the relationship between different female social classes through scenes in which ladies break the class barrier to comfort— and occasionally, to be comforted by—"their less fortunate sisters."[6] Though some of these novels conclude, as tradition decreed, with marriage, they augmented or replaced the tenement-tale device of the providential male with redemptive—and given the era, rather daring—descriptions of cross-class feminine encounters and friendships. Women's removal from wage work, still a dominant theme, deflected public attention from industrial abuses.

Nevertheless, saving the working girl was no longer exclusively the province of men, as these novels, like so many women reformers of the period, argued. In the new feminine fiction, as in reform writings by women, a privileged woman's contact with her counterparts in sweatshop, mill, or department store, whether as investigator, benefactor, or crusader, symbolizes her responsibility to the female downtrodden.

The discussion of such matters in early-twentieth-century fiction was part of a woman-fueled effort to ameliorate the sufferings arising from the poor employment conditions and limited education of working women. As one champion of cross-class friendship put it, women needed to "stand by other women as men stand by men" (Jones, 214). Women had been agents of charity from the early 1800s, but the end of the century saw a proliferation of feminine efforts to "elevate" the urban poor by imbuing them with middle-class culture, a kind of "social housekeeping."[7] According to this view—which was central to the early professional stages of feminine social welfare activities—woman was an intuitive reformer who could civilize society the way she did the home. As a "guardian of culture," she was "naturally inclined to . . . guide young women on the path to adulthood" and create in the social settlement an extension of the upper-class home to which she was accustomed.[8] Certainly the 1889 founding of Hull House provided a haven for young working girls seeking more opportunities for education and social-ization than the streets provided. What the Polish immigrant Hilda Satt found in Jane Addams's social experiment, she recalled years later, was an "oasis in the desert," mercifully free of the noise and odors of her shirt factory job and the discomforts of her family's cramped Chicago flat.[9] Complete with parlor, drawing rooms, library, and music room, Hull House fostered assimila-tion and cultural awareness through books, music, and lectures on everything from English literature to factory conditions.

Satt was in many ways the woman reformer's ideal working girl; she was anxious to receive the culture offered by the settlement houses and working girls' clubs. These organizations attempted to turn untutored working girls into good female citizens, an ideal often expressed through the phrase "edu-cated motherhood" (*Stranger*, xix). Of course, such philanthropists, in their "solicitude for the upbuilding of [working-class] character,"[10] were not ad-dressing what one women's historian terms the "inequities built into the capitalist system" (Ryan, 234). Yet, like their less traditional sisters who formed the Women's Trade Union League (WTUL), these women were attempting to bridge the class gap.

Marie Van Vorst, a novelist, reform journalist, and daughter of New York society, expressed the cross-class impulse well when she reminded her privileged sisters of the corrosive effects of class disdain. "I belong," she wrote, "to the class of women who, one day by chance out of her carriage, did she happen to sit by [a working woman's] side in a cable car, would pull her dress back from the contact." There would, she remarked regretfully, be "no look of sisterhood."[11] Maud Nathan, president of the Consumers' League of New York, urged awareness of woman-fostered injustice to women. In a 1906 essay she appealed to women purchasers to alleviate the poor conditions endured by women wage earners. Her suggestions ranged from boycotting stores that overworked and underpaid their saleswomen to insisting on labels that guaranteed goods would "not profit those who have stolen from the wages of overtime work of helpless working girls."[12] Although she alluded to both consumers and workers in class rather than gender terms, Nathan's real focus was the "responsibility which rests on the women who spend for some of the existing abuses and evils surrounding the women who work" (646).

Voicing another period idea, Marie Van Vorst felt it her duty to become the "mouthpiece for [the working woman] to those who know little of the realities" of labor (*Woman*, 168). The same idea flowered in the era's many undercover articles by women journalists who were concerned about the womanly working class and scented a good story as well. Explaining her decision to become an undercover domestic servant, Lillian Pettengill explained: "I am likely to wait long before one of her class pictures to the public the conditions of . . . industrial life."[13]

Van Vorst and Pettengill were following a precedent set in previous decades by reporters who freed themselves from the restrictions of the "woman's page," to which they were routinely assigned, and covered the female workers of the slums instead. They were also following in the footsteps of Nellie Bly, the flamboyant late 1880s journalist who did incognito work in Pittsburgh and New York department stores and factories. Bly, however, attracted far less attention for those articles than for her undercover pieces on the Blackwell's Island women's lunatic asylum, and her journalism smacked more of stunt work than reportage. Lillie Wyman and Mary Gay Humphreys wrote extensively from their interviews with working women, as did the labor investigators Helen Campbell and Clare de Graffenreid. But few other women before the 1900s were moved by journalistic, reformist, or artistic motives to Bly's adventuresome reportage.

By 1899 the tide had turned. In the same year that Margaret Sherwood, a Wellesley professor and *Scribner's* contributor, published fiction about an heiress posing as a salesgirl in her father's department store, the sociologist Annie Marion MacLean went undercover to gather data about the salesgirl's world. Sherwood's fictional heroine is so unsettled by her experience that she retreats into her wealth; but MacLean's conclusions were published in an important scholarly journal and set a trend for female undercover investigation. Very soon magazine and book publishers were catering to the widespread curiosity about these reverse Cinderellas.

Dressing herself in the female worker's clothing and adopting her mannerisms, Marie Van Vorst labored in New England shoe factories and southern textile mills as "Bell Ballard." "The Woman Who Toils" was a 1903 magazine series; Van Vorst coauthored an expanded version with her sister-in-law Bessie, who adopted a worker's identity in factories in Chicago, Pittsburgh, and the western New York town of Perry. Billed as the "Experiences of

Two Ladies as Factory Girls," the Van Vorsts' book soon gained international attention. It was published in Great Britain with frontispiece photographs of the two in work garb (see the illustration opening this chapter), and it was even translated into French. When Marie's *Amanda of the Mill*, a novel relying on her South Carolina experiences, was published soon after, she could claim an intimate acquaintance with the cotton mill in which it is set.

Though they did not describe the variety of jobs mentioned in *The Woman Who Toils*, Inez Godman's 1901 *Independent* essay on trading the role of the woman who keeps a maid for that of the maid herself, and Pettengill's *Toilers of the Home* (1903), culled from her two-year experience as a domestic, gained a large readership. Pettengill, who urged that servants be treated with more respect by their female employers, may well have influenced *What Diantha Did* (1910), Charlotte Perkins Gilman's novel of a lady-turned-servant who founds a domestic workers' cooperative. Also claiming public attention was Dorothy Richardson's *The Long Day* (1905), a highly literary narrative of its genteel author's adventures in unskilled jobs and working girls' rooming houses, now considered a classic.[14] Toward the end of the decade, "Diary of an Amateur Waitress" (1907) appeared in the liberal-minded *McClure's*. Its author was Maud Younger, who, though not from the working class, later founded a San Francisco waitresses' union to help combat the treatment from employers that she chronicled in her diary; for example, "[It] is not pleasant to have a stranger doubt whether you are respectable."[15]

Not to be outdone by a rival, *Everybody's* magazine ran a series of pieces based on Rheta Childe Dorr's undercover work among finery-loving Portuguese women in a Fall River, Massachusetts, cotton mill. (Dorr also did a stint in a department store and published her response to her treatment in "Christmas from behind the Counter," which appeared in the *Independent* six years after the Inez Godman piece on domestic servitude.) The articles and memoirs of lady-workers continued to be popular well past World War I. By the Progressive decade, however, women like Anna Garlin Spencer and Dorr herself had returned to the more traditional mode of investigative reporting, joining the economists Edith Abbott and Helen Sumner in the well-documented and wide-ranging analyses that replaced narratives like Pettengill's and Younger's.

The middle- and upper-class women who published the results of their undercover work pointed sympathetically to the chasm between their lives, in which cotton-mill, pickle-factory, or glove-counter work was a data-gathering interlude, and those of the women who remained behind. The women novelists of the day explored the tension in such encounters between class and gender identity, between sororal impulse and class condescension, and last but not least, between women as workers and as ladies. The conflict between condemnation and acceptance that informed the cultural debate about wage-earning women was quite evident in tenement tales. To understand how this conflict shaped an equally important literary response, it is necessary to locate the fiction of Wharton, Freeman, and their contemporaries in the context of the feminine debate on the gentrification of the woman worker. These writings, some by the working woman's philanthropic sponsors, some purportedly by culture-craving workers, and others by middle-class investigators who disbelieved in uplift, eloquently reveal the impulses toward sisterhood with, as well as contempt for, the woman worker.

One apostle of the lady's mission, Wharton's sister-in-law Mary Cadwallader Jones, looked to the leisured women who managed the working girls' clubs not only to provide a friendly space but to shape the working girl's morality as well. In her essay "Woman's Opportunities in Town and Country" (1894), which may have inspired the *House of Mirth* segments on the club work of Gerty Farish, Jones wrote to urge the female upper classes to "stretch out [their hands] to make life happier and more full of meaning, *and free from temptation*, for the girls and women who have to work for their living in our great stores and factories" (207). Like her fellow philanthropist Grace Hoadley Dodge, Jones argued that contact with "ladies whose life and education [were] in . . . wealthy homes" (209) inspired those whose characters so urgently needed forming. Writing on the Dodge contribution in the early 1900s, when the club movement was still popular, Lillian Betts concurred. She applauded the civilizing influence of the movement and, reasserting its role in the moral education of the shop girl, attributed its "power in thousands of lives" to "the process of character building through accretion and elimination."[16]

What needed eliminating, of course, was the unrestrained behavior that burgeoned in the workplace, the tenement street, and the dance hall, at union-sponsored social events and unchaperoned lectures. Betts cited the example of tobacco factory girls, their homes "in one of the worst sections of the city" (148), who, before joining a neighborhood club run on the Dodge model, were "mentally . . . in a state of nature" (147). After exposure to "earnest, refined women" (138), even these toughened types elevated their conduct. "Can anyone doubt," gushed Betts, "the readjustment of ideas, the revelation of beauty, the new birth of values, because of the vision of a larger world lying beyond factory, workshop, office, school-room?" (159).

By the time fiction began dramatizing such meetings, both inside and outside of the club milieu, working girls' clubs had flourished so much that in New York City alone 18 centers had attracted almost 10,000 women, a popularity that certainly rivaled, if not surpassed, the city's female trade union activity. The leisured ladies who donated seed money also administered programs that balanced lectures on historical and political subjects, discussions on hygiene, and essays on ideal womanhood with courses on homemaking and child-rearing skills. The clubs embodied a philosophy about the wage-earning woman that transcended her immediate situation; though engaged in workplace activities, she was one who craved the self-improvement that training in "the pursuit of womanly virtues" could provide.[17]

To her philanthropic supporters, then, the working girl was a lady in disguise, or at the very least, a tabula rasa on which the code of genteel conduct could be imprinted—provided she had not succumbed to the temptations of the town. Cautioned Dodge, "[N]ever put yourselves in any way in a man's power" or "pass the bounds of maidenly modesty or reserve."[18]

The best examples of the belief that the worker as incipient lady could be taught to conform to nineteenth-century notions of proper feminine behavior by avoiding spiritual impurity are provided by *Thoughts of Busy Girls* (1892), written under the Dodge aegis and, despite her protests to the contrary, her editorship as well.[19] By the late 1890s she had instituted discussion groups for the promotion of the "three Ps": "Purity, Perseverance, and Pleasantness" (Reitano, 130). In *Thoughts of Busy Girls*, under titles such as "Purity and Modesty: Two Words of Value," essayists espouse a philosophy of self-control, mannerly behavior, and "the desire to please people" (55). Acknowledging that some girls succumb to provocative dress, waywardness, or the anger at poor wages that leaves them open to bad men, these young writers warn against dissatisfaction with one's lot. Just as the authors of Victorian conduct books and domestic fiction cautioned their affluent female audience to "make [themselves] malleable to the will of others," these writers preached the working girl's self-subjugation.[20] Thus the ideal working girl is not the wage earner but the future "comforter and helper in fighting the battles of life" (18), a phrase domesticity ideologues employed to describe wives of the middle and upper classes.

By the early 1900s club members themselves began to challenge the club structure, and elite women assumed less powerful roles. But by their very presence, the affluent women disseminated traditional beliefs about femininity. The clubs disguised the impossibility of attaining true economic power—much less what the lady class enjoyed (if mainly through male largesse)—by pursuing a program of "manipulation in the interests of inducing . . . ladylike behavior."[21] In this they contrasted with the Women's Trade Union League, whose elite female sponsors, though criticized as conservative or condescending by radical organizers, embodied an alternative cross-class interaction. Even the social settlements, more dedicated to cultural assimilation than the WTUL, intermittently supported women strikers and argued for slum improvements.[22] Still, the girls' club movement represented the culturally acceptable way of "improving" the working woman—one that surfaced in cross-class fiction as well.

No discussion of the era's gentrification thinking would be complete without a brief scrutiny of its most famous attack on such thinking, Dorothy Richardson's 1905 narrative *The Long Day: The Story of a New York Working Girl*. The daughter of a physician and a trained journalist herself, Richardson set out to become an insider in the world of urban manual labor. Her willingess to adopt a worker's identity set her apart from a Grace Dodge or a Mary Cadwallader Jones. She did share their belief that working women envied, even if they could not emulate, ladylike conduct, the mannerly and controlled behavior that, in spite of her attempts at disguise, Richardson brought to her months as a worker. Yet her work experience only reinforced her conviction that women of the lower classes made themselves ridiculous by aspiring to gentility. That conviction permeates her novelistic narrative of Rose Fortune's life in a hall bedroom in a cheap lodging house, a paper-box factory, and a steam laundry.

Characterized by impressively detailed observation, a beautifully polished style, and unusual skill at capturing workplace personalities and situations and thus conveying lived experience, *The Long Day* was greeted with enthusiasm. Most found it a moving account of women's struggle to earn their daily bread.[23] Few heeded the complaint of the labor organizer Leonora O'Reilly that the book pictured working women in an unflattering way.[24] Countered Rose Phelps Stokes—herself a journalist and working women's advocate who, before her marriage to a member of the wealthy Phelps Stokes family, had toiled as a factory girl to support her immigrant family—"[N]o one wishing to know the New York working girl's condition should be without a copy of this book."[25] Nor is this praise too fulsome: *The Long Day* is one of the most fully realized accounts of female urban survival in American narrative art. But the same qualities that make it so powerful—the lucidly analytical voice, the fidelity to the details of female economic deprivation, the cleverly literary style—reveal its limitations. Like other journalists who sought out such otherwise alien feminine experiences, Richardson took factory employment as a research task while on the staff of a city newspaper, the *New York Herald*, and her angle of vision is that of the tour guide in a tawdry section of the city. Her surface objectivity about a work experience she shared and then left does not conceal her condescension. While she is inside her own experience as a worker, she still sees others from without.

Though always conscious of the superiority that family and education conferred upon her, as she entered imaginatively into the economic life of the worker Richardson came to understand the slogan of so many of the city's female breadwinners, presented twice in her narrative: "WORK OR STARVE! WORK OR STARVE!" (5). When depicting unskilled women as being at the mercy of the job market, *The Long Day* sympathizes with their limited prospects. Richardson found them capable of friendship but saw little else to admire. At the core, indeed, hers is a contemptuous vision. To her middle-class eyes, the appearance of working women ranges from the slovenly to the flashy and announces their low intelligence, poor memories, "degraded literary tastes" (300), and general inability to improve themselves. She peppers her book with depictions of those whose "coarse, bold, stupid" (31) faces or "weak chin[s]" (61) mark them as socially and intellectually inferior. Even when she praises the few women who join a "decent" look (218) to an admirably quiet manner, she undercuts such praise by calling them uncharacteristic.

Both fascinated and repelled by the rowdy behavior she witnesses at the workplace, she is more interested in a feud between Irish and Italian paper-box workers—which erupts in oaths and hand-to-hand struggle—than in the close, cacophonous workplace that exacerbates such tensions. She loads her descriptions of working women's calmer interactions with sarcastic reflections on their limited verbal repertoire and uneducated speech. The brash but friendly girl who, not knowing her name, yells out "Good morning, Carrie!" Richardson acidly terms a "quick-witted toiler" (65). She casts as a Dickensian grotesque another box-factory coworker, the irrepressible Phoebe, whose invariable response to taunts from other women is "Hot a-i-r!" (66). And she lets Phoebe damn herself by claims to refinement that in their very recitation prove its impossibility: "The ladies I'm used to working with," remarks the untutored girl, "likes to walk home looking decent and respectable, no difference what they're like other times" (68). To Richardson's further sardonic amusement, the paper-box workers give themselves new names they consider refined, speak of chums as "lady-friends," and, with no guide but their childish imaginations, mistake the trappings of aristocracy for true breeding.

Convinced that class-bound working girls never shed their characteristics and preferences, it is doubly interesting that the chief suggestion Richardson makes for improving their lot is reminiscent of Grace Dodge: give working women the vestiges of a middle-class home, such as a parlor for receiving male visitors, and they will behave better. By offering so genteel a suggestion for a class of women whom she sometimes pities but never truly respects (not to mention her assumption that working women will rush to embrace the parlor over the saloon), Richardson subscribes to the gentrification she claims to distrust. In addition, although she reserves this rescue for one not in need of it, herself, she fictionalizes the ending of her narrative by describing Rose Fortune's providential escape. It issues from meeting not a potential husband but a "nice" girl who urges her to learn clerical skills and helps her out of her factory existence. Although few of the working girls' clubs could promise such upward mobility, they certainly preached the elevating feminine encounter.

The ideology of the worker-lady transformation was formulated by the working girls' clubs, modified but not challenged by the settlement house movement, and largely rejected by WTUL members; it was best summarized by the society woman Bessie Van Vorst in *The Woman Who Toils*. "The Perry [N.Y.] factory girl," she opined, "is separated from the New York society girl, not by a few generations, but by a few years of culture and training" (69). Although on the surface Richardson scorned this idea, like so many of the era's female reformers she felt that the working woman's character needed building. She thus joined the Grace Dodges of her day in viewing the working woman as a flawed version of the leisure-class female. Indeed, both Richardson and Dodge revealed their distaste for what the urban historian Alan Trachtenberg terms an "exchange of subjectivities."[26] Despite their avowed aims, many of the women who either as benefactors or investigators encountered the female working class or, equally important, as novelists envisioned it, were uninterested in hearing laborers' voices or exploring their culture. Like Dodge and Richardson, such women preferred to see the working girl from the perspective of the lady, thereby providing themselves with a "screen of protection" (Trachtenberg, 275) from the feminine membership of a potentially dangerous social class. Consciously or not, privileged observers—the women novelists of the early 1900s prominent among them—did little to squelch the controversy about the fitness of feminine work. Whether grafting ladylike behavior onto the woman worker or demonstrating its impossibility, their cross-class texts embrace a vision of the working girl as a lady in disguise or, to her discredit, no lady at all.

Had they looked to the immediate literary past, women writers of the 1900s would have found others who viewed the wage-earning woman through an aristocratic lens. But a decade earlier the working girl's female imaginers produced no disadvantaged heroine yearning for uplift. Women writers of the 1890s attributed her position in the world of work not to the accidents of birth but to financial reversal. Edith Wharton's 1892 story "Bunner Sisters" is set in the 1870s, a time when post–Civil War dislocation had left once-bourgeois women to fend for themselves; her aging, shopkeeper siblings cling to "the bottom rung of the middle-class ladder."[27] They need not attend a Grace Dodge lecture to understand the virtues of cleanliness, dignified attire, self-abnegation, and cheerfulness in the face of adversity. Allying themselves, if only in imagination, with the one well-to-do customer among the lowly neighborhood clientele who furnish the rest of their meager income, theirs are the values of decayed gentility: the quiet ritual of teatime, the few good heirlooms, the appreciation of Longfellow and the Bible. As it is, they are thrust into the unseemly necessity of self-support and, though they never complain, must even do piecework to supplement the scanty profits from their shop.

All that the sisters, particularly Ann Eliza, the altruistic older one, have left is a quality of character that elevates them, or so Wharton would have it, above the uneducated, dime novel–devouring women who surround them and whom they courteously befriend. The Bunner women's very innocence of the sordid world that encroaches on them—most notably, genteel-seeming men who would marry simply to rob them—proves their undoing. This Wharton tale, not published until almost 25 years after it was written, was rejected by *Scribner's Monthly Magazine* as too depressing.[28] Certainly the trials to which she subjects her fragile characters surpass those in *The House of Mirth* and *Ethan Frome* (1911), produced when her reputation was secure. At sea in a world of social and moral inferiors, the sisters are no more able to fend for themselves emotionally than they are financially. The renunciatory elder sister, Ann Eliza, gives up her own preference for and income to a Mr. Ramy so that Evelina can wed him. She finds her sister months later at her door, dying, destitute, and cast off by a husband who took drugs and beat her. No small part of that degradation is that Evelina had to do millinery work to survive, a perception that later informs the story of Lily Bart as well.

Wharton's focus is on the social tragedy of women who have lost caste and are condemned to self-support. Her early tale teaches that ladies should never marry ill-bred neighborhood types, as Evelina's death from the effects of marital mistreatment demonstrates. Nor does Ann Eliza, her funds exhausted by her sister's funeral and facing destitution herself, find masculine rescue. She is in distinct contrast to Miss Smith, the shabbily genteel protagonist of an 1890 tenement story by the male writer H. C. Bunner (a name coincidence suggesting Wharton's rejection of his plot?) who finds happiness in marrying her semiliterate downstairs neighbor. Rather, Ann Eliza tries to enter the burgeoning feminine work force and seeks department store employment, which even by the 1890s was infused with a false gentility and considered one of the few wage jobs a native-born woman could take. But as in "The Real Thing" by Wharton's friend Henry James—published the year she attemped to publish "Bunner Sisters"—the phony aristocrat can find employment in a superficial commercial culture because he fits the part better. Ann Eliza Bunner is the real thing, but she cannot compete. Though it is, in Wharton's vision, to her credit, Miss Bunner's upbringing did nothing to toughen her. With neither youth nor shrewd self-marketing, she has only breeding, of no use in the mercantile world.

By the end of the century, coincident with the philanthropic dissemination of the ladylike ideal, the feminine literary perception that ladies who supported themselves were tragic underwent modifications, although Wharton herself would reinvigorate the idea in her later work. A novel that exemplifies the increasing recognition of the debt women reformers owed the female working class is Margaret Sherwood's *Henry Worthington, Idealist* (1899). It is titularly the story of a college professor with an "inherited sense of responsibility toward the world" (2) that flowers for a time in his opposition to his university's acceptance of money from a Mr. Gordon, the unscrupulous owner of a department store chain. The novel soon shifts to Worthington's female counterpart, Gordon's daughter Annice. Dissatisfied with being one of the "women who spend," Annice goes to work at Smith's Department Store—which is notorious for mistreating its workers—after discovering that her father is the owner. She takes the pseudonym of Anna Whitney and finds a ragged berth in a typical six-bed room at the Merton Home for Working Girls. Subduing her revulsion at a place she feels turns women as "gray and dirt-coloured and miserable and sordid" (70) as itself, she receives a character reference from the matron. Evidence of the same moral watchfulness that Dorothy Richardson would resent when she masqueraded as a worker, the letter attests to Annie as a "sober, honest, worthy young woman" (74) and enables her to obtain employment at Smith's.

There Annie studies the shop girl with a vengeance. She is outraged at her beginner's salary of $2.00 a week, her lengthy workday and forced overtime, the hardness of her work, the unfriendliness of the floorwalker, and the fact that, though chairs are provided for clerks, they are fined if they use them. She who had kept a maid begins her economic education when she meets "the girls with dark-ringed eyes" (66) who served as clerks in her father's place of business.

But with that quickness to impugn the female wage earner that even her champions evidenced, Annice is offended by her moral and sartorial sins. Those whom Grace Dodge saw as reclaimable, Sherwood's daughter of privilege finds to be the moral and cultural opposite. The shop girls at Smith's are "shrill" (67) young women with "unabashed eyes . . . and bleached yellow hair" (94), given to vamping male customers with "Did you want anything in our line, Sir?" (94). Annice's insight into these girls' unenviable economic situation all but vanishes in her refusal to acknowledge a sisterly bond with any of them. Any, that is, but Mary Burns, who, sensing that they are the only "old-fashioned" (77) salesclerks in that flirtatious atmosphere, takes "Annie" Whitney under her wing.

At this point in the narrative, Sherwood subordinates social protest to an homage to domestic sentimental tradition. Like Wharton, she focuses on orphaned siblings of reduced fortune. Though she has adjusted to the work world in a way that poor Ann Eliza Bunner did not, Mary Burns mirrors Ann Eliza's devotion to a younger sister she would like to liberate from breadwinning. And once again the male is the serpent in the economic garden: years before Mr. Gordon had swindled Mary's father and reduced the Burns sisters to the desperation of self-support. Annice, ironically ignorant of this sin of her father, responds as an heiress and philanthropically offers financial help.

In her novel charting its heroine's journey from heedless to socially conscious heiress, Sherwood had an opportunity to make a more democratic use of the Burns sisters. Their family's economic betrayal by a department store magnate could have mirrored the plight of all working women swindled by wretched pay and greedy employers. But such an insight evades Sherwood, and Annice Gordon as well. Instead, the Burns women represent the antithesis of the worker, who is "common" in both senses of the word. Like the Misses Bunner, they embody a vanishing ante-urban ideal of "up-country" womanhood, "virginal, old-fashioned, sweet" (123). Thus when Annice offers financial assistance to a woman in need, it is to her alter ego, Mary Burns, rather than to the bleached blonde or the "Jewess" (94), two other women with whom she also toiled. But this philanthropic plot thread is cut rather than allowed to unravel: the Burns sisters, from first to last superior to the charity-accepting class, refuse Annice's offer. They then drop out of the plot as Annice, exhausted by the difficulties of earning a living among the uncouth, seeks the safety of her wealth and marriage to Henry Worthington, whose own attempts at disassociation from the Gordon money prove as ineffectual as his bride's. When the novel was published a critic in the *Literary World* wryly commented, "[W]e do not see that society was much the better for their [efforts]."[29]

What emerges from this treatment of interclass friendship is a reluctance to follow it through, much less develop an agenda for reform. Yet, unlike Wharton, whose self-supporting city spinsters look back to their preurban youth, Sherwood thrust her lady-workers into the industrial marketplace that, by the end of the nineteenth century, defined the lives of all wage-earning women.

In the next 10 years, women novelists would be less reined in by nostalgia for the preindustrial past than Sherwood and the early Wharton. Though not without prejudices of their own, the new writers produced instead a fiction of feminine transformation. As Wharton deepened her examination of the woman who has lost all save good manners, the majority of female writers, struggling against their own condescension, made the woman who had been born rather than fallen into the laboring class central to the text.

"I stifle in class isolation," explains the settlement house resident Hilda Lathrop about her decision to live among the poor. Her quest for meaning is the fulcrum of *A Listener in Babel*, published in 1903, four years after the Sherwood novel, by Vida Scudder, another Wellesley professor and contributor to leading journals. Sounding the note of social responsibility for the women "by whose labor I live . . . weaving, sewing, selling, giving away their . . . womanhood" (63), the semiautobiographical (Scudder spent summers in a Boston settlement in the mid-1890s) Hilda, possibly named after the Hull House resident Julia Lathrop, forsakes a luxurious life to move into Langley House. The settlement is a thinly veiled Boston version of the famous Chicago venture; a Miss Abbott holds college extension classes on literature, much like her real-life counterpart Jane Addams, as described by Hilda Satt. At Langley House Hilda listens to a "Babel" of philosophies; visiting businessmen, religious leaders, anarchists, charity workers, lawyers, labor organizers, and, very briefly, women workers offer solutions to the problems of the day.

As a woman with more commitment to a socially useful life than Sherwood's Annice Gordon, Hilda puzzles through these conflicting social welfare theories, initially adopting a Grace Dodge model of benevolence. "I wonder if it wasn't worth while coming to live in [the settlement], just to introduce Wordsworth into a steam laundry in summer" (224), muses Hilda when Katie Donovan, the laundry worker to whom she has taught the Lucy poems, thanks her with a "smile of pure delight" (223). Certainly the Donovan girl is all that a working girls' club could desire. But with a bow to documentation, Scudder notes that Katie is debilitated by a work-induced cough and by having to iron 2,000 linen collars a day in a steamy laundry. For all her support of women's movements, the fact that neither she nor Hilda finds a contradiction between reciting poetry on the job and keeping one's wits about one there demonstrates that Scudder did not have firsthand knowledge of the 10-hour day. Some workers, such as the 1920s writer Anzia Yezierska, did combine days of manual labor with evenings of amassing knowledge. But Katie's ability to do so is far more typical of Scudder's Wellesley undergraduates than of laborers who must guard against distractions from their mechanical work lest, like those Dorothy Richardson encountered as an incognito laundress, they lose fingers in the mangles or risk similar injury. Scudder seems unaware of such considerations.

Nor is reverence for literature the only lesson Miss Lathrop teaches the settlement house girls. After reciting a poem extolling the joys of the hereafter, Hilda reminds her girls that earthly suffering, particularly in the form of steam laundry and garment-trade work, has an end. Before that Christian finale, however, there is earthly consolation. She instructs the girls who long to visit beautiful places that "there's another round world that every one of us has to ourselves." Katie, described quite realistically as "docile but puzzled" (228), gropes toward the answer: working girls should simply imagine the world they cannot have.

When someone less malleable, the Russian candy-maker Sonia—whose heavy accent shows that her Americanization is incomplete—challenges the promulgation of Dodge-like resignation by commenting that she cares for freedom and economic justice rather than fantasies of beauty, Hilda realizes the limits of benevolent instruction to the female masses. By the novel's end she has evolved a plan for a female cooperative community, prompting the claim by one critic that the novel is an early feminist work.[30] Her long-range plan is to teach the unskilled the weaving, dyeing, and printing talents that would help support a community of female artisans. Although Scudder, a John Ruskin disciple, does not elaborate on the difficulties of teaching unskilled women the high craftsmanship of the English artisan, presumably such a community would be run along the lines of a Pre-Raphaelite crafts community, or like the reformer-poet-artist William Morris's 1890s Kelmscott Press, whose activities ranged from designing type to espousing a philosophy of artisanship as the expression of pleasure in labor.

Hilda's plan translates vocational experiments of the day into a plan to help women workers—but only by creating an upper class within the laboring one. In her section of *The Woman Who Toils*, Bessie Van Vorst, employing the class-bound language of so many of the era's women reformers, suggests that American factory girls—who in another work she argues should be culled from those laboring only for "pin money"[31]—could form a "new, higher, superior class of industrial art laborers" (*Woman*, 162). Hilda's plan evidences a similar lack of insight. In contrast to the ideology behind the newly founded Manhattan Trade School for Girls, praised by Rheta Childe Dorr for "giving the working girl a chance" to equalize her vocational position with men through technical training,[32] Hilda's ideal is an elite group reclaimed from the ugliness of the slums to be handmaidens of a new movement—working-class versions of herself. Nor will this worker-artisan, feminine advance guard be organized on strictly sororal lines. The newly matriarchal Hilda will be the one first to study and later to teach the skills to lift the better women workers out of factories. In the meantime, Katie (who will nonetheless continue to call her Miss Lathrop) will do research on modern industry—a worker turned lady-investigator of workers. Oblivious of the condescension implied, Hilda will hire another settlement girl, Maggie, as her servant, a job more satisfying to Maggie than the garment trade for its proximity to her new mistress.

Hilda's decision to transform Katie and to "save" Maggie rather than the militant Sonia issues from her desire to elevate the malleable rather than embrace the cross-class cooperation that would limit her to a subordinate role. In this Hilda embodies a problem Scudder herself never solved. She fully supported the Women's Trade Union League, whose well-off sponsors, in addition to supporting strikes, "believed that an individual could transcend her social background by becoming self-sufficient and relating to working women without self-consciousness" (Dye, 55). But Scudder did not achieve such transcendence. She identified with educated women, whether on campus, at clubwomen's meetings, or, for brief periods, in the social settlement. Remarked one biographer, Scudder "was unable to renounce her comfortable life to live in either a settlement [with any permanence] or a utopian community."[33] Like Hilda Lathrop, who responds gratefully to Katie Donovan's protective warning that her teacher would "die" if she had to live on a worker's wages, Scudder was apologetically "exhausted" by direct contact with poverty, the "confinement of the city," and the "squalor" of working women's home and job surroundings (*Listener*, 233). She praised Tolstoy's mission to the poor and wrote constantly of the ill effects of class separation, but she preferred, and elected, a life among women of her class to a Tolstoyan one among the workers.

Scudder's philosophy of removing young women from drudgery to do craft work symbolizes her evasion of all she found harsh and ugly about the working woman's lot. Despite her intellectual adherence to the Women's Trade Union League, her fiction reveals a squeamishness about female manual labor. When the novel was published, a *New York Times* reviewer perceived it as a story of the "ladies of the settlement," not the working girls who visited there, and there is justice to this interpretation.[34] Though less judgmental about the morality of working women than a Margaret Sherwood, Scudder elevates without entering into their experience and embraces a utopian form of noblesse oblige, not one of sisterhood.

Scudder averted her gaze from feminine work. Mary Wilkins Freeman, whose fiction even prior to her one industrial novel was termed "harshly naturalistic" in its attention to the economic rigors of the lives of New England women, did not.[35] Before *The Portion of Labor* was published, Freeman was already known for her bleak stories of self-sufficient Massachusetts women. Many of her protagonists are gritty rural spinsters who survive, with varied degrees of success, by selling the products of their gardens, beekeeping, and quilting or by running boardinghouses. However slender their profits—some of these women are near starvation—their defining belief is in self-reliance through self-employment. "A Kitchen Colonel" (1891), for example, contrasts the independent spirit of one such protagonist with the listless defeatedness

of her women boarders who work in the local shoe factory. The wearing down
of women on the assembly line, noted in passing in that short story, became
the basis of *The Portion of Labor*.

Members of the army of Randolph, Massachusetts, factory operatives
who earn 50¢ a day gluing shoe linings—and as the novel proceeds, are
forced to take a wage cut—Freeman's women are geographically and emotionally distant from the Boston settlement house refugees of Scudder's fiction. Randolph had been involved in the shoe industry since the 1850s.
Though the town did not figure significantly in labor protests, Freeman was
well aware that, like her heroine Ellen Brewster, the women of Massachusetts
had been involved in intermittent protests about poor pay and conditions from
the beginning of the century.[36] They "participated fully," notes one historian
of the industry, in the many strikes organized by the Boot and Shoe Workers'
Union "and often proved more determined than the men to remain out until
they had won their point."[37] Freeman may have been familiar with the activities of Mary Nason, who in 1895 played an important role in the Boot and
Shoe Workers' Union, particularly in a number of its local strike activities in
which, like Ellen Brewster, she roused men as well as women to collective
action. Nason also apparently attracted the notice of solidly respectable
women's organizations; the Women's Christian Temperance Union lent its
support to the striking women of her union.[38]

Around the time Freeman's novel was published, Marie Van Vorst in *The
Woman Who Toils* described the kind of Massachusetts shoe factory in which
Ellen Brewster could have been expected to work: a tinderbox workplace
covered with oil-soaked refuse; glue-filled air that stifles the women, near
whose machines foremen fling new piles of work with unceasing rapidity.
Thus when Freeman's Ellen observes her coworkers, egged on by a foreman
who alternately chides and ogles them, speed up production as if they were
extensions of the machinery they operate, she reminds them that a "girl isn't
a machine" (360). Looking at Sadie Peel and Hattie Wright, young women
who outside of the shop are quite pretty, she is further dismayed to see how
quickly their faces, hair, and clothing become smeared with the dirt of the
pastebrush. The ceaseless pace of their labor and the lack of a place to clean
up turn them all into "slatterns" (359), a plaint echoed by Van Vorst in her
shoe-factory narrative. Whereas Van Vorst marvels that women endure such
a life, Ellen takes action. In a rousing oration to the women she works with—
and then to the workmen who are drawn to listen, "as iron filings to a magnet"
(477)—Ellen proclaims that it is the capitalists who have made times hard
and who should suffer. Her powers of persuasion would have been the envy
of Mary Nason, for there is little evidence of women leading a mixed strike
in this period.[39] Ellen's words inspire a strike action, and—proof of management's fears of her—she is blacklisted and reduced to home piecework.

The very qualities that make Ellen so potent a leader set her apart as
well, prompting Freeman to raise the issue of ladylike behavior so central to

cross-class women's texts in the 1900s. Ellen is fighting on more than one front. In addition to battling for the workers, she is struggling to choose between a life of labor and one of ease. From childhood on she has been in her class but not of it, possessing what one *Bookman* reviewer praised as "unusual delicacy of organization above others of her blood."[40] This sensitivity, presumably the mark of one of nature's noblewomen, joined to a beauty characteristic of the romance heroine, has made her the darling of a would-be benefactor, Cynthia Lennox. A rich woman related to the owners of the Lloyd factory, she offers Ellen a Vassar education and the upward mobility that accompanies it. The factory owner, Robert Lloyd, finds Ellen so much his equal even without an education that he asks only to marry her and remove her from his factory to his mansion.

Recognizing that militance is the antithesis of the cross-class leap her saviors expect of her, Ellen for a time resists philanthropic and marital rescue in the name of the sisterhood of labor. Lloyd's taunt that she prefers a "lower" to a "higher" life prompts her to ask: "Is Vassar College any higher than a shoe factory? . . . Instead of being benefited by the results of labor, I have become part of labor. Why is that lower?" (389). But the pressures to join the lady class prove stronger than herself, and Ellen takes what Freeman deems her rightful place with the elite.

Just before she decides to marry Lloyd, Ellen recants her militance. She addresses the strikers again and, with as much vehemence as she had recently urged the opposite course, successfully urges them to accept Robert Lloyd's terms, clearing the way for their return to work and her acceptance of the owner's marriage proposal. In Freeman's earlier fiction, her heroines often renounce marriage for a frugal, work-centered existence. As one more comfortable with a rural economy, she could praise a marginally genteel spinster for deciding to retain her independence. But, despite a surface sympathy, she could not approve a similar impulse in that permanent class of wage-earning women who, by their very work grievances, challenged "feminine" renunciation with a crusading fervor that united them not only to each other but to militant men as well.

To meet the dual threat of unwomanly conduct and class revolt, Freeman undoes the shoe workers' strike, invoking the outmoded suggestion, which they improbably follow, that they consider themselves artisans, not wage workers. She further sacrifices logic when she turns worker's complaints into a biblical-sounding paean to the dignity of work. Not surprisingly, her novel was attacked for its lack of verisimilitude, particularly evident in Ellen's turnabout behavior. In an attempt to impose a consistency on the text that it otherwise lacks, recent critics have contended that it is "as a woman" (Bardes and Gossett, 127) that Ellen, compelled by love for Lloyd, leaves the world of work. Yet that observation does not explain Freeman's conflicting impulses to make a heroine of a committed "girl of the people" (350) and then to deny her work identity entirely. Such conflicting plot elements suggest more than a reluctance to give power to the women Ellen leaves behind. Rather, the conflict indicates that writers were having difficulty reconciling the contradiction between born workers and born ladies.

Attempts to dismantle the model of the gentrified working girl without abandoning their basic elitism come from very different directions in Marie Van Vorst's *Amanda of the Mill* and Wharton's *The House of Mirth*. Both writers were born to old New York wealth, and both were interested in what Wharton called female "lives bounded . . . by the low horizon of the factory" (*Fruit*, 22). Wharton, however, preferred to make short tours of woman-filled New England factories and to engage in conversations with her philanthropist sister-in-law over Van Vorst's strenuous incognito activity in shoe factories and cotton mills. Interestingly, both wrote other novels in which the respective protagonists have little difficulty making the transit from worker to lady and lady to worker. The heroine of Van Vorst's *Philip Longstreth* is the object of her employer's largesse and, in turn, plays "lady bountiful" to an unwed mother in her plant. Wharton's *Fruit of the Tree* employs the Sherwood model of a well-born woman who, when her family loses its wealth, supports herself uncomplainingly. Justine Brent becomes a nurse to mill hands and, in another familiar plot device, eventually returns to her rightful class by marrying a mill owner. Yet the doubts about cross-class transformations suppressed in these texts surface in stronger works by Van Vorst and Wharton, novels that critique cross-class fiction.

Van Vorst offers *Amanda of the Mill*, set in the South Carolina cotton mills where she was an undercover worker, in support of her belief that if a gentlewoman can become a common toiler, any worker, given the training, can make the opposite journey. *Philip Longstreth*'s factory heroine is notable for her beauty and refinement, but Amanda is "a mill-labourer like the rest" (105). The mill owner's wife—a symbol of Van Vorst returned in her real identity to play the savior—adopts and spirits away Amanda, the backwoods child she glimpsed on a mill tour; this "rescue" is presented as cause for optimism. For thanks to "the best teachers France and England could supply" (172), Amanda returns after a dozen years with all traces of the mill "blot[ted] out" (173). Presumably even more inspiring is that Amanda returns to help the other workers as a combination of "Sister of Charity and . . . Lady Bountiful" (264), saving mill women "from wrong" (250).

The mill women seem like animals, however, to one whose modesty barely covers the elitism of her admission to one of her new class that she has only been "civilized" (250) herself for 12 years. Her own sister has become a promiscuous drunkard. She makes some tentative attempts at contact with her former coworkers but seems aware of the irony of attending a strike meeting disguised as a worker. She has so lost contact with her class that her only redemptive act is to take one of these women as her servant. After she marries the new inheritor of the mill, she abandons, at his urging, any other plan she may have had to rescue the workers, content to let him apply the wisdom he learned as an activist-gentleman in reduced circumstances.

Undercutting even the sometime philanthropy in which she had engaged, Van Vorst suggests that men of good breeding who have worked with their hands, not their feminine counterparts, are best suited to the task of class reclamation.

However egalitarian Van Vorst's announced agenda, her own class allegiances produced a novel whose low opinion of the feminine masses could not permit her heroine, once elevated, to return to them. The novel is no testament to the power of a cultural experiment to elevate those miserably exploited by the manufacturing class.

Class barriers form the subject of Wharton's *The House of Mirth* as well. The novel was a best-seller in 1905 and 1906 for its "fascinating glimpse into how the very rich amuse themselves" (Ammons, 26)—from their opulent, calculating marriages to their flirtation-filled gambling and house parties. But its enduring value lies in its critique of the "American mythology of decorative and idealized femininity."[41] For in this novel of monied New York manners, women are ornaments and the rigidity of the idle-lady code precludes their economic independence and spiritual growth. On the surface the life of the protagonist, Lily Bart, is a cosseted round of opera evenings and sojourns at country estates. She limits her social usefulness to a visit to a working girls' club, where, in Wharton's clear-eyed reference to the lady bountiful, Lily makes the generous financial contribution that enables her to save one girl's health and to "look . . . down . . . from above, from the happy altitude of her grace and benevolence" (287).

Lily herself becomes a poignant victim of the monied upbringing that has schooled her in uselessness. Her misplaced confidence in the ruthless Gus Trenor, a lustful financier who demands sexual payment for investing her slim capital, compromises her. Unwilling to make a mercenary marriage, whether to a plodding scion of old or the pushing upstart Ned Rosedale, she loses the confidence of her wealthy friends and relations and plummets into the millinery trade, shabby lodgings, and an "accidental" drug overdose.

In Wharton's vision, a lady may fall, but a worker cannot rise. It is impossible to picture a Freeman or a Van Vorst heroine received in the Van Osburgh circles frequented by Lily Bart in her better days, or Sherwood's once-genteel Burns sisters and Scudder's settlement house Katie viewed with anything but contempt by all save the slightly comic girls' club advocate Gerty Farish. Even Gerty's club efforts in behalf of the sickly typist Nettie Crane— who, in a standard subplot, has been betrayed by her "gentleman"—hardly produce social ascension or cultural enlightenment. Rather, Nettie recovers her health at the kind of "Holiday House" for working girls that Wharton's own sister-in-law Edith Jones helped support and eventually weds a forgiving man of her own class.

Yet if Wharton's worker is no lady, the reverse transformation suggests an alternative connection between women of the two classes. On the surface Wharton criticizes Lily for embodying the selfishly idle woman, who was so often the target of women reformers like Maud Nathan and Marie Van Vorst in *The Woman Who Toils*. For in her salad days, apart from a condescending visit to a girls' club, Lily's contact with the female laborer is limited to drawing back her skirts when she meets the charwoman scrubbing the mansion house stairway. (In *The Fruit of the Tree*, Wharton again depicts the pampered type in the person of Bessie Westmore, who, viewing conditions in a mill she has inherited, feels ill and flees.) But Lily's horror of the charwoman reveals deeper impulses: fear of her own possible fate and flight from the nightmare of lost caste. Like her impulsive donation to the girls' club, her reaction embodies her recognition, unwilling and only half-acknowledged, of the economic kinship between vocationally unskilled ladies and workers. For, her reputation lost, Lily's descent into what Wharton refers to in horror as "the underworld of toilers" (286) is that of any member of the female elite whose investments have vanished and whose chastity has supposedly been lost. In Lily's world women are forced to be "economic parasite[s]," and single women hunting for plutocratic mates—or married ones seeking solace in adultery— must keep up the pretense of morality.[42] But as the Gus Trenor episodes demonstrate, Lily Bart is almost as vulnerable to destitution and male sexual predation as the seduced—and betrayed—Nettie Crane. Just as Nettie must go into a kind of exile after she is compromised by a "gentleman," so must Lily.

Out of their common vulnerability comes the potential for interclass communication more egalitarian than any described thus far. Late in the novel a reduced Lily—the elitism that informed her philanthropic days cold comfort to her now—encounters Nettie Crane, who is providentially married and the mother of a child. When Nettie recognizes her suffering and takes Lily home to comfort her, their brief interaction suggests redemption not by the lady but of her. Nettie's concern contrasts with the response of Lily's cold society "friends" who, unwilling to see in her fall the potential for their own, scapegoat and desert her. Had Lily not been despondent, Nettie's wistful "I only wish I could help *you*" (315) might indeed have been of value and even given Lily the confidence to open a hat shop and achieve economic self-sufficiency, as she had planned. In a larger sense, Lily's taking Nettie's baby in her arms—an egalitarian act she hallucinates in her dying moments as well—heralds an erosion of class prejudice in an understanding of the bonds uniting all women.

In a moving passage describing Lily's entry into that maternal world, Wharton transcends the lady bountiful narrative and demonstrates the qualities that endow her work with a universal significance: Lily, smiling, holds out her arms to Nettie, who, "understanding the gesture," lays the child in them. "The baby, feeling herself detached from her habitual anchorage, made an instinctive motion of resistance; but the soothing influences of digestion prevailed, and Lily felt the soft weight sink trustfully against her breast. . . . As she continued to hold it the weight increased, sinking deeper, and penetrating her with a strange sense of weakness, as though the child entered and became a part of herself" (315–16).

Yet Wharton's denial of the possibilities inherent in sisterhood leads her to resurrect the very differences that the scene questions. Nettie is, finally, too awed by her onetime benefactor to know how to help. Lily, despite her plight, is too accustomed to such awe to accept the hand of friendship. Alfred Kazin remarks that Wharton "could only love those who, like herself, had undergone a profound alienation [from her class] but were bound to [it by] native loyalties and taste."[43] Thus the charwoman Lily snubs proves to be worthy of it, for she is a blackmailer. Only Lily's willingness to buy the letters possessed by an immoral representative of the lower orders saves the reputation of (an immoral) member of her own circle. More important, Lily's entry into the ranks of the wage earners is colored by her creator's sense that it is a social desert with no one but "dull" and "colorless" (282) working girls whose economic deprivation is an emblem of their soullessness.

To the era's familiar animus against the unaesthetic life of laboring females, with their "exaggerated hair" (*House*, 282) and colloquial speech, Wharton joins a disdain reminiscent of Dorothy Richardson. Like the author of *The Long Day*, Wharton points to the vulgarity of those who cannot appreciate the lady in their midst. Rather than descend to their level, Lily, like Wharton, is offended by their "insatiable curiosity" (286) about the rich. Thus the fact that she becomes "an object of criticism and amusement to the other work-women" (284) is both vindication of her inability to do the work required and evidence of her superiority to those who can.

Despite her reduction of working women to mercenary or malicious drudges—and her willingness to make only partial exceptions to that rule, like Nettie Crane, who recognizes her betters but is, after all, a woman with a sexual past—Wharton recognized the fragility of women who were trained for no useful work. Although this recognition did not replace the elitist vision of interclass communication central to her colleagues' texts with a more egalitarian one, she illuminated the economic vulnerability of the lady class in a way no other cross-class writer did. In this she differed from Van Vorst, who linked Amanda's strength to her newfound class privilege. Still, both Wharton and Van Vorst, without rejecting gentrification ideology, suggested its limitations for worker and lady alike.

The second decade of the twentieth century dealt the deathblow to the fiction discussed in this chapter. Ladies continued to appear in working girl novels; even in the socialist writer Arthur Bullard's *Comrade Yetta* (1913), an imperious WTUL leader takes a working girl into her home. But in a period of "worker solidarity" fiction, elitist uplift was condemned and the redemptive power of lady bountifuls denied or restricted to financial contributions. Even woman's rights advocates not in tune with the new strike mood modified the cross-class plot, as in a 1910 novel by Charlotte Perkins Gilman, *What Diantha Did*. Gilman's undercover heroine takes a servant's job, but only secondarily to spread her influence among domestics. She is more interested in freeing women of her class from clubwomanship to enter the world of professional work. Though Diantha forms a girls' club and a servants' cooperative—as in a Scudder novel, the feminine upper class again shapes the lower—she uses the newly instructed coop members to liberate the lady, or at least the respectable matron, empowering the very women who once sponsored feminine philanthropy.

During its heyday the cross-class novel represented an alternative to the interclass scenario of shop girl and scoundrel found in male texts, from the antebellum George Lippard to the tenement writer Julian Ralph. What is more, on the rare occasions that turn-of-the-century men considered the female redeemer or the need for ties between the worker and the lady, it was with the conviction that upper-class women were ineffectual at best. In Harold Frederic's *The Lawton Girl* (1890), the pampered town heiress who expresses interest in the women employed at her father's iron mill loses it almost immediately, in distinct contrast to a male reformer who argues for economic justice for female as well as male factory hands. Owen Kildare, another novelist who pictured working-class life, included in his autobiography an anecdote about the wisdom of feminine cross-class separation. At the height of his fame, he attended a society party with Mamie, the real-life worker sweetheart he venerated. There she became the recipient of "illy veiled sneers and insults" from those Kildare satirically calls "her sisters." She demonstrated such restraint with those who looked at her as if she "were an escaped beast from the jungle" that, Kildare concludes, it is the self-reliant working girl who should be teaching manners to the lady, though she could spend a more pleasant time among the working classes.[44]

Centering their texts on female interactions across the class divide, women writers—one of whom, Edith Wharton, produced a lasting work of literature—challenged the antifeminism of the above descriptions. They translated the period concern with feminine social responsibility into plots marked by serious discussion of the undercover investigator, the club and settlement movement, and even the strike. If they acknowledged the gulf between the lady and working girl, they tried to bridge it as well, widening the focus of the debate on wage-earning women to encompass issues not explored by male writers. However haltingly, they questioned substandard conditions for women workers, envisioned a community of women inspired by the ideas of an upper-class benefactress, and enabled working women to spearhead strikes by male as well as female laborers. All of this is a far cry from the world of easily corrupted shop girls, their women friends either immoral or absent, of the male-generated tenement tale.

Women authors shared the cultural prejudices of their male predecessors, although they emphasized the working girl's social inferiority rather than her sexual availability. A low opinion of the female wage earner inspired tenement writers to weave stories that end in the moral guardianship of the neighborhood marriage or the fall into (unremunerative) prostitution; a parallel distrust informed women's texts. Their novels preach about a female underclass so prone to workplace temptations, militance, and vulgar conduct that uplifting rescue is for the few. When the heroine is not already a lady, disguised as a worker to gather data before returning to her accustomed sphere, she is an aspirant to gentility—either her female benefactor's protégée or her male employer's mate, or both. On the rare occasions she attempts a return to her class, she discovers its impossibility. Class-based disdain for working women affects the converse transformation as well. When a lady falls into the working class, there is little possibility that the experience can teach, much less ennoble her.

Despite attempts to document the conditions of industrial womanhood, these women writers could not shed the ideology of uplift. Nor could they imagine that, through her own efforts or those of her class, the female bread-winner could better her own life. As to true sisterhood, even Wharton, who came the closest to a vision of the "common bonds created by womanhood" (Reitano, 123), rejected it in the name of class distinction. In all the cross-class texts, as in the tenement tale, cultural bias colored the efforts to record the mores of the feminine workplace, reflected the controversy surrounding women and work, and restricted respect for the wage-earning woman. To the problem of rendering a representative working girl in a positive way O. Henry and, a far greater talent, Theodore Dreiser, followed by the strike novelists of the 1910s, now turned their attention.

Dulcie in her furnished room, drawn by Jay Hambidge, from O. Henry's "An Unfinished Story," published in *McClure's* (August 1905)
New York Public Library, Astor, Lenox, and Tilden Foundations

4

Defenders of Her Life:
O. Henry and Dreiser

I'll take my eight a week and hall bedroom.
                                        "The Trimmed Lamp" (1906)

Anything was good enough so long as it paid, say, five dollars a week
to begin with. . . . Things would go on . . . until Carrie would be
rewarded for coming and toiling in the city.
                                        Sister Carrie (1900)

WHEN WILLIAM SYDNEY PORTER—O. HENRY—WROTE "ELSIE IN NEW
York" (1905), one of over 20 tales of working womanhood he penned, mostly
for the *New York Sunday World*, that journal was only too pleased to have
him entertain its half-million readers with his characteristic blend of realism,
irony, and sentiment.[1] His literary stock has fallen, but in his time it was
thought he "breathed new life into the short story."[2] Even the redoubtable
Nation magazine called his style "[s]mart to the verge of genius." To this day,
his work remains in print, and few short-story writers have ever been more
popular with the American public.[3] Prolific, established, and well paid, he

was sought after not only by the *World*, then the largest paper in America (Current-Garcia, 38), but by the all-powerful *Saturday Evening Post*, which he took pleasure in turning down for their cavalier treatment of him in earlier days.[4] In the early 1900s, the same years that Theodore Dreiser's *Sister Carrie* (1900) was condemned and unread, O. Henry was lauded—and financially rewarded—for his pieces on the shop girls and boulevardiers, waitresses and brokers, typists and "swells" who comprised his New York "four million," the title of one of his successful story collections.[5]

In characteristic fashion, "Elsie in New York" centers on a questing protagonist whose surprise encounters and ironic reversals provide an object lesson in the vagaries of urban life. As a working girl tale, the story employs the "virtue tested" conventions central to the mass-market story of the lower-class woman. Yet this narrative of a fur cutter's orphaned daughter, who "start[s] out in the world to seek her fortune" (723) and rapidly ends up in the clutches of a designing businessman, has an unconventional element as well. In the controversy about the unfeminine working girl, Elsie's creator is squarely on the side of her defenders. He even argues that her so-called protectors only injure the working girl in the name of elevation. Critical of these self-appointed moral guardians, whether in literature or life, he casts a cold eye in his tale at a feminine philanthropy akin to that celebrated in the cross-class novel. In "Elsie" he takes particular aim at the female watchdogs of the era's protective associations, who saw the dangers of white-slave rings in every employment bureau and job advertisement. He satirically depicts those like Grace Dodge—who by the early 1900s had expanded her redemptive activities to found a society to aid working girls newly arrived in the city,[6]—as black-clad social meddlers from the "Association for the Prevention of Jobs" (723). In his scenario, these warped do-gooders work out their antipathies by dissuading impressionable girls from seeking work in the wicked city. "Beware of any one who offers a job" (723), warns one of these grotesques, frightening Elsie so thoroughly that she sees moral peril where she once saw legitimate job openings. No wonder she is fair game for the advances of a vulpine fur-shop owner who is last seen preparing to seduce her. Comments O. Henry acerbically, thanks to "Associations, and Societies," the working girl is "lost thus around us every day" (726).

The "darling of the Sunday-supplement reader" (Current-Garcia, 156), O. Henry successfully targeted a mass audience by marketing an increasingly familiar American type in plots whose clever use of coincidence both amused and surprised. As he had done with the cowboy and the con man, the Texan and the derelict, the lover and the aristocrat, he packaged the working girl so that her spirited response to the vicissitudes of urban life made a good story, and one that did not offend the public or the genteel censor.

In his working girl novels, O. Henry's contemporary Theodore Dreiser aimed for a similar, if more elevated, readership. Though he was knowledgeable about the mass market from his years as a reporter on big-city newspapers and an editor of the women's magazines *Ev'ry Month* and the *Delineator*, in their time *Sister Carrie* and *Jennie Gerhardt* (1911) never enjoyed the success accorded an O. Henry tale.[7] *Sister Carrie*, his first novel, was condemned for its "social feminine vagrant" and its focus on the "miserably low life of Chicago and New York"; it netted $68.40 in royalties.[8] Though the book won more critical approval when it was reissued seven years later, "even at that day," noted Dreiser ruefully, "the outraged protests far outnumbered the plaudits" (qtd. Lingeman, 464). By the time *Jennie Gerhardt* was published in 1911, his journalistic career was lucrative enough; but his second work of fiction, although praised by everyone from *Bookman* reviewers to H. L. Mencken, sold respectably at best.

Perhaps Dreiser erroneously assumed that the sympathy for the valiant shop worker or laundry girl that O. Henry's tales elicited would be felt for the same girl after she became a woman. In any event, *Sister Carrie* and *Jennie Gerhardt* daringly extended O. Henry's critique of the forces marshaled against the woman wage earner. O. Henry "hover[ed] on the outskirts of social commentary," "complet[ing] a picture" of the struggling labor heroine rather than condemning the deprivations that shaped her choices.[9] Dreiser, who elevated the working girl story into art, defended the moral compromises involved in her urban survival. Even more unsettling to period readers, he declared the purity of the woman who made them.

Their differences aside, these two champions of the working girl were rare enough before the strike fiction of the century's second decade; both also possessed what one student of Degas's portraits of laundresses called his "humanizing vision."[10] Departing from the moralism that informed even the most sympathetic contemporary fictions, O. Henry and Dreiser moved toward presenting the woman worker's struggles and aspirations from her point of view. They transformed her longings and desires—for finery, for excitement, for love, for security from want—from the emblems of her corruptibility into the symbols of her aspirations. If Dreiser transcended O. Henry in his understanding of the economic, social, and psychological forces that shaped the working heroine, they were united in the impulse to rebut her judges and uplifters, to comprehend rather than censure. To a certain extent, they challenged the stereotypes of the immoral workplace and the culpable or sanitized labor heroine that were perpetuated even by her supporters and were standard fare until the rise of the strike novel.

The fact that O. Henry and Dreiser cast the blue-collar woman as heroic for entering the world of work reveals their literary limitations as well as their strengths. Because they saw the female wage earner in gendered terms, they were unable either to imagine her response to her work as other than escapist or to politicize her resentment in organizing her peers in opposition to their employers. Nor, though both painted survivors rather than victims, could they locate woman's resilience in her workplace self rather than in her after-hours pleasure seeking. Nonetheless, they produced a more convincing treatment of her desires and aspirations, her values and opinions, than did any practitioner of the tenement tale or the cross-class novel. By the time *Jennie*

Gerhardt appeared—a year after O. Henry's death—the strike novel was widening the woman worker's possibilities for literary heroinism and political expression. Until then, however, few American writers were more effective in proclaiming her right to be.

O. Henry's descriptions of the working woman's privations and temptations have a sympathetic particularity that anticipates Progressive-era surveys like *Making Both Ends Meet: The Income and Outlay of New York Working Girls* (1911) by Sue Ainslie Clark and Edith Wyatt.[11] That work joined a wealth of other ones, including Clara E. Laughlin's on the urban "work-a-day girls" and Elizabeth Butler's on the shop women of industrial Pittsburgh, in offsetting charges about the low morals and flighty characters of working women by offering vignettes of those whose weekly wage could hardly cover room rent and food.[12] By quoting prototypical working girls who could not "live on hopes an' virtue" (Laughlin, 154), such surveyors offered the economic defense of the female moral lapse that would be the watchword of Progressive reform literature in the 1910s. Writing just before the period of Progressive fascination with ameliorating social conditions through detailed study, O. Henry was no crusader. But he brought a documentary specificity to the working girl's battle against circumstances rather than her capitulation to them; to her fear of sexual bartering ("An Unfinished Story" [1905]); to her dual sense of isolation and security ("The Skylight Room" [1905]); to her excitements (the Lower East Side Clover Leaf Social Club in "The Coming out of Maggie" [1904]); and to her joy of fellowship ("The Third Ingredient" [1909]).[13]

Adept at giving a piquancy to his tales of female seekers in pinched circumstances yearning for some pleasure, romance, or validation beyond their grasp, O. Henry was as sought after by the liberal monthlies *McClure's*, *Cosmopolitan*, and *Everybody's* as he was by the mass-circulation papers. *McClure's*, which published a number of his tales, was earning a particular reputation for exploration of urban economic problems, and "undercover" articles on women toilers by Maud Younger were part of its new agenda. Pieces by the *Everybody's* contributors Bessie and Marie Van Vorst and Rheta Childe Dorr on the factory girl were also part of the reform inquiry into the conditions of the immigrant and native-born poor. Even before the Progressive onslaught on social ills, such journals printed Harvey O'Higgins's lightly muckraking fiction on the overworked Irish servant or working girl mistreated by her alcoholic family and Myra Kelly's humorously sympathetic portraits of disadvantaged Jewish schoolchildren on the Lower East Side. Yet most stories, even in these periodicals, still favored "American girl" heroines, "female characters exemplifying the highest ideals of chastity . . . blue-eyed rectitude . . . [morally inspiring] feminine virtue" (Lingeman, 157–58), in romance plots that differed only in geographical locale. When it came to mass-market magazine fiction about the independent working girl cut loose from home ties or about the bourgeois guardianship of the family on whose table she waited, few but O. Henry turned their attention to the "independent feminine wage earner" ("The Ferry of Unfulfillment" [1903], 375). When such a heroine made one of her rare appearances, as in Emma Walton's 1903 *Everybody's* story "The Point of View," she was used to underscore the value of shedding a finery-obsessed worker's life for that of a respectable wife. The commentators of the day made a point of allying the working girl's desire for silks, beads, and ostrich-plumed hats with a propensity to flighty conduct if not to downright sin.

Walton's humorous tale of a seamstress about to marry in no way contradicts such prejudices. Despite its light tone, the story takes the familiar detractor's part in condemning the provocatively attired working girl whose identity the heroine presumably has left behind. It opens with an account of the prospective bride ruining her flashy clothes in an eager tour of her new house. When Walton's heroine is unruffled by having lost a glove and ruined her shoes, it is a harbinger of marital respectability, for it signals readers that this working girl has joyfully entered the domestic sphere and rejected unchaperoned evenings and gadabout dress.

In addition to "An Unfinished Story" (published in *McClure's*), a number of O. Henry's stories that appeared in the *Sunday World*—but could well have found their way into the more reform-minded *Everybody's*—take on the dress issue and reverse the condemnation of the working girl implicit in so many mass-market magazine stories. That Maida, the winsome glove-counter protagonist of "The Purple Dress" (1905), thinks constantly of clothing is "evidence of her perpetual longing for pretty things" (732), not the sign of an unregenerate nature. But it is more than that as well. For Maida dons the garb of self-display not, as the working girls' detractors feared, as one who promiscuously exchanges sexual for material favors, but as an urban hopeful on a quest for the marital grail. Nor in O. Henry is her search a mercenary one. Maida's is the innocent optimism of youth, and her aspiration to move the head clerk to a marriage proposal is the sign of that optimism. The privations she has endured, and the fact that she cannot own the purple dress if she is to pay her room rent, reveal her longings, not her mercenary connivances. She shares the Walton heroine's awe of wedlock, but nothing in her love of self-display precludes it.

His skill at dramatizing the struggle rather than the defeat of the common working girl, hungry for both food and city excitement, is evident in "An Unfinished Story," his famous examination of her meager wage, hall bedroom, and scanty diet. The clichéd plot concerns Dulcie, the young woman bedeviled by a $2.00 room rent and a $6.00 weekly wage, the 60¢ price of lunch and the $1.00 cost of dinner, who must choose between jam and crackers and a night on the town with one Piggy, who "hung about the shopping districts, and prowled around in department stores with his invitations to dinner" (689). The angle of vision is far more the girl's than the moralizer's. When, to reward herself for the week's end, Dulcie stops off to buy an imitation lace collar with her last 50¢, no social guardian reproaches her for her frivolity. As if castigating her critics, O. Henry asks, "[W]hat is life without pleasure?" (688).

He mounts a similar defense of her existence in a third-floor back room in a West Side brownstone. By the 1900s self-supporting working women not living with their families—a significant minority had come to the metropolis from rural locales—were ungraciously termed "women adrift" because they lodged or boarded outside of parental control. Fear of the promiscuous activities that might result from the lonely freedom of their rooming-house lives caused as much alarm as if women adrift were the majority, and discussions of "the lodger evil" and "the furnished room problem" abounded.[14] By 1910 over 168,000 women boarded or lodged in Manhattan, and O. Henry's heroines are definite members of this population.[15] They inhabit the kind of small drab room that, in the eyes of less friendly or more alarmed observers, would have at best earned the pity of those familiar with Jacob Riis's searing photographs of their garrets and at worst branded them as uncouth and even immoral, like Henrietta in Richardson's *The Long Day*. When Richardson, the incognito journalist who authored the book, visited Henrietta, her rowdy coworker, she came only to condemn.[16] Like many who projected their disapproval of the self-supporting woman onto her lodgings, Richardson saw only "squalor" (124) in the tasteless decorations and "cheap" (130) lithographs Henrietta had hung up to brighten her poverty. She evinced little surprise when, expressing the great fear of supporters and defenders alike, she revealed that this working girl received men in the place.

One of many such rooms observed in O. Henry's fiction—tiny skylight, cramped, poorly lit, poorly heated, and poorly furnished—Dulcie's little lodging in "An Unfinished Story" also sports the "violent oleograph" and "gilt china vase" (689) that offended Richardson and the ladies who "shop[ped] in carriages, and did not understand" ("Purple Dress," 732) the worker's tastes or her privations. Rather than being a pathetic or embarrassing reminder of caste or a locus of iniquity, the room asserts her right to be. It is a testament to her independence and survival skills and represents her small victory over anonymity as a department store girl indistinguishable from any other who "sold . . . edging, or stuffed peppers, or . . . trinkets" (688). The cluster of cherries Dulcie has tied with a pink ribbon marks not her limited aesthetic sense but her valiant pursuit of beauty in an unlovely environment. Her rice powder—risqué to a girls' club observer—is necessary for her self-respect. And the famous general in the print on her wall, whom she humorously offers jam and crackers when she decides against a strings-attached dinner date, is the guiding father she has erected as a bulwark against the city's pitfalls. Drawing strength from the little world she has created, Dulcie is the quintessential urban toiler, asking to make enough to keep her world intact, with a bit left over for a lunch of pineapple fritters or even a blue kimono.

To skirt the censors, the story does contain the warning that, like the eponymous Elsie, Dulcie and her kind are in danger should their wages be cut off. Also, the designing Piggy, his porcine unattractiveness reminiscent of the bloated final customer of Crane's fallen Maggie, is a reminder of the repellent quality of bartered sex. But those, such as Theodore Roosevelt, who were moved by Dulcie's financial plight might have been surprised at the subversiveness that O. Henry, who was fond of saying he "modeled Piggy on himself" (Stuart, 175), brought to Dulcie's story. On one level he was exorcising his guilt about his manipulative womanizing by projecting it onto the Piggy character. On a deeper level, he was divesting the shop girl's fall of its doomsday implications. For the whole piece has a matter-of-factness about female urban survival that both belies Dulcie's damnation and points to a way of seeing that few other writers, besides Theodore Dreiser, had the courage to embrace. Because the overriding feeling is admiration for Dulcie, the story implies that she would be much the same girl, indeed unchanged, were she to accept aid from a Piggy. In any case, the reader is left with respect for her, whether her next step is "false" or not.

Other O. Henry stories, featuring more savory men than Piggy, refute the many who condemned the working girl's receptiveness to the sexually fraught meetings endemic to the urban social scene—across a shop counter, in a park, on a ferry ride to Coney Island, at a dance hall. O. Henry rebutted the watchdogs of the Committee on Amusement of Working Girls, who feared the new arenas of "diversion, flirtations, and displays of style" where girls worked out their desire for escape from the work routine.[17] Observing these pleasure seekers, Hutchins Hapgood deplored the propensity to speak to strange men that made them "swashbucklers in petticoats" (Peiss, 131). But O. Henry's savvy heroines "will not settle for any two-bit masher" (Blansfield, 98). They negotiate the sexual dangers of the urban milieu by balancing self-protection with what O. Henry humorously terms the "drawing of a matrimonial prize" ("Trimmed Lamp" [1906], 828). There is little harm in the ambitions and hungers that fire their willingness to converse with strange—but affluent—men. They meet masculine attentions with a seasoned wariness, not, as in the tenement tale, a tarnished innocence. Thus Florence, the self-possessed, tenement-dwelling protagonist in "Brickdust Row" (1906), initially greets the "I love you" of a well-spoken excursion trip stranger with, "That's what they all say" (796). In "The Ferry of Unfulfillment," the "Girl from Seiber-Mason's" department store, "glancing up with capable coolness," fields a man dressed "in the best of clothes" with, "Ain't there any way to ever get rid of you mashers?" Only when he disarmingly responds to her taunt ("I'm not one of that kind") does she decide "it might be good to hear a little of what he had to say" (375).

O. Henry, it should be remembered, wrote for magazines and publishers that wooed a family audience and disavowed the frank treatment of sex. Lacking Dreiser's boldness, he colored the working girl's quest for experience accordingly. His heroines are willing to seek their romantic fortune in talk with unknown men but are prudent enough to fend off those with no matrimonial intentions. (Some, like the heroine of "A Lickpenny Lover" [1904],

even err on the side of prudence and pass up bona fide offers out of disbelief.)
Attuned to popular taste, O. Henry was not above using the pretested device
of the providential male rescue and injecting it with the coincidence that was
his hallmark. In "A Skylight Room," the stranger who comes to the typist
Elsie Leeson's aid is the very man she came to the city to seek. Nor did O.
Henry shun the dime-novel finale of the cloak model who maritally snares a
millionaire Texan, as in "The Buyer from Cactus City" (1900).

But all of his stories contain the sexual-political perception that, waiflike
or self-reliant, unattractive or compellingly pretty, working women must negotiate their interactions with men, must decide for themselves what the
possibilities are. For plain, 29-year-old Hetty Pepper in "The Third Ingredient," the future is a succession of hall bedrooms and the role of "Shoulder"
(31) for younger, more attractive women until they marry and leave the
Vallambrosa Rooming House. For the unattractive heroines of "The Brief
Debut of Tildy" and "The Coming out of Maggie," both published in the
World in 1904, it is basking in unexpected attention from men. For Nancy
in "The Trimmed Lamp" it is a sensible, working-class fiancé. Sounding the
rare tragic note, for poor Eloise Vashner of "The Furnished Room" (1904) it
is suicide; but counter to stereotype, she is driven to it by loneliness rather
than the remorse of the fallen woman.

What O. Henry remarked of his shop-girl portraits applies to all his
toiling heroines: "It is not the salesgirl *in* the department store who is worth
studying; it is the salesgirl *out* of it" (Stuart, 140). His remark is not totally
accurate, for he endows the banter of those like Maida and Grace ("The
Purple Dress") with a humorous understanding of the role of the workplace
in "creating a common identity."[18] Respect for their talk of clothes and diver-
sions, of impending bills and handsome men, is notably lacking in Richardson, who found only ignorance and maleducation in factory girls' chatter, and
Bessie Van Vorst, who remarked contemptuously, "[I]n all they say there is
not a word of value."[19] Nevertheless, O. Henry's remark about his portrayals
suggests the limits of his art, which merits the enduring reproach that his
characters are types, "described by representative traits rather than individual
qualities" (Blansfield, 87). He legitimizes the woman toiler only in her desire
for escape, her longing to enjoy the fruits of the city that extracted her youth.
His heroines do engage in a wide range of jobs, from the lowest paper-box
factory and restaurant work to the more desirable shop work to the stenogra-
phy and typing work that, given the opportunity, might help them ascend.
And by the sheer multiplicity of his stories, the working girls who people
them acquire a reality that even the marital denouements he resorts to do not
negate. Still, as in Jacob Riis and Marie Van Vorst, Julian Ralph and Edith
Wharton, O. Henry conveys no sense that the working woman could develop
a personal, much less a political, consciousness, discover or define herself
through her shared experiences, develop competence, resent ill treatment,
or decide to revolt.

Accepting the numberless young women who labored outside the home as a permanent presence in the commercial life of the city, O. Henry brought a new tolerance to the literary depiction of them. But like other imaginers, he shied away from their workplace existence to focus on their after-hours conduct. Unlike his contemporaries, he did not preach moral regulation, though, with the exception of "The Trimmed Lamp"—which climaxes with a passage on the kept woman's unhappy lot—he made sure his heroines do not forsake work for any but the marital path. O. Henry's toilers wish, prudently, "to be set in some home and heart; to be comforted, and to hide behind some strong arm and rest, rest" ("Ferry," 375). One purple dress satisfies their vanity, and they seek not sumptuous meals but the solid assurance that there will be food "during a cold, dull winter" ("Springtime à la Carte [1905]," 635). Whatever their discontent with their taxing employment, they recognize that their dreams are just that and pragmatically greet the prospect of the next day's work. Thus did O. Henry validate his heroines' yearning for life, finding in it no threat to middle-class morality. It was left to Dreiser to remove those limits and elevate yearning to art.

Sister Carrie begins in the Chicago of 1889, the city and time of Dreiser's own reluctant laboring at a succession of jobs akin to the factory work of his heroine. By 1900, when his book was published, Carrie's migration from village to metropolis had been undertaken by one-third of all urban working girls, those young, single women whose transit signaled hope for a "better thing [that] would eventuate" from "coming and toiling in the city" (15). In O. Henry that "better thing" is just as often the marginal independence of the wage earner who scrapes by. But in Dreiser's "modern Dick Whittington tale,"[20] Carrie Meeber rises to stage celebrity and, her morally rocky climb notwithstanding, validates the dreams of the feminine masses whose hopes extended that far but whose prospects did not.

Her introduction to the metropolis is hardly propitious. Unskilled, she can find employment only in a Chicago shoe factory, a "clacking, rattling" (36) place of the kind Dreiser periodically reported on in his journalistic pieces. There she encounters the female urban pragmatists who, in their self-protective savviness, anticipate the shop hands, waitresses, and lower-rung salesclerks of O. Henry's fiction. Prone to romantic chatter but reconciled to their lot, Carrie's coworkers attend the "balls of the Plasterers or Woodworkers Union" (55) and encourage or discourage flirtations according to their fancy.

In its naturalistic attention to what a genteel era considered seamy details, Dreiser's detailed rendering of the shoe-factory setting—the nervous pace, the spatial segregation by gender, the alienating sights, sounds, odors, and intermittent sexual harassment—surpasses the surface realism of O. Henry's allusions to the work floor and the shop counter. Nor is Dreiser content with giving us only details. He describes a certain adaptation to the imprisoning work world. Reminiscing years later about his sisters' response to their low-paying jobs in Chicago in the 1880s, he referred to their constant talk of "[c]lothes and men."[21] In this Carrie's workmates, like the Dreiser sisters, mirror laboring women for whom "it was easier . . . to repress complaints against the rigors of their jobs and to focus on the rites of courtship and the opportunities to socialize with their friends in the workroom."[22] Dreiser, more interested in Carrie's unhappy observation that her "idea of work had been so entirely different" (40), stops short of scrutinizing her coworkers. But he does record at some length these women's confidences, exchanged out of earshot of the suspicious foreman and under cover of surrounding noise. Such conversations reveal how they tailor their life goals to a weekly wage of $5.00 and the energy left over from their time spent in a workplace where "[n]ot the slightest provision had been made for [their] comfort" (39).

In "The Transmigration of the Sweatshop" (1898) and "Christmas in the Tenements" (1902) Dreiser humanizes the women whose lives too "often reduced [them] to the conditions of mere machines."[23] He does not moralize about Carrie's coworkers or about their real-life counterparts. Thus while opponents of the nondomestic woman deplored her desire for pleasure and her uplifters sought to replace her quest for pleasure with self-improvement, Dreiser pointed to the "problem of finding clothes and amusement on fifty cents a week" (Carrie, 55). His journalistic comments on "store girls, shop girls, girls who serve as servants the year through" ("Christmas," 151) apply to Carrie's underprivileged workmates as well. For them to crave diversion at a Bowery dance hall is not to sin but to "desire to obtain something of that which they see," of "that other world of show and beauty which is ever flashing before their straining eyes" ("Christmas," 152).

Dreiser was the first American novelist of stature to defend a working girl's yearnings for the "new consumer capitalism" of an increasingly city-oriented America.[24] In one important scene, Carrie enters a large department store to seek the kind of sales work alluded to in such O. Henry tales as "The Trimmed Lamp" and "The Ferry of Unfulfillment" and is distracted by the grandeur of the place. Rather charming in its naïveté, hers is a wide-eyed homage to its "remarkable displays of trinkets, dress goods, shoes, stationery, jewelry" (22). The full effect of such displays was so enhanced by the recent improvements in lighting and use of space that even jaded bourgeois matrons who could afford what Carrie could not found it a capitalist pleasure palace. Yet Dreiser makes it clear that her response, "touched with . . . desire" (22) for the beauty of metropolitan wares, embodies not the mercenary impulse of which shop girls were accused but the impulse of a culture that embraced the *grand magasin* and all the other "free-floating possibilities of a commodified world" (Bowlby, 61). Recognizing the lure of an economy that thrives on creating desire, he paints the landscape of materialism that lures Carrie and her sisters as one in which there is nothing that "she could not have used—nothing which she did not long to own" (22).

If, like her fellow toilers, nothing in his heroine's shoe-worker existence enables her to do more than yearn for the beauties of city life, she is no Dulcie, satisfied with a dance hall evening, a cheap lace collar, a good meal. In her imagining of urban joys, Carrie's "wild cerebrations . . . exhausted the markets of delight" (30). The contrast between her fantasies and the drabness of her life highlights the lure of an "urban scene . . . pulsating with an energy to which she can respond only by wanting."[25]

The adolescent Dreiser's resentment of manual labor caused him to be dismissed from five successive Chicago jobs[26] and no doubt shaped his approval of Carrie's rebellious dissatisfaction with shoe work, which she found "distasteful" and even "nauseating" (39). Part of Dreiser wanted to validate the longings of all hungry working women. "[T]hese people are human beings," he felt impelled to state in "The Factory" (177). Another part accepted Carrie's revulsion at her toughened and "common" (55) workmates, whose very tolerance of the noise and dirt, the spying of the foreman and the advances of the male coworkers, made them "clattering automatons" (36).

Much has been written on Dreiser's "inconsistent mechanism."[27] He was pulled between naturalism, which viewed men and women as being at the joint mercy of circumstance and instinct—Dreiser dubbed it "chemisms"—and social Darwinism, a vision of humanity in thrall to or triumphant over grinding social and economic forces. The conflict is evident in his portrayal of woman's work. Dreiser sees Carrie's coworkers as victims, on the one hand, of "material conditions" (39), and on the other, of their own lack of imagination. He alternately pities these drones whose "minds are apparently so hopelessly inadequate to the task of living well" ("Factory," 176) and focuses on Carrie, the triumphant exception. Like all of his protagonists, particularly his working-class ones, she "yearn[s] in a world of limits"[28] but brings to her economic problems a "mental rebellion" (55) absent in the mass of women workers. Further revealing his ambivalence about work and the feminine character, his fiction articulates what his journalism implies, that the blame for a mechanical life, one that Carrie finds "hard and low" (40), should be placed on the worker herself—thus his unflattering references to Carrie's fellow workers' mindless amusements, coarse, ungrammatical banter, and innate vulgarity and his insistence on her separateness from them. In a throwback to the tenement tale, he all but casts her as a princess among the serfs.

On one level, Dreiser bows to prevailing attitudes about the unfeminine workplace, a conviction that shapes his portrait of Jennie Gerhardt as well. He softens his criticism of the machine girls with the perception that, despite the spiritual starvation of their factory lives, they display woman's sympathetic nature; they coach the standoffish Carrie on how to improve productivity and how to fend off advances from fresh men. But like Julian Ralph and J. W. Sullivan before him, Dreiser deplores the constricted existence Carrie flees; the women left behind become part of his condemnation.

O. Henry would have applauded Dreiser's shoe-factory girls' informed wariness of track-crossing "gentlemen" ready with money and promises. For Dreiser, the typical woman worker lacked the vision or drive to reach for the "great, pleasing metropolis" (*Carrie*, 29) personified by affluent salesmen like the flashy Drouet, or like Carrie's second lover, the smooth-talking saloon manager Hurstwood. Dreiser takes the urban pragmatism of O. Henry's wage earners much further. It is the day after the jam and crackers and employment have run out, and the Dreiser heroine must survive. He divests her decision to live with Drouet, and later Hurstwood, of the dire quality of studies like Elizabeth Butler's *Women and the Trades*, her Pittsburgh survey of poor girls forced by ill pay to trade the house of commerce for one of prostitution. Nor does Carrie find in the generous Drouet what George Kibbee Turner's *McClure's* pieces on easily swayed Chicago shop and factory girls would have predicted: a "cadet" for a brothel who lures, ruins, and channels her there with terrifying efficiency.[29]

In a reversal of period fiction and the thinking that informed it, Carrie neither ends up broken by street prostitution nor endures the assorted punishments that moralists hoped would chasten working women tempted to sell their sexuality to lascivious men. One of her lovers supports her financially when she first engages in amateur acting. The other, though hardly the altruist in his desperate New York days, urges her to take up such work professionally, and she does so to great acclaim.

In presenting his heroine as a stage success, Dreiser, the younger brother of a songwriter who introduced him to the places where theater world and demimonde intersected, was aware of the reputation of acting as the work arena of the morally suspect woman. Yet, as David Graham Phillips did in his book *Susan Lenox: Her Fall and Rise* (written 1911; published 1917)— the story of a streetwalker who climbs to Broadway celebrity—Dreiser may have endowed Carrie with the qualities of the courtesan but he desexualizes her with references to her untarnished nature. "Her sexual allure is completely that of the archetypal Victorian heroine," writes Sheldon Grebstein, "comprised of innocence, purity and helplessness."[30] If references to these qualities dominate Dreiser's discussion of the postlapsarian Carrie, such idealizing affects his vision of her theater work as well. Her new vocational role is really a tribute to her longing for effortless fame rather than arduous perfecting of her craft. Even an early description of her theatrical ambitions suggests this: "Ah! to be rid of idleness and the drag of loneliness—to be doing and rising—to be admired, petted, raised to a state where all was applause" (177).

Unwilling to examine her as a worker at a trade more financially profitable than stamping out shoes and more emotionally profitable than living with Drouet or Hurstwood, Dreiser describes her as one removed from any association with work. In this he again resembles the tenement novelists, particularly Edward Townsend, whose *A Daughter of the Tenements* he scornfully reviewed in an 1896 issue of *Ev'ry Month*. Both Townsend's Carminella and Dreiser's Carrie achieve stardom easily, although Townsend barricades his heroine against charges of immorality with a guardian mother and an upwardly mobile suitor who weds her to ensure her respectability. Dreiser clearly diverges from that plot strategy, but to idealize his laboring heroine he too divests her theater climb of toil.

Despite its ambivalent attitude about woman's labor, *Sister Carrie* is a tribute to working womanhood. Its heroine is rewarded for "coming and toiling in the city," just as she had wished. She outwits those who wish to manipulate her, sheds economic dependency on lovers and exploitative employers, and escapes the ravages of conscience that destroy Crane's Maggie and countless other literary girls who go wrong. Dreiser certainly separates himself from sentimental rewarders of the working girl like Laura Jean Libbey; in the final chapters of *Sister Carrie*, his newly prosperous heroine is still searching, still yearning for happiness. Yet in the powerful scene toward the novel's end in which "Carrie Madenda," sitting in her plush suite with all the trappings of her new success, does not even recognize the nameless man stumbling in the snow outside as the broken, out-of-work Hurstwood, Dreiser reshapes the Libbey myth of feminine escape from poverty and seduction. Ironically, he does so not by denying that myth—his winsome heroine rises while her "seducer" falls—but by anchoring it in psychological truth. For here is Carrie, safe from the struggle of working girlhood. Both her prosperity and disinterest in the troubles of the poor—"We'll have to take the coach tonight," she responds to the "sight of someone falling down" outside (495)—are the measures of her survival.

Such scenes notwithstanding, *Sister Carrie* initiated a defense of the woman worker that explained away her moral compromises and removed her from the labor that necessitated them. A year after his first novel was published, Dreiser began *Jennie Gerhardt*, in which he continued to defend those compromises. Daunted by personal and professional difficulties stemming from the chilly reception of *Sister Carrie*, he did not complete it until 1910, when his discussion of Jennie's labor passivity, compared to the new fiction of female militance, was beginning to be dated. Again, his novel is set in the recent past, this time 1880, a period when, like the fictive Gerhardts, his family experienced the economic strain of their immigrant father's inability to support them forcing the women out to work. As in *Sister Carrie*, he argues that sweatshop-level work, not being a kept woman, strips a woman of her youth and dignity. This time his sexually unorthodox heroine possesses not unladylike ambition but the qualities of a blue-collar "angel of the hearth." Unlike Carrie, the simple, loving Jennie is no study in the "psychology of desire" (Lehan, 16). What she yearns for is the dual role of dutiful daughter and compassionate sister. That she takes work as a hotel cleaning woman and home laundress—and later as a domestic in a rich Cleveland home—does not negate her capacity for "exemplif[ying] feminine values."[31] "[T]he nature of children, the order of a home," comments Dreiser, "were . . . her province" (*Jennie*, 406).

Jennie's work scrubbing steps at a downtown Columbus hotel and doing the washing of a prominent guest there is, if anything, evidence of the compliant spirit associated with traditional womanliness rather than of a Carrie-like determination to better her prospects. Though the Gerhardt women are city dwellers seasoned enough to seek cleaning jobs outside the home, Jennie soon settles for taking in laundry work, a throwback to women's tasks in a preindustrial age. She does not think to seek permanent work as a hotel laundress, though women routinely held such full-time jobs in large urban centers, as Dreiser, a laundry-wagon driver attracted by the women he worked with in 1890s Chicago, well knew. Indeed, his very awareness of the public perception of these women may have prompted him to keep Jennie uninvolved with them.

One study of laundresses in nineteenth-century France argues that middle-class culture insisted on seeing such women "in exclusively sexual . . . terms," a feeling many Americans also harbored.[32] The fantasy, which bore some relation to reality, was that women who delivered men's garments to their rooms (the site of Jennie's own seduction by her employer, Senator Brander) worked in intense heat in semiclothed conditions, reinforced each other's need for alcohol to cope with their work, and were among the most immoral of the female working class. In 1905 Dorothy Richardson labored for a time in a New York laundry and gave a less racy description of American laundresses. But she alluded to their sexual availability and deplored their slovenliness, their love of drink, and, to her unsympathetic eyes, their work culture characterized by slang, shouting, and complaints.

Although he uses Jennie's laundry work as a symbol of the fate of many unskilled, impoverished women, Dreiser censors her involvement in it. He does not give Jennie's work even the few pages of description he allots to Carrie's shoe-factory labors. In lieu of a description of her work, her creator almost calls up the fantasy of the sexually available laundress. To soften the harsh truth that, to make a living wage, Jennie has only herself to sell, Dreiser emphasizes that she is "barren of the art of the coquette" (35). She does not "fully understand [Brander's] meaning" (37) when he proposes a liaison; though she accepts his proposal, she "enjoy[s] it all innocently" (43)—the second of Dreiser's chaste Chicago sinners.

Interestingly, even as Dreiser completed this early part of his novel, female militancy, though not a fixture on the organized labor landscape, was becoming more noticeable. As early as 1903, 35,000 women had marched in the Labor Day parade in Carrie Meeber's Chicago. By 1906 laundresses in San Francisco were rebelling against their notoriously low wages and the Shirtwaist Strike of 1909, the largest women's strike of the century's first decade, was not far off.[33] But Jennie, lacking even Carrie's limited curiosity about her work surroundings, is a study in complete isolation from the workplace, which at least fires Carrie with dissatisfaction with her job and companions. Working with her mother—which, in a book dedicated to reversing many sentimental assumptions, is no safeguard against the "corruptions" of work—Jennie desires only to replicate domestic duty outside the home.

Neither immoral nor militant nor materialistic, Jennie is "true womanhood" forced to wash dirty shirts and floors. In her beauty and loving kindness she is nature's noblewoman, the peer of any "lady in disguise" in works by Marie Van Vorst or Mary Wilkins Freeman. Indeed, if *Sister Carrie* parodies the damnation–or–male rescue formula of the tenement tale, *Jennie Ger-hardt* satirizes the fairy-tale plots of *Amanda of the Mill* and *The Portion of Labor*, in both of which a toiling protagonist, remarkable for her beauty and self-sacrifice, escapes wage work through friendship with a philanthropic female and marriage to a capitalist male. Jennie soon attracts the amatory attentions of an employer, but there is no magic wedding for this lower-class woman. Her first employer, Senator Brander, dies before learning of the impending birth of their illegitimate daughter. After the child is born, Jennie arouses the interest of another affluent man, the millionaire scion Lester Kane, whom she meets when working as a maid at the home of his wealthy friends. In a Dreiserian slap at Kane's late-Victorian hypocrisy, she is induced to live with him provided she pose as Mrs. Kane.

Obviously, Dreiser parts company with the Van Vorst school of fiction, which took a hard line on feminine sexual transgression. He sanctifies Jennie's love affairs in the name of womanly self-sacrifice. Just before the liaison with Kane, she reflects on her need to "make her family happy . . . [and to] give Vesta [her daughter] a good education" (159), linking such goals to a vague hope of marriage to him. Dreiser further champions her aspirations through criticizing the snobbery that prevents Kane from marrying her. Such class-bound thinking is personified by Lester's sister Louise. Typically, in a male author's vision of women's interclass relations, she is a spiteful snob who disdains Jennie for her lowly origins and prevents her from rising in the world. So does Lester himself, who bows to family pressure and eventually marries within his own class, leaving a characteristically unembittered Jennie to seek solace in the two orphan children she adopts.

Sentimental as this plotting is, it is a radical rejection of the oft-voiced prejudice that women's encounters with the work world made them uninterested in motherhood and prone to "refuse [its] responsibilities."[34] Still centered on a defense of her "pre-eminent femininity" (*Jennie*, 128), Dreiser concludes the novel by shifting the discussion from her sexual to her maternal conduct in the wake of Kane's departure and her daughter's death. Punished by his rejection and Vesta's passing—two reasons the novel was considered less controversial than his initial one—she atones through a nunlike dedication to caring for the young. Even without this atonement, however, Jennie is the "moral center" of the novel "in a way that Carrie is not" (Yglesias, viii). Yet the cost of defending so saintly an example of working womanhood also suggests Dreiser's ambivalence about the female work world from which he liberated her.

Apart from Dreiser and O. Henry, there were not many to defend the innate purity of the labor heroine who was seasoned at fending off the Piggys or initiated into sexuality by the Drouets. Another rare attempt was the brief portrait of a cannery worker, Lizzie Connolly, in Jack London's 1909 novel *Martin Eden*.[35] (His 1913 *Valley of the Moon* marries off the virtuous working girl and evades the issue.) The earlier London work was poorly received, for its pessimism displeased audiences used to the spiritedness of his Yukon and South Sea tales. Lizzie is one of the few characters in the work not imbued with philosophical gloom. Not one to wait for male notice, she vies for the affections of Martin, a working-class novelist who becomes increasingly remote as he achieves wealth and fame. His emotional energy is taken up first by Ruth, a society girl who scorns the lower orders, and later by a despondency about life's futility that leads to his suicide. Early in the narrative, still infatuated with the lady class, he responds to the "cannery girl" in the language that was second nature to her condemners. He feels only "spiritual nausea" at the seduction attempts of the "tawdry" Lizzie, with her "cheap ribbons" (87) and "bold black eyes" (88).

As in *Jennie Gerhardt*, harlot becomes saint. Deserted by his elite love interest, Martin, as will Lester Kane in his last days, recognizes the working woman's moral superiority. Lizzie confesses that she has "kept straight all these years" (476) but is willing to sacrifice her virtue—and even her life— for him. Her offer, with none of the financial strings that attach to the sexual trading of both Dreiser heroines, elevates her above the status-minded Ruth in much the same way that Jennie's renunciation of Lester proves her superiority to the money-loving Louise Kane. But London's portrait of a Magdalen manqué, although a slap at the lady bountiful novelists, highlights the boldness of Dreiser's chaste working-class sinner. For shorn of its sacrificial drapery, Lizzie's is a willing sexuality that confirms period prejudices about the immoral working girl. In portraying Carrie and Jennie, Dreiser, on the other hand, carefully associates them with an innocence impossible to apply to London's "passionate and inviting" (85) woman of the people.

Despite this difference, London joins Dreiser, O. Henry, and their colleagues in tenement and cross-class fiction by locating working womanhood in a sexual arena. Significantly, the radical journalist Mary Heaton Vorse prefigures a different kind of attention in "Experiences of a Hired Girl" (1901), finished the year after *Sister Carrie* but never published.[36] Nora, an Irish immigrant, tells of her servant's life in a semiliterate manner guaranteed to alienate even liberal magazines like *Everybody's* and *McClure's*, to which Vorse, like O. Henry and Dreiser the journalist, usually contributed. A labor sympathizer and, later, an organizer of one ILGWU precursor, the Amalgamated Clothing Workers of America, Vorse produced light romances to support herself while she covered events like the 1912 Lawrence textile mill strike. Just as she contrasted with O. Henry and Dreiser in her activist reportage, her Nora is a vocal antithesis to their heroines. Like Jennie, she belongs to the 1900s' largest category of women wage earners—domestic servant, numbering almost one-third by contemporary estimates.[37] Totally work-centered, Nora, unlike Jennie, has no trust in the employer class to which she is in thrall. She reflects on the rigors of her life to inform "Mrs. Drake" about them. (The story is cast in epistolary form.) A spokeswoman for all maids, she voices her opinions about the "ladies" and "gentlemen" for whom they toil, employers who are emotionally distant and ruthlessly exacting about household detail. Although she is too harried by the demands of her tasks to envision collective action, given Vorse's labor agenda, Nora's very dependence on her employers' whims demonstrates its need. In short, as a literary working girl, she is—in marked contrast to Dulcie and Carrie, Elsie and Jennie—someone new.

O. Henry and Dreiser challenged prevailing attitudes about the morally tempted woman wage earner by writing fictions that legitimized her longings for the products, excitements, and money-purchased security of the consumer culture she toiled to serve. Recognizing her struggle for a fair wage and a hall bedroom, the two men asserted her right to an existence on her own terms, without redemption or apology. They chose neither to assimilate their working girls into workplace culture nor to inspire them to sisterly solidarity, political action that would soon inspire Arthur Bullard, James Oppenheim, and Theresa Malkiel. O. Henry, unsympathetic to trade unionism, satirizes the strikers who prevent his beleaguered Elsie from securing New York employment. Still in his presocialist phase, Dreiser termed a garment strike manifesto a "queer circular" (Pizer, 399) and painted Hurstwood sympathetically for taking a scab's job during an 1895 streetcar strike modeled on a violent Brooklyn one that raged the same year.

Dreiser's working girl defense centered on exculpating his "fallen" heroines; O. Henry's milder one was based on the premise that their social lives were no threat to middle-class morality. O. Henry lacked the profundity to endow a worker heroine with interiority, much less the consciousness of economic injustice or the need for collective action. Alive to those issues, Dreiser nonetheless sought refuge in a protective mentality that removed the exceptional working girl from degrading toil rather than envisioned her workplace as the site of personal change. Much like the tenement and cross-class novelists, his fiction, though it was the apex of a pyramid whose base consisted of those routine works, was divided between compassion and condescension, between locating his heroines at work and rescuing them from its influence.

Although they did not transcend the debate on the working girl's character, O. Henry and Dreiser posed a far more significant challenge to late-Victorian orthodoxies than did their colleagues or predecessors. Reversing literary formula, they refused to cast the working girl's vulnerability as ripeness for corruption—or uplift. O. Henry embraced plots of manly rescue, but not exclusively. As many of his heroines remained behind the counter as exited the shop with fiancés. Dreiser also used the providential male but found him flawed and finally inessential. His working girls, alone but not adrift, anchor themselves. Both men inaugurated the movement from sympathy to admiration, from validation to empowerment, that fiction in the "decade of strikes"[38] would, with some success, take farther.

Illustration from "A Meeting of the Girl Strikers" by W. T. Banda, published in
McClure's (November 1910) just before the end of the Shirtwaist Strike
New York Public Library, Astor, Lenox, and Tilden Foundations

5

Comrades or Helpmeets?: Female Militance in Strike Decade Fiction

I won't shut up. . . . We ought to strike.

Comrade Yetta (1913)

I'm a fool—nothing but a woman—I'll never be Joan of the Mills anymore.

Pay Envelopes (1911)

IN 1906, 16-YEAR-OLD BRONX-BORN ELIZABETH GURLEY FLYNN, WELL acquainted with urban poverty and the left-wing socialism she was convinced would eradicate it, joined the newly formed Industrial Workers of the World (IWW).[1] She hailed it as "a militant, fighting, working-class union."[2] As she recalled in her autobiography *The Rebel Girl*, the IWW met her need for a secular religion to aid the masses and empowered her as a public speaker. Soon, under IWW auspices, she was traveling across the country to study factory conditions, organize local strikes, and serve as delegate to the national convention held in 1907 in the city of Dreiser's nonmilitant heroines, Chicago.

Already an accomplished orator, Flynn inaugurated her activist career with a series of New York speeches and a speedy arrest for blocking traffic with her agitational eloquence. Soon after the arrest, her militance—and precociousness—prompted Theodore Dreiser, then an editor of *Broadway* magazine in search of "any personality that makes a stir in the city," to interview her for a biographical piece.[3] He entitled the article "An East Side Joan of Arc" and praised her "ardent" socialism (Flynn, 65), although, as in his other journalistic pieces on famous women, he focused more on the singularity of her career choice than on her political agenda. Whatever his true attitude, the emerging female activism Flynn represented would be as absent from *Jennie Gerhardt* as it was from *Sister Carrie*.

Even as Dreiser completed his paean to the private stoicism of the laundress Jennie, across the country laboring women's public unrest revealed that Flynn's brand of activism was becoming more commonplace than Dreiser's writings implied. Between 1905 and 1915, 100,000 women in the clothing factories of Chicago and New York joined workers in Philadelphia, Rochester, and Cleveland and walked off their jobs. San Francisco tobacco strippers, Chicago telephone operators, Aurora, Illinois, corset-makers, Roxbury, Massachusetts, carpet weavers, and Troy, New York, collar starchers all agitated for improved working conditions.[4]

In the New York City Shirtwaist Strike of 1909–10, the largest women's strike up to that time, over 70 percent of the strikers, or 20,000 women, boycotted their work for an unprecedented 13 weeks. As with the less spectacular women's strikes of the day, the "Uprising of the 20,000" produced limited employer concessions. Many strikers, still out when it was declared over, found it an incomplete victory; between 1,000 and 3,000 women and men went back to work with no gains at all.[5] Nevertheless, because easily one-quarter of the nation's women wage earners were in the garment and textile industries by the time of the uprising, the strike was immensely important.[6] It signaled that young, largely immigrant women could not only take on an oppressive sweatshop system but also rebel against male unionists like Samuel Gompers, the powerful head of the American Federation of Labor (AFL). Before the uprising, Gompers considered women neither "organizable [n]or dependable" (Flynn, 56); afterward, he grudgingly revised his opinion. Thanks to the newly militant female rank and file, the International Ladies' Garment Workers' Union (ILGWU), though it continued to deny women top leadership positions, was transformed from a craft association into a modern union.[7]

Offered minimal support by male colleagues but solid help from the Women's Trade Union League, denounced by the commercial press yet applauded by the more liberal journals, the garment-trade women of New York City, depending on the observer, embodied the menace or the vitality, the unnaturalness or the heroism, of feminine working-class protest. Some Americans were no doubt more offended than moved by the well-publicized mass meetings, parades, and antiscab stratagems of the "Great Uprising." But in the public mind it was that strike, in the words of an article on the ILGWU organizer Clara Lemlich in *Collier's* (one of the few mainstream journals to commend the event), that transformed many a "Ghetto coquette" into an "orator."[8] As the era's plentiful fiction on the type attested, the familiar controversy over the "unwomanly" female wage earner had taken on a new urgency.

From 1900 onward the growing AFL, the emerging Socialist party, and the resultant struggle to upgrade wages, hours, and safety conditions in the masculine workplace focused more attention on the male trade unionist than on his unskilled feminine counterpart. Still, Americans were increasingly aware that more women wage earners were engaged in or spearheading strikes than at any time in American history. The public met the new feminine militance with an apprehensive curiosity, mixed at times with sympathy when roused by headlines about police clubbing women strikers. Whether the activist was Flynn, the Shirtwaist Strike fomenter Clara Lemlich, the onetime cap-maker and dedicated garment-union organizer Rose Schneiderman, the former machinist and Socialist party candidate Kate Richards O'Hare, the working-class "soul" (Tax, 97) of the interclass Women's Trade Union League Leonora O'Reilly, or the host of unsung labor Joan of Arcs who emerged during the prewar period, even writers aiming at the bestseller lists were turning to a new kind of working girl. Commercial presses published widely reviewed novels on the female trade unionist. For the most part, they were received as "social documents of value as well as striking art," tales of "vividness and convincing truth."[9] Often inspired by and favorable to the New York Shirtwaist Strike, such novels included Arthur Bullard's *Comrade Yetta* (1913) and, its title a reference to the populous poor, James Oppenheim's *The Nine-Tenths* (1911).[10]

The era saw, and novels recorded, other famous examples of woman's labor protest. One notable example was the Lawrence textile strike of 1912, in which 25,000 Massachusetts men, women, and children participated. Encouraged by IWW votaries Flynn and "Big Bill" Haywood, who ran special meetings empowering them to stand up to husbands and male workers opposed to their participation, women served on strike committees, discussed tactics, took over the picket lines, and stayed in jail rather than pay the fines.[11] When the mill owners capitulated to the protesters, the IWW journal *Industrial Worker* singled out women strikers and strikers' wives for their instrumental role. Grandly remarked Haywood, "[T]he women won the strike."[12] Given the widespread opinion that women should not strike, a backlash was inevitable. Lawrence became the subject of a widely discussed 1916 novel by the American author Winston Churchill. Ironically, though his book was lauded for its verisimilitude, his anger at the event itself and women's role in it prompted him to revise history by downplaying their participation. Popular female writers such as Margaret Deland and Zona Gale, though not as adulatory as a Bullard or as censorious as a Churchill, were also quick to include episodes of womanly militance in their fiction, which updated the cross-class feminine novel of the previous decade. Like their male colleagues, they too chose sides in the new controversy about the "unwomanly" striker.

As the debate on the character of women workers was modernized to include the burgeoning phenomenon of the feminine mass strike, laboring women found that they were agitating on more than one front. The Shirtwaist Strike leaders Lemlich and Yetta Ruth, who jointly inspired the novelistic portrait of Bullard's Comrade Yetta, endured picket line harassment, arrests of dubious legality, and brutal prison treatment to protest conditions for garment-trade women. As badly as male workers were treated—as late as 1914 the majority of wage-earning men, both in and out of the clothing trades, did not earn a living wage—women experienced exploitation of far more harshness.[13] Punished or fined for the slightest infraction, they were turned away if five minutes late to work, charged for the electricity that ran their machines, made to pay for breaking a needle, and timed when they left to go to the toilet. Paid much less than men for similar work, at constant risk of sexual harassment, they suffered repeated indignities.

There were other ways in which they were embattled. They had to combat the charge, leveled by everyone from pillars of society to IWW members, presiding judges to trade union ideologues, that to unionize, in the words of an AFL official, "defeminize[d] and unsex[ed]" them.[14] Echoing the separate-sphere apologists, pin-money theorists, and those who accused women of stealing men's jobs, most of the unions in the AFL prohibited women members. The anxieties about competition that fostered such attitudes were only exacerbated by women's new assertiveness. Many working men responded by viewing women in the "accepted bourgeois framework" and "falling back on arguments about women's natural behavior and the sanctity of the home."[15] As late as 1914 the AFL annual convention almost passed a resolution against the participation of women in the paid work force, despite paying lip service to its female representation and the presence of a tiny number of AFL organizers, such as Mary Kenney and Annie Fitzgerald. Between 1910 and 1920, of the 450 delegates elected by the New York City ILGWU, the union of the Shirtwaist Strikers themselves, "only 25 were women" (Basch, 48). Union membership was never high among working-class women; an estimated 74,000 belonged in 1910. Although many of them were "alienated by male hostility" (Foner 1964, 225), the new female firebrands and their supporters countered the charges of antifeminine conduct in a variety of ways. The very existence of the WTUL, a Chicago- and New York–based alliance of affluent and working women, heralded a new confidence in female union building. Alice Henry, who edited the WTUL paper, *Life and Labor*, between 1910 and 1915, urged the proliferation of all-woman locals so that the female rank and file could receive "the splendid training that is conferred when persons . . . work together for a common end."[16]

Those who urged the working woman to organize had great faith in their personal ability to move the female laboring masses. The IWW warrior Flynn, for instance, responded to her Wobbly husband's expectation that she relinquish a "man's job" for motherhood with a refusal to be consigned to the hearth. "I knew," she candidly explained, "I could make more of a contribution to the labor movement than he could" (Tax, 152).

Flynn was alluding to her talents, not her gender, but others relied on the argument that, as a chronicler of the Shirtwaist Strike, Helen Marot, remarked, "women make the best strikers" (qtd. Baxandall, Gordon, and Reverby, 190). Marot compared striking to child-rearing and acting as a domestic "rock of Gibraltar" and shrewdly employed the rhetoric of femininity as proof of her contention. The same "self-surrender to a cause, emotional endurance, fearlessness and entire willingness to face danger and suffering" (192–93) made the "spirit of martyrdom" (192) as natural to the 600 woman strikers arrested for picketing as it did to domestic womanhood. Yet perhaps the most common argument was that, as even Gompers, faced with the fact of the Shirtwaist Strike, reluctantly averred, women with little or no trade union experience were agitating for the 52-hour week, an end to forced night work, and equal pay for all women who did the same kind of work (Comstock, 20). Not all women's grievances were honored by manufacturers. The era's greatest female labor tragedy, the Triangle Shirtwaist Factory fire of 1911, in which 146 workers, mostly women, perished, would not have occurred had employers moved to correct the safety hazards of which strikers had warned. Nevertheless, despite the mixed results of their new activism, the movement to jettison Victorian attitudes toward women's labor—and their labor protest—was under way.

By its very choice, whether veiled or outright, of the most publicized working girl protests of the day, fiction helped initiate a new phase in the old debate. In the 1880s and 1890s, as part of the rise of the economic novel with its heightened attention to social problems, strike fiction had studied masculine labor discontent with a "dawning sympathy for the working man's demands."[17] Though still fearful of organized labor, many novelists "began to see a connection between . . . the angry [male] worker and his alienating, uncreative work" (Blake, 56). But because the female activist did not play in this fiction even the modest part she played historically, she provided no model for the next century's strike novelists. Whether referring to or interweaving the events of notable strikes, the new novelists claimed an authenticity hitherto absent in all but a handful of past works—from the rare anti–Lowell mill novel through the respective New England and southern factory tales of Mary Wilkins Freeman and Marie Van Vorst, all works that displayed only a sketchy understanding of the factory scene.

Furthermore, the new female strike novelists responded to the fact of womanly militance rather than to the recent creations of Crane and Dreiser, O. Henry and Edith Wharton. They broke with the tradition of the apolitical working girl, despite a lingering romantic preference for the unusual or exceptional heroine. But now, as Flynn said of Emma Goldman, it was "agitational vibrance" (50) rather than her beauty or refinement that distinguished the labor heroine; in works less friendly to a Flynn or a Goldman, her transient fascination with the new militance characterized the heroine. Another subgenre linked to the theme of feminine labor, the Progressive novel of white slavery, updated the formula of the workplace innocent at sexual risk. But even that form disavowed a connection to previous "wicked city" fiction by a muckraking claim to absolute truth, buttressed by statistics on brothel wages and conditions and, in one best-seller, an appendix containing a grand jury report on the white-slave traffic.[18]

From Arthur Bullard to Zona Gale, the very acknowledgment of the female labor firebrand involved an altered attitude toward woman's manual labor. Proclaiming their right to strike, these fictive Clara Lemlichs were obviously proclaiming their right to work as well. In virtually all of the strike decade's fiction of feminine militance, however, there was a counterimpulse as well. In the more radical writers, it turned the female comrade into the helpmeet; relegated her to secondary status within the union or the Socialist party, and marriage to a fellow activist. More conservative fiction, whether by male foes or by women who doubted trade unionism, extended domestic ideology to the activist sphere, minimizing or trivializing Flynn's rebel-girl militance. In contrast to their predecessors, the authors of the new strike fiction did reverse sexual stereotypes. But mired in the working girl controversy, they were at odds with feminine equality in the workplace, the union hall, and the home.

Women had risen up, if sporadically and in small numbers, from antebellum times, sometimes in tandem with men. Female operatives joined male mechanics to strike for the 10-hour day in New England in the 1840s and 1850s. Both sexes agitated during the New York City cap-makers' revolt of 1874. So too in the Great Uprising of 1877—in the first nationwide strike in American history, midwestern women cigar-makers and store clerks struck in sympathy with railroad men. In the late 1830s in textile-producing Lowell, Massachusetts, the 1860s in the shoe town of Lynn, Massachusetts, and in the New Jersey factory towns of Paterson, Passaic, and New Brunswick in 1874, women marched alone. Despite discouragement from union leaders during the rise of the AFL in the 1890s, women formed short-lived protective associations, local assemblies, working women's associations, and, as early as 1870, the first national union of women workers, the Daughters of St. Crispin. By the 1880s several hundred of those whom the *Chicago Tribune*, with its readers' concurrence, had dubbed "shouting Amazons" (Foner 1964, 194) were agitating in Chicago for the eight-hour day. By the 1890s they were entering the burgeoning, pre-ILGWU United Garment Workers (though not in leadership roles). Finally, in 1900, they laid the groundwork for the Women's Trade Union League, the first national body dedicated to organizing women workers, and for their truly mass strikes in the new century's second decade.[19]

Although women had accumulated a history of protest, until the 1910s strike fiction did not recognize it. Only fiction of the labor press, such as W. H. Little's *Our Sealskin and Shoddy* (1888), which includes a strike by a fledgling "Sewing Girls' Protective Association," even acknowledged the existence of such organizations.[20] The book was first serialized in a journal published by the Knights of Labor, the first national union and one with over 50,000 women members and 113 all-woman locals at its height in 1886.[21] But the novel's attitude mirrored that of the Knights themselves, who, though they urged women to organize against exploitation, envisioned their role in the movement as "one not directly dependent upon their status in the labor market" but as one filled by the "housekeeping wives of laboring men."[22] *Our Sealskin and Shoddy*, like many early strike novels, falls back on a denouement of employers being receptive to workers' grievances. It thus resolves the contradictions between working and home-loving female Knights by denying women's centrality in their own battles.

The novel centers on the employer-heiress Mamie Symington, who, disguised as the worker Betty Broadbird, is the one who actually masterminds the protest—with help from a patrician mill manager who decides on the girls' grievances. The talk of union is thoroughly defused, and the girls are freed to redirect their energies to marriage. Other Knights of Labor novels give women even less latitude. Women are either on the organized labor sidelines (*Breaking the Chains* by T. Futton Gantt [1883–84] or "heroine[s] of the washtub" perfecting the homebound role of the "lady Knight" (Frederick Whittaker's *Larry Locke: Man of Iron* [1887]).[23]

Fiction with a wide middle-class appeal, most of it antilabor, took greater steps to sever the connection between women and strikes. John Hay's *The Breadwinners* (1883), inspired by the Great Uprising of 1877, omits any mention of the part played by female strikers, or even of what one newspaper deplored as the "very active part taken by the women, who are wives and mothers" (qtd. Foner 1964, 173).[24] They taunted the military sent in to quell the protests in places as far apart as Ohio and West Virginia, but in Hay's version, "Every woman went for her husband and told him to pack up and go home" (Hay, 241). Relatives of would-be mill strikers in Rev. Beverly Warner's *Troubled Waters* (1885) stave off a similar disaster by reminders of the "misery, starvation, [and] uselessness of past strikes."[25] The seamstress-with-a-past at the center of Harold Frederic's *The Lawton Girl* (1890) shares this sentiment. Distressed at a factory uprising, pictured as the eruption of an irrational mob, she disavows her class allegiance and risks her life to warn the owners. Even when, as in Francis Hopkinson Smith's *Tom Grogan*

(1895), the Herculean heroine is sought out by a male union, she rejects it as corrupt. It is men, not the otherwise feisty ghetto women, who strike in the sweatshop tales of Abraham Cahan, as well as in Edward King's *Joseph Zalmonah* (1893), an account of the Jewish attempt to found a New York City cloak-maker's union. In King's book, women feebly assent to men's protest plans. Contrary to actual events, they are no more than human scenery in the battle to found the United Garment Workers. The one woman who is politically effective, an affluent theatrical wife with designs on Zalmonah, is as much siren as socialist. Killed off—then considered literary justice for the adulteress—she supplies further evidence that nineteenth-century American fiction found womanly militance morally unacceptable.

By the early 1900s muckraking exposés of the underside of big business by Charles Edward Russell, reporter-novelist David Graham Phillips, and that scourge of the Standard Oil Company, Ida Tarbell (who also praised the womanly solidarity of the Shirtwaist Strike), helped create a climate receptive to fiction on workers' rights. The socialist Isaac Kahn Friedman found a publisher for *By Bread Alone* (1901), his novel of the Chicago Amalgamated Steel Workers' Union uprising, in the forward-looking McClure's Company. Upton Sinclair's novel on the meatpacking industry, *The Jungle* (1906), inspired by the Chicago stockyards strike of 1904, was published under the solid Macmillan aegis.

Both strike novels found a broad audience that, if it did not applaud the strike argument, bought the books expressing that view. It is all the more significant that, in Friedman's novel, the steel-town heroine wants to escape her limited existence, not aid her male relatives' attempts to shut down the mill. A similar inattention to women's workplace agitation characterizes Sinclair's succès de scandale. Sinclair glosses over the fact that women, who accounted for over 10 percent of meat workers and had their own local, supported male strikers.[26] Sinclair's Jurgis Rudkis, who moves from slave to scab to strikebreaker, finds that, through a socialist dedication to working collectively toward a new economic order, he can "be a man" (Blake, 72). In thrall to a literary tradition that erased female labor activity, Sinclair denies this enlightenment to Jurgis's wife Ona. Though also an oppressed stockyard worker, she is cast as incapable of political awareness. Jurgis finds the political light; she falls victim to employer seduction and remorseful death and is the vehicle for the stereotyped message such well-worn plot devices represented.

Even at the height of the next decade's muckraking fervor, in the few Progressive-era novels that mention women's strikes—Reginald Wright Kauffman's best-seller about "the social evil," *The House of Bondage* (1910) is the most important—women are similarly powerless to ward off the seducer. By the 1910s he is no longer an uptown rake or a lustful boss, but the "cadet" of a sinister vice organization whose tentacles reach into the Lower East Side and the country village alike. Regardless of the seducer's new guise, in Kauffman's vision his wiles are far more attractive to the Lithuanian garment worker Carrie Berkowicz than the 1909 Shirtwaist Strike, in which she is briefly involved. Given that even muckrakers like Kauffman associated labor protest with anarchic male activity, it is not surprising he had difficulty taking Carrie's commitment seriously.

If early socialists were too caught up with masculine grievances—and white-slave novelists with their idée fixe—to envision feminine protest, there were works in which heroines received a quick political education that enabled them to resist the enticements of the pimp or the threats of the subcontractor. Unfortunately, the most outspoken novel of the strike, *The Diary of a Shirtwaist Striker* (1910) by the onetime sweatshop worker Theresa Malkiel—told in the first person from a striker's point of view—was published only through the socialist press and read by few not allied to the movement. Omitted from Walter Rideout's fairly inclusive *The Radical Novel in the United States* (1956), it sank to an obscurity from which labor scholars have just rescued it.[27]

Malkiel was a dedicated socialist whose marriage to a radical lawyer did not lessen her efforts at reform. Had her *Diary*, "dedicated to the nameless heroines of [the] Shirtwaist Strike," been noticed in its day, it is interesting to speculate on its possible influence. For the heroine, Mary, not only scoffs at the charge that "it ain't lady-like to go on strike" (*Diary*, 95), but she walks on countless picket lines, brawls with the police, and does a workhouse stint, all standard in Shirtwaist Strike fare by male authors. In a departure from their treatments of grass-roots women's strikes, Malkiel also has her spokeswoman convert a paternalistic fiancé, an artisan distrustful of "foreign" strikers, to the cause.

Choosing a nonimmigrant protagonist to suggest that the strike is American rather than merely Jewish or Italian, Malkiel infuses Mary with a growing consciousness of solidarity with women of her class. This new awareness is formed in opposition to a number of male figures: Mary's employer, her initially disapproving father and fiancé, and the socialist men who discourage women from fighting back. Attending a fund-raising meeting with Lemlich, Mary strengthens her oppositional identity through a realization of the limits of cross-class sisterhood. No grateful would-be "lady" of the Freeman and Van Vorst type, she rages: "The way [those rich women] directed their opera glasses at us!" (*Diary*, 119). Over the three-month period of the strike she "undergoes a process of moral and political apprenticeship, reappraisal, and change" (Basch, 64). She learns to "to bury . . . personal feelings when the welfare of the other girls is at stake" (*Diary*, 200). Nor does her newfound spirit of "hail to us girls" (210) prevent emotional fulfillment. She will marry her Jim the day the strike is officially settled, remain at work, and espouse her newfound theories as well.

Malkiel's vision of the Uprising of the 20,000 was uncompromising in its certainty that women must neither trade marriage for the struggle nor relinquish their trade union membership or leadership roles. Ironically, the popular press at the end of the decade published only novels by socialist women who shared Malkiel's approach—to the Triangle Factory fire and women's subsequent organizing activities in the garment trades. By then, public interest in women's strikes had cooled. Furthermore, Zoe Beckley's *A Chance to Live* (1918), whose heroine vacillates between organizing and renouncing strike activity, more properly belongs to the postwar cadre of works on woman's new individualism, to be treated in the next chapter.

More typical of superficially radical but commercially viable treatments of the working girl's bildungsroman were those by male authors, like Arthur Bullard's *Comrade Yetta*. In the years prior to its 1913 publication, Bullard edited the socialist daily, the *New York Call*, which serialized Malkiel's *Diary* a few months after the strike was settled. During the strike the paper printed special editions to raise funds for the out-of-work shirtwaist-makers and pay homage to leaders like Clara Lemlich. At a time when only the police beatings of girl strikers gained public sympathy for female protesters, the *Call* praised Lemlich, then 18, as the "frail little girl with flashing black eyes" who stood up at a Cooper Union meeting on 22 November 1909 and successfully moved for a general strike.[28] The way in which Bullard empowers his heroine by playing on associations with Lemlich, only to abandon the similarity as she moves from sweatshop worker to socialist journalist to wife, reveals much about his attempt to reconcile the female firebrand's right to political action with what he believed was her antithetical destiny as a woman. For all his belief in women as labor comrades, Bullard exemplifies the Victorianism of the few prostrike novelists whose work was accessible to the average reader.

Early in *Comrade Yetta*, Yetta Rayefsky, an orphaned Jewish immigrant unused to questioning her treadmill existence as a Lower East Side vestmaker and boarder with relatives whose greed is exacerbated by poverty, finds enlightenment. Bullard's handling of the scene marks a rejection of the seduction thinking pervasive in treatments of the female naïf from the tenement tale through the white-slave novel. Yetta, who "had never heard the life of the working class discussed before" (78), goes to a skirt-finishers' ball, unaware that it is a strike meeting as well. As a series of WTUL, socialist, and garment union speakers illuminate the oppression of her life, including her misperception that because she is a "speeder," or quick worker, she profits accordingly, she eagerly receives the new truths. She sees that she is "[c]heated at home by her relatives, and at the shop by her boss" (78).

Although she enters the "ball" a vulnerable sweatshop girl whose craving for dance hall romance makes her prey for the prowling local cadet, Harry Klein—Bullard's bow to white-slave thinking—she leaves an incipient activist. Shedding Klein and decades of American seduction literature, the awakened working girl rises to speak, the very "champagne which was to have been [Yetta's] utter undoing [giving] her courage": "If there's a union in my trade, I'll join it. I'll try not to be a slave. I can't fight much. I don't know how. . . . That's all I got to say! . . . I'll try not to be a slave" (83–84).

Like her sisters in militance who people the narrative, Yetta moves from the sexually vulnerable sweatshop girl to the self-strengthening woman whose dual drive is to "fight" and to "know." Soon a labor ball of fire, she inspires a shop walkout, as did Lemlich in 1906 when she formed Local 25 of the ILGWU. Three years later the first major women's strike gains force, and Yetta—again like Lemlich—becomes a WTUL organizer.[29]

During the strike Yetta expands her contacts with politicized working women and their supporters. She encounters a host of impassioned girl pick-eters—young Jewish and Italian women ready to go without food or warm clothing and intent on following the rules for pickets, chief among them the order to "plead, persuade, appeal, but . . . not threaten" the scabs entering the boycotted factories.[30] As she embraces the spirit of martyrdom lauded by contemporary observers friendly to the strikers, she meets WTUL leaders; New York heiress Mabel Train, for instance, is modeled on the founder of the WTUL, Margaret Dreier Robins. Yetta welcomes the aid of affluent women reformers, as did Lemlich with WTUL luminaries, but in a break from such philanthropic influence unimaginable in a Van Vorst or Scudder novel, she throws it off to advocate change in her own way. Before that break, again in the Lemlich mold, she drums up support from women's organizations whose air of privilege she resents. She pickets, is violently harassed by hired thugs, and is arrested—though not, as Lemlich was, 17 times!—and, like Lemlich and another prototypical striker, Yetta Ruth, is sent to the workhouse. She emerges a celebrity of sorts and rededicates herself to the strike action.

What the real-life Yetta experienced afterward has not been recorded. When the clothing manufacturers offered a settlement and helped force the strike to a close, many women did go back to a shorter work week and increased wages. But the employers blacklisted Lemlich and others deemed troublesome. Yetta Ruth, though awakened to the power of collective action, may well have found herself worse off economically than when the strike began. Through her socialist affiliations, it is known that Lemlich found political work, but she had difficulty making a living and lost her job with the suffrage forces in an unknown dispute. She fell into obscurity, although she was later given an honorary pension for her services to the ILGWU.

Rather than dramatize the fate of these women, Bullard sidesteps the issue of their poststrike lives, as if unsure of how to depict the romantic and workplace experiences of sisters in militance once the excitement, but not the need for continued resistance, has died down. He turns the novel into a tract on socialist woman as helpmeet, a role in which he casts Yetta, who joins the staff of the *Clarion* (Bullard's *Call*) and the party as well. Though drawn to a freethinking college professor from Mabel's circle, Yetta, after much soul-searching, finds her romantic identity in marriage to a man of her own class, the *Clarion*'s editor, Isadore Braun.

The alliance cements her dedication to the nonviolent agenda espoused by party regulars, who sought to "make socialism relevant to the existing problems of American workers" (Weinstein, 6). Though there were fierce internal divisions in the major unions about socialist influence, the party remained a power until the coming of the First World War. Furthermore, in a presuffrage age, no other political party "fought as consistently for the full enfranchisement of women" (Weinstein, 54). In its heyday around the time of Bullard's novel, one-tenth of the party's 120,000 dues-paying members were women (Rideout, 50). But if in theory the party was more enlightened than trade unionists, it remained opposed to all-woman organizations and generally refused women full political acceptance.

The fate that Bullard has in store for Yetta is representative of this refusal. Exchanging her interest in industrial unionism and in editing the newspaper's "Labor Page" for a socialist version of domestic womanhood, she mends what Bullard sees as the split between the "modern" and the "other"— the "hereditary woman within her" (433). She becomes the editor of the *Clarion*'s "Mother's Column," as if a woman's acceptance of that role denies her participation in all but a woman's club version of socialism. In her assessment of the book, the author of *Women and the American Left* (1983) finds Yetta in every way her husband's comrade.[31] Yet to this reader Yetta inhabits a socialist separate sphere. Although there is nothing to reproach in Yetta's plan "to win Socialism for the babies" (445), little remains of the woman who had wanted to empower the tubercular Mrs. Cohen, a widow whose children were more immediately threatened than future generations of socialists when she was fired for her "slow" output. In her firebrand days Yetta had leapt to the sweatshop podium and commanded: "Nobody'll go back to work . . . unless [the boss] takes Mrs. Cohen" (120).

In defusing Yetta's militance, Bullard employs a sexual division of intellectual labor. Though with her husband she is a delegate to an international socialist convention, domestic concerns have become her political platform. Not even suffrage, which her sister socialists agitated to include in the party platform, interests her now. It is not that woman's concerns with home and child are narrower, but that Bullard is fixated on keeping political womanhood womanly.

Bullard, then, begins a defense of working girl activism only to end by Victorianizing the woman striker. Much of *The Nine-Tenths*, by the onetime social worker and utopian socialist James Oppenheim, appears to be on a reverse trajectory, although he ultimately resolves the split between contending types of womanhood in a manner similar to Bullard's. He allows the prim schoolteacher Myra Craig to be drawn into the Shirtwaist Strike long enough to imbibe the heady spirit of feminine freedom. But he is careful to distinguish her from the militant women she meets and to shunt her into marriage to Joe Blaine, a printing-plant owner turned radical editor. It is Blaine who registers events, not any of the women characters, whether Myra, or another woman to whom he is drawn, the seasoned professional organizer Sally Heffer, or Rhona Hemlitz (Clara Lemlich), whose trial he covers.

That Oppenheim highlights male consciousness of a largely female labor event has gone unremarked by period and modern reviewers alike. They prefer to interpret the book, to cite Walter Rideout, as the "most nearly complete fictional account of the Uprising" (62). Blaine's factory is the site of a fictive version of the tragic Triangle Factory fire, which Oppenheim has preceding the Shirtwaist Strike. This rearrangement aside, it is true that Oppenheim includes everything from the Lemlich-charged Cooper Union meeting to the exact words of the draconian Judge Cornett (Judge Cornell), who sentenced the girl picketers for "being on strike against God" (265). Missed by those who have commented on the novel as a kind of "photography"[32] of female activism is that Joe Blaine rejects the "easy comradeship" of Sally Heffer, who "would never be dependent" (289), in favor of the ultrafeminine and fitfully political Myra, who would provide "peace, relaxation, diversion" (290).

Myra, who participates in strike duties out of loyalty to Joe, is the "angel of the hearth" updated for socialist purposes. She is involved in labor events when her mate is shorthanded but, instinctively seeking the kitchen and not the study, is the "daughter [and] mother" (312) when the battle is done. At the finale, her decision to marry Joe marks the end of a "barren, fruitless life" (215), presumably the kind led by rebel girls. Her outlook broadened by her role of eyewitness to women's history, it is as a helpmeet, not a comrade, that Myra embraces motherhood. Leaving labor organizing—and work outside the home—to men, she will thus prevent the "race" from being "endangered" (232), language reminiscent of the industrial physician Azel Ames and his traditionalist disciples. Even as Oppenheim's surrogate Blaine reports on the admirable actions of those like Rhona-Clara, whose workhouse "martyrdom . . . could be used as a fire and a torch to kindle and lead the others" (279), he distinguishes between true women and the zealots who "man" the barricades.

Collected under the title *Pay Envelopes* and also published in 1911, Oppenheim's short stories are more critical of the female comrade in arms.[33] His disapproval of strong women—not, as in *The Nine-Tenths*, his ambivalence about them—informs tales that, in their emphasis on primal gender roles, oddly anticipate Hemingway. Whether the assorted working-class wives, many doubling as workers, crave mastery or suffer from it if their husbands are brutal, their subordinate status is not a social circumstance but a law of nature. In "Meg," a supposedly "fearless, self-reliant" (56) factory woman wilts at a command from her ne'er-do-well worker husband. When the workman's wife in "The Cog" urges her steelworker husband to strike and, because he is master, is not heeded, she is grateful that he has taken control, even though he can only escape poor working conditions by quitting his job.

Finally, "Joan of the Mills," who is "free, strong, almost masculine" (168) and a self-appointed agitator with "defiance, energy, leadership, and . . . direct drive" (152), gives it all up when she falls in love with a worker she had come to recruit. Her thoughts of the strike forgotten in the urge to renounce her virginal Joan of Arc identity, she relinquishes her place on labor's front lines to the worker she has inspired. She remains home to mother his young son and reflect on the "power [that] bid her mate with this man—following him through all the world" (169).

Pay Envelopes makes explicit what is implicit in *The Nine-Tenths* and *Comrade Yetta.* Woman can take political action, but to find the "womanhood . . . within her" ("Joan," 175), she cannot sustain it. In comparison with the working girl philosophy of earlier writers, however, the composite vision of Bullard and Oppenheim is an advance, for it acknowledges female working-class might, whether such power is relinquished or not. Woman is no longer a face in the male labor crowd, but a student of anticapitalist resistance whose university is the workplace or strike hall. No employer's threat or thug's violence, only her own craving for a home and husband, causes her to step down from the soapbox.

But clearly, socialist writers felt compelled to reassert the "woman's nature" argument. (Even Malkiel invoked it to an extent.) What of those whose personal or political conservatism already predisposed them against the female firebrand? Did they even consider women in the labor struggles of the period? Three conservatives provide representative answers. By the second half of the decade, when the woman striker was a more familiar and less daring subject, Winston Churchill, Zona Gale, and Margaret Deland, at some cost to verisimilitude, wove her into novels that were received as well as their earlier best-sellers. Churchill had found immense success with historical romances like *Richard Carvel* (1899). He customarily outsold Crane, Norris, and Dreiser combined.[34] By marketing dramas of village life or marital discord as effectively as Churchill recycled historical subjects, both Gale and Deland routinely sold 100,000 copies of their books. Gale, known as early as the strike decade for her studies of both the harmony and grimness of American village life, would win a 1921 Pulitzer Prize for the play she adapted from *Miss Lulu Bett* (1920), her poignant novel of a fenced-in midwestern woman.[35] A typical Deland book on middle-class feminine dissatisfaction, *The Iron Woman* (1911), "appeared to almost hysterically favorable critical reaction."[36]

When they turned their attention to female work, to some extent these writers replicated the split between the working girl's male and female imaginers. That split was observable between tenement writers and cross-class novelists and in the difference between an Oppenheim, who minimized labor sisterhood, and a Malkiel, who championed it. In the same way, Churchill rejected feminine solidarity while Gale and Deland flirted with it. Nevertheless, they were all traditionalists, and their similar handling of wage-earning women proves more important than their gender difference.

In roman à clef fashion, Churchill's *The Dwelling Place of Light* (1917) is a recognizable account of the 1912 Lawrence, Massachusetts, textile strike, a long and ultimately successful walkout, primarily for higher wages, staged by 25,000 immigrant textile workers.[37] Among other protest notables, Churchill includes Antonio Antonelli, the fictive surrogate of IWW organizer Arturo Giovannitti, who was jailed during the strike. His account of women's involvement includes a passage on the death of an unnamed Italian activist, in actuality Anna Lo Pizzo, who was killed following one of the biggest demonstrations. The police wrongly and deliberately blamed the IWW, which the antistrike Churchill carefully omits. A number of other passages refer to the woman-run soup kitchens, which were crucial in feeding the striker's children and keeping spirits high. Most important, Churchill's white-collar heroine, the mill owner Ditmar's private secretary Janet Bumpus, has a transforming encounter with the immigrant Gemma, in real life strike committee member Rose Cardullo. The Italian girl, whose eyes, in Churchill's unsympathetic reading, "glittered like the points of daggers" (322), for a time inspires the malleable Janet, who has joined Gemma's picket line. Yet, transferring her allegiance from her employer to a commanding male strike leader, the ever-subordinate Janet sees herself as a kind of "office wife" to the men inevitably in charge.

The era's numerous reviewers, who differed on the book's quality but not on its accuracy, had no difficulty decoding the "smoky, polyglot [New England] settlement" (*Dwelling*, 1) teeming with Poles, Slavs, and Italians, and other recent immigrants as the scene of the Lawrence happenings.[38] In recent years, an authority on American strike fiction mistook the book for an account of the 1912 Lowell strike, in which there was minimal female participation (Blake, 100). Such an error is understandable, for it has been observed of Churchill that he "wrote of new things in the old vein," and women do not figure prominently in his version of Lawrence.[39] Genteel Janet Bumpus, though reduced to being a "working girl of the mill city" (56), has far less in common with Anna Lo Pizzo or Elizabeth Gurley Flynn than with the heroines of Mrs. M. L. Rayne's *Against Fate* (1876), or Lillian E. Sommers's equally sentimental *For Her Daily Bread* (1887). These novels also feature native-born heroines whose reduced circumstances and high school or secretarial educations thrust them into transient contact with inferior "foreign" women. Whether a family friend helps lift these onetime ladies out of the working mire or an employer has more sinister plans, Rayne and Sommers decry the fact that a girl from good family must work at all.

They also invoke the nativism that surfaced off and on in American history from the Civil War onward. As John Higham points out, Lawrence signaled "a new foreign threat," awakening a "conservative alarm."[40] In Churchill's thinking, Janet initially disdains the mill's "bestial" foreigners to seek help from the class to which she should have belonged—only to be seduced by the mill owner Ditmar. Then, in a fury at his perfidy that foolishly prompts her to identify with the mill workers, she is lured again by Rolfe, a charismatic IWW leader, to donate her typing services to the strike committee and her energies to the picket line.

Plunging his WASP heroine into an immigrant mass strike allows Churchill to deplore the "modern, chaotic society" (Schneider, 264) that has generated such unrest. He soon sabotages her quest for a dwelling place of light, but his subordination of the strike to Janet's doomed spiritual search— she dies bearing her employer's illegitimate daughter—does not fully account for his erasure of womanly participation in Lawrence's parades, marches, mass rallies, and clubbings by police. Anyone as acquainted with the strike as Churchill was could not have been oblivious to the female presence on the human chain, that "moving sidewalk," writes one women's historian, "that wove around all the mills of Lawrence in an unbroken line" (Wertheimer, 365), involving from 5,000 to 20,000 workers, women and men. Save for a two-page scene with Gemma, all the labor strife, including, in a fantasy of IWW anarchy, an Italian striker's assassination of Ditmar, is conducted by the "dangerous" male disciples of the IWW. In the supreme act of writing women out of the strike, Elizabeth Gurley Flynn, so instrumental at Lawrence, is never mentioned.

It is likely that Churchill transferred militance to men precisely because the Lawrence protest, at least in the short run (a national depression in 1913 produced massive unemployment in the textile town), was a woman-produced success. In the context of the strike, Churchill's clichéd story of the fall of the genteel worker who becomes her employer's castoff symbolized his saddened realization that the American girl raised to be superior to the factory and the strike was ill equipped to survive in it. Unable by training or conviction to sustain the troubling new kind of feminine behavior personified by Gemma and her kind, Janet can only perish. Although Churchill made efforts to disguise the fact, the potent, violent Gemmas were here to stay.

Gale and Deland minimized working women's history in a different fashion. The two have been cast as novelists of the "new woman," that once-controversial social and literary type in search of independence, a profession, and equality with men. She had been in vogue since the 1890s, when she generated responses ranging from ire that she was a "hen that doesn't sit"[41] to admiration for her attempts to widen the bourgeois role. By the strike decade she was a predictable figure in the fiction. She invariably espoused, but did not usually act on, advanced views about marriage and suffrage. More than most heroines of this genre—whether by the British authors Mona Caird (*The Daughters of Danaus* [1894]) and Sarah Grand (*The Beth*

Book [1879]) or the American writer Constance Cary Harrison (A Bachelor Maid [1894]), who "could not bring herself to describe factory work in her inventory of women's new occupations"[42]—Cosma Wakely of Gale's A Daughter of the Morning (1917) and Freddy Payton of Deland's The Rising Tide (1916) seek to learn what they share with women engaged in labor protest.[43]

Before consigning their heroines to comfortable marriages, these two novels include scenes in which their supposedly rebellious "new women" address (and in Freddy's case, are briefly jailed with) women of the striking classes. Such cross-class encounters, one interpreter has claimed, reveal privileged women's new "social responsibility" as well as their "feminist commitment to women."[44] This reader would argue that the scenes in question marginalize the laborers sought out by these would-be female trailblazers and merely extend the philanthropic woman's novel discussed in chapter 3. Cosma, a country girl whose knowledge of the urban immigrant woman is limited to a series of briefly held factory jobs—a stint at work that a critic argues is "sisterhood" (Maglin, 99) in action but that occupies a miniscule part of the text—claims that she felt like she was "every factory girl in New York" (135). On the heels of that extravagant assertion, she eagerly accepts the good offices of her employer's wife, a philanthropist of the Vida Scudder ilk, who whisks her off to a finishing school cum college where she can mix with the right sort. Less a representative of woman's upward mobility (Cosma, fleeing a loutish rural fiancé, was no penniless immigrant to begin with) than of the capitalist largesse that has enabled her to attend school, the now-educated Cosma claims she wishes to devote herself to women's causes. Before making an alliance to a man of wealth, her only stabs in that direction are to undertake research on Chinese labor with her affluent fiancé. Then she returns, once, to her former haunts to encourage the women on strike to understand the employer's viewpoint, hardly the actions of a radical.

Deland's Freddy, though scornful of her well-to-do family's injunction that she give up "her feminist nonsense and agree to marry" (Blake, 101), is also more sound than fury in her support of the working woman. She walks on a garment workers' picket line and is arrested for it, activities Deland views as satirically as she does the scratching, biting little Italian immigrants who cause an "unseemly scuffle" (262) when taken to jail. Soon weary of the activist's role, Freddy is a patrician whose interclass feminism, like Cosma's, is limited. The garment-trade organizer Rose Schneiderman attended a suffrage convention around the time of the Deland novel. Had she heard Freddy's lectures to factory women on the ballot as bringer of increased wages, her advice would have been the same she gave at the conference. "[H]elp the working woman. [D]o not ask her to come out and help you get woman suffrage. . . . [G]o to her and offer her your help to win [it]."[45]

For all the speeches and grand gestures, the Cosmas and Freddys, as do most "new woman" characters, exemplify what Caroline Forrey has termed their creators' "inability to imagine any satisfactory new roles for their newly awakened heroines" (53). Poised between the Victorian and the modern ages, these questing, narcissistic protagonists are unable to envision the kind of cross-class bonds that, despite the skepticism of some working-class organizers, the WTUL leader Margaret Dreier Robins forged with trade union women during the Shirtwaist Strike. Gale and Deland consign their female working-class militants to the status of Hollywood extras in a silent film. Yet, even glimpsed as undifferentiated faces in the crowd, these rebel girls have a fixity of purpose lacking in "new women" like Cosma Wakely and Freddy Payton.

Prior to the American entry into World War I in 1917, writers on wage-earning women attempted to erase or trivialize her newfound militance, to transform her from a comrade into a helpmeet, or, less commonly, to render in fiction the ardent, empowered types like Elizabeth Gurley Flynn and Clara Lemlich. Whatever the political allegiance—or chauvinism—of the imaginer, during the strike decade, both in life and art, the female militant was a fixture on the labor landscape. Thus when Bertha Aarons, a Lemlich figure with a minor role in *The Children of Light* (1912), Florence Converse's muddled homage to patrician socialists, steps to the podium, neither author nor reader expects—or gets—a Dutch Kitty or a Maggie Johnson. Nor does she exemplify the type Dreiser but a few years before defended for her average conscience, O. Henry genially presented as a husband hunter whose workplace was "her forest,"[46] and Freeman and Van Vorst caused to renounce her militance almost as soon as she discovered it.

In a few texts and in the opening sections of many others concerned with the new feminine activism, the woman wage earner revealed an energy absent in her earlier incarnations as sweatshop Cinderella, harlot, or paragon of gentility. Focused where her predecessors had been flighty, predatory, mercenary, or escapist, she was no longer fearful of the workplace, no longer hanging on, making do, waiting for rescue. Still, because old prejudices interfered with new empowerment, the response of commercial press fiction to woman on the labor barricades was one of vacillation. If the Comrade Yettas were worlds away from the childlike victims of turn-of-the-century fiction, they were less full-fledged activists than women who subordinated political to domestic activity.

World War I "shattered such organization as the Socialist movement had managed to develop" (Blake, 90–91). It also brought an end to the American literary preoccupation with feminine militance, at least until the resurgence of proletarian fiction in the Depression era. By 1922 the occasional socialist, such as Elias Tobenkin in *The Road* (1922), continued to extoll the union activity of a garment-center earth mother. (Significantly, she ends up in the Soviet Union, a worker's state receptive to her views.) Even earlier, however, by the closing years of the war, it was not the Tobenkins but those like ambitious Anzia Yezierska who dominated the novel of female industrial labor. Now the working woman climbed from sweatshop humiliation to middle-class respectability. As they urged assimilation, not defiance, and upward mobility, not solidarity, the novelists of the new individualism provided closure to the lengthy debate on woman's work. From Yezierska on, it was every working girl for herself.

Hairdresser's Window, a John Sloan homage to the working-class woman as celebrity, 1907
Wadsworth Atheneum, Hartford. The Ella Gallup Sumner and Mary Catlin Sumner Collection © 1992 Wadsworth Atheneum

6

Upward Struggles:
Fictions of Feminine Mobility

Unwilling dressing, lonely breakfast, the Subway, dull work . . . the
boss's ill tempers . . . no love, no creative work. . . . So went the days.
The Job (1917)

"Ach! God from the sky! I'm so burning to live—to work myself up
for a somebody! And why not?"
Hungry Hearts (1920)

WHEN AMERICA ENTERED WORLD WAR I, WOMEN GAINED ACCESS TO
"men's jobs" in industry, and, its new expansion quickened by the war, to
the business world as well. Audiences for the fiction of what the socialist
author Zoe Beckley in *A Chance to Live* (1918) termed "the firebrand girl"
no longer found the woman striker a compelling figure.[1] As one wage earner
in the Beckley book points out, the "war's making all kinds of chances for
smart young women" (248). The novel features a conversation between the
sweatshop militant Nena Rabinovitch and the ambitious heroine, Annie Har-

gan, who has left the shop and glowingly describes her promising typing job. To Nena's injunction that working-class women remember the martyrs of the Triangle Factory fire and agitate to prevent similar tragedies, Annie replies in the working girl's new voice: "Why don't you get loose from the factory, Nena? There's loads of chances to get along, once you've made up your mind to dig at night school and give up going places. . . . Why do you waste your time trying to get girls to go on strikes? Why don't you tell them to get out of it all—and why don't *you* get out of it?" (141). Given Beckley's agenda, Annie must awake to the selfishness of such sentiments. By novel's end, she has renounced narrow individualism to join Nena's radical settlement, the "People's House."

In the war years, however, Beckley was out of step with an America increasingly accustomed to press coverage of women "doing the work of men" and "thriving on the new job."[2] The decade of the firebrand had come to a close. Its demise was hastened by the need for—and recognition of—woman's abilities in the skilled manufacturing work previously considered so unsuited to the feminine intelligence and physique.[3] As wartime employment opportunities diverted the impulse to militance, few but the *New York Call* found Beckley's call to renewed radicalism other than utopian.[4] Equally significant, the "red scares" of 1919–21, bolstered by Gov. Calvin Coolidge's strikebreaking actions and antilabor sermonizing in Massachusetts (Brown, 80–81) weakened the labor movement, forcing the unions to adopt a more conservative posture than in the days of the Shirtwaist Strike.[5]

Despite the red-baiting, by 1920 nearly 400,000 of the over eight million members of the female work force were union members, four times the number of ten years earlier.[6] Among women working in the eastern garment trade and female workers in many other manufacturing jobs affected by the economic decline in the aftermath of wartime prosperity, the woman's strike was not moribund.[7] Yet neither the postwar increase in trade unionism nor the existence of scattered job actions equaled the feminine militance of the Shirtwaist Strike era, much less attracted the kind of public notice enjoyed by the strikers of 1909. Women craving leadership roles were certainly no closer to positions of power within the unions than they had been in the strike decade. (It was not until the 1930s that, despite continued male dominance elsewhere, women came to the fore as leaders of the AFL-inspired Congress of Industrial Organizations [CIO].)[8] Throughout the 1920s the female rank and file was more likely to fight to retain places they had earned during the war or seek employment elsewhere than to engage in workplace rebellion in the name of feminine unity.

Rather than rely on the sisterhood of workers, a number of the postwar investigators recorded that dissatisfied women, uninterested in unions, made their own spirited complaints to their employers regarding insufficient wages, unsanitary conditions, and ruses employed to cut their weekly pay. In *Working with the Working Woman* (1922), a well-known narrative, Cornelia Stratton Parker approvingly quotes a representative interchange between "Sadie" and her New York City dress-factory boss. "Well, miss," he queried, "what [do] you expect to get here?" "What I'm worth," replied the confident girl.[9] In the course of her research, Parker sampled a number of feminine occupations, including laundry, candy factory, brassworks, and garment work. She discovered that in all of these fields women who thought their work too hard, although aware of strikes in the clothing industry and elsewhere, preferred to change jobs—frequently.

In a further sign of the times, more ambitious native-born women who wanted "to read papers on the lecture platform" (Parker, 90) and Jewish and Italian immigrants bent on assimilation through attending lectures "at the New School for Social Research" (Parker, 27) saw these jobs as transitional. Enduring the exhausting day to gain culture or language skills by night, they set their sights on the white-collar world, in which, by 1920, 90 percent of all typists and stenographers were women. By the middle of the decade, over 500,000 women workers were employed in clerical positions.[10] (Even the Russia-bound heroine of the socialist Elias Tobenkin's 1922 strike novel *The Road* had "been dreaming of office work since she was a little girl," only to be sidetracked—and radicalized—by the need to support her illegitimate child.)[11] Anticipating their movement from salesclerk to buyer, the children of recent immigrants also looked to department store work, where Edna Ferber's Ray Willets (originally Rachel Wiletsky) successfully competed with the native-born anxious to be freed from home duty.[12]

Other ghetto daughters, like Anzia Yezierska's heroines, aspired to public-school teaching. By 1920 that profession was the standard "woman's reward" for acquiring a college degree. Of the one-third of collegiate women trained as teachers and 75 percent already in the field, almost half were from immigrant—and often Jewish—origins.[13]

Of course, few wage-earning women of Yezierska's generation, whether immigrant or native-born, had the iron will of her career-bound protagonists. But by 1920, when over eight million women (23.6 percent), were in the nation's work force (Brown, 81), a woman had only to have completed high school—particularly if she had received some business training there—to have access to opportunity. For the first time, women in clerical and sales positions outnumbered those in factory jobs or domestic service. Department stores added entry-level training programs—one newly hired Ferber heroine spends two hours a day in the store school of instruction—to bolster the reputation of sales as the "Cinderella of occupations."[14] In sum, for working-class women positions in the white-collar and sales worlds represented an escape from the factory. If in this climate of hopefulness that escape often proved less satisfying than anticipated in terms of promotion opportunities or wages,[15] the new ambitiousness did not inspire the resentment leveled at woman's wage-earning predecessors. The new aspirations, in fact, helped to "reweave the working girl back into the fabric of socially approved womanhood."[16]

A new generation of "undercover" observers, rejecting the elitism of

Dorothy Richardson in *The Long Day*, found the ordinary wage earner an adventurous type, undefeated by monotonous work or poor pay. In contrast to the pitiable grotesques and vulgar hoydens peopling the undercover narratives of two decades before, the new eyewitness historians found a spiritedness in working women that transcended the fatigue of running a foot press "7,149 times by the meter" (Parker, 63). Discarding dismissive ethnic and class-based stereotypes and insulting phrases, the new narrators cast no aspersions on the working girl's colorful attire and dance hall evenings. Whereas Richardson linked the feminine workplace to privation and immorality, the new undercover writers saw challenges, not suffering. Women's finery and dance hall nights were no longer the emblems of her moral flaws but represented her ability to dominate life. She earned praise for how well she clothed and enjoyed herself on a tight budget, and she embodied a dignified spirit in the face of a spirit-dulling job. Most important, the new observers suggested that it was time to remove the stigma from women's work.[17]

More pragmatic allies of the woman wage earner, attuned to continuing injustice, argued that only economic betterment would remove that stigma. To that end, 1920 saw the birth of the Women's Bureau of the Department of Labor. The successor of the World War I–era Women in Industry Service,[18] it was formed to help survey women's pay scales and working conditions and to push for woman's right to a minimum wage, an eight-hour day, and equal pay for equal work (Tentler, 78). In its most effective period, 1920 to 1925, the bureau bolstered the idea that, in the words of its chief, Mary Anderson, a former garment and shoe worker, the woman in industry "was an important asset to the nation" (Brown, 79). Although the bureau was appalled that the mistreatment of women laborers that Van Vorst had exposed two decades earlier in *The Woman Who Toils* still existed, it also pointed with pride to the fact that "four pages were required to list all the [wartime] jobs in which women substituted for men" (Chafe, 65). By its very existence, the bureau affirmed not only that woman was a fixture on the labor landscape but that wartime job mobility should be possible "even to the uneducated" (Kessler-Harris 1982, 227). Wrote one advocate of the female jobseeker, improved access to jobs was making women "known to themselves."[19]

Through the creation of assertive labor heroines determined to struggle upward rather than remain in drudgery, in texts whose very titles imply the new concern with self-development—*The Job* (1917) by Sinclair Lewis, *Hungry Hearts* (1920) by Anzia Yezierska, and *Broken Barriers* (1922) by Meredith Nicholson—the new authors showed women coming to personal power through work.[20] They applied the determination of their strike-oriented predecessors to a new model of "acquisitive individualism" (Kessler-Harris 1982, 226). A wide range of period novelists, most of whom found neither woman's work nor her ambitions unfeminine, centered plots on two types of women: immigrants trying to escape the factory, and American daughters trying to establish work roles for themselves. These chroniclers of her new aspirations included writers as diverse as Anzia Yezierska, the muse of the

Yiddish-accented sweatshop girl who would "make myself for a person";[21] Sinclair Lewis, whose insular small-town heroines quickly adapt to an office world they never made; and Theodore Dreiser, who sympathized with the woman whose ascension plan is thwarted.

The new authors no longer questioned the propriety of the female workplace, only whether its satisfactions equaled, much less replaced, those of the home sphere. Many propelled their heroines on an Algerian path. Some, dismayed that even well-bred young ladies had "to battle for their bread" (*Barriers*, 10), uneasily sought refuge from the new truths. Others pointed to the consequences when reality fell short of expectation. Yet, whether authors embraced feminine upward mobility, fled from its implications, or exposed it as mythic, all illustrated its new centrality.

As these writers charted the shift from rebellion to aspiration, from collective to individual action, the debate on the propriety of woman's work did not so much disappear from their works as take a different form. Now woman's ambition rather than her workplace presence generated new doubts and defenses. What price did the immigrant woman, defiant of Old World imperatives, pay in her search for assimilation and economic security? How did a woman, immigrant or native-born, transcend what one eyewitness called the "changeless monotony" of the white-collar sweatshop.[22] Conversely, did success at work, as opponents of the career woman contended, handicap her "in the winning of a mate"?[23] And if, as one banking executive argued, "business and matrimony [do] not go together" (qtd. Lehrer, 127), could the new fiction overcome the reluctance to permit a woman both love and work? In answering such questions fiction both criticized and celebrated the working girls who prompted them.

In the 1920s, remarks one student of Anzia Yezierska's self-transforming heroines, "it was plausible for a young woman who dreamed of success to articulate it without seeming alien to a culture that had only recently acknowledged women's independent aspirations."[24] The new sense of place was not confined to the working girl. Another aspiring type was the career woman, that postsuffrage successor to the 1890s "new woman," who embraced the theory of vocational fulfillment but did not always live by it. By the 1920s women had gained greater access to the university, graduating to "a seemingly bewildering array of choices" (Brown, 150). Between 1890 and 1920 the number of professional women increased over 200 percent—triple the rate of male advancement. From 1910 to 1920 the number of women in professions as diverse as chemistry, architecture, and law doubled. The feminine entry into the professions, however, was hardly massive. By the 1920s only 5 percent of America's doctors were women, as were 1.4 percent of its lawyers and judges. In both law and medicine, as in business, academia, and even the woman-shaped world of social work, women were far less likely than men to advance to high positions.[25]

In postwar fiction, particularly by female authors, women could beat the professional odds. But these authors followed the prewar lead of the "new woman" authors Mary Austin (*A Woman of Genius* [1912]), Elia Peattie (*The Precipice* [1914]), and Mary Roberts Rinehart (*K* [1915]), whose respective heroines triumph while engaged in the arts, as a head of a government children's bureau, and nursing, professions that call for more "feminine" intuitiveness than "masculine" intellection. Equally significant, in a continuation of the interclass elitism informing fiction at the beginning of the century, the "new woman" novel, titularly opposed to restraints on professional choices, skirted discussion of the class barriers that impeded it. At times, from the vantage point of the working-class writer Anzia Yezierska, "new women" from the privileged classes, personified in her 1920 story by the WASP Miss Whiteside, thwarted those they saw as competitors from the laboring classes. Yezierska may have met such treatment when, as a scholarship student, she earned a Columbia Teachers College degree (ironically, in domestic science, a field she abhorred). In "Soap and Water" (1920), her fictive alter ego Shenah Pessah certainly encounters condescension from Miss Whiteside, a woman dean at Columbia. A symbol of feminine professional success, she is an elitist foe of the sweatshop (and sweaty) immigrant Shenah, whose teaching placement she blocks. So, too, with the exception of one kindly soul who comforts the despondent Shenah, do the social workers and vocational counselors who tell Yezierska protagonists in search of career advice to "rise slowly from [factory] job to [factory] job" ("America and I" [1923], 30). Lewis and Ferber's career-hungry women do not set their sights on Columbia University degrees or on acceptance by what Yezierska calls the "icebergs of convention" ("Soap," 175). Instead, they find modest positions in libraries or work their way up from the office pool or the shop floor to reach minor executive positions in hotel or department store hierarchies. Yet, if these working-class variants of the "new woman" take their advancement where they find it, they too remain outside the social and professional circles frequented by women collegians from "good" families.

Whatever their view of the chasm between affluent and blue-collar career seekers, writers from Yezierska to Lewis found more in common between those women than between the working girl and the flapper, the archetype of 1920s female rebellion. Like the female professional, she was more likely to be a bourgeois daughter than a working one. As early as 1915, Alfred Stieglitz captured the privileged type in a surrealistic photograph of Georgia O'Keeffe's rebellious young friend Dorothy True. Superimposed on her black-stockinged leg is her gamin face. Her bobbed hair and dark, lipsticked mouth are self-consciously naughty responses to the dullness of life as the daughter of a successful Portland paper manufacturer.[26] As if responding to Dorothy True, a 1921 *New York Times* article, "Mrs. Grundy on the Job of Reforming the Flapper," deplored the "new morals and ethics and dress of our Younger Generation."[27]

At issue was a pampered young woman with ready access to automobile rides and invitational dances. With her scanty dress, forward manner, and pursuit of a life on the dance floor, the flapper was the target of moral reproaches about "sex mad womanhood" that were previously leveled at the factory and shopgirl.[28] As working girls became more culturally acceptable, the flapper, an affluent product of the postwar loosening of manners and morals, made her own bid for independence.

It was one that had little to do with the vocational ethic of the feminine work force in the 1920s. If the flapper threw off restraint, "kept her legs in plain sight," and was "brazen and at least capable of sin if not actually guilty of it" (Yellis, 44), like the hardworking white-collar girl, she embodied a new demand for recognition as an individual. Yet this "dancing daughter" (the title of a 1928 Joan Crawford film) had the luxury of a life dedicated to pleasure, unlike working women earning their daily bread or pursuing job advancement.

In actuality, many working-class women no doubt shared the flapper's desires, whether for sexual freedom, romance on their own terms, or just a hedonistic night out. By the 1920s such desires were powerfully heightened by motion pictures. Yet, as Dreiser's moviegoing factory girl in *An American Tragedy* (1925) and a minor servant character in Sinclair Lewis's *Main Street* (1920) demonstrate, the working girl who could feed her fantasy life with movies in which she saw "lovely fellows in dress-suits and Bill Hart and everything" would never meet those fellows in person.[29] As early as 1917 Winston Churchill's working girl novel *The Dwelling Place of Light* had deplored the power of the "ephemeral brightness of the screen" to fill impressionable women with impossible romantic fantasies.[30] Other opponents found greater dangers. Not only did movies with titles like *Flaming Youth* (1923) and *Wine of Youth* (1924) inspire emulation of the flapper, but they disseminated a view that women, far from eternal victims of masculine lust, could be lustful themselves.[31]

Still, it is significant that in the new Hollywood working girl films—on domestic service in *Her Winning Way* (1921), the factory in *When Destiny Wills* (1921), and the department store in *Manhandled* (1924), starring Gloria Swanson—as well as in the pulp magazines still hawking the Laura Jean Libbey formula, the optimal ending was marriage, usually "to the rich boss . . . or the handsome hero with the bright future" (Rosen, 81). In these films, whether teasingly chaste or cunningly wayward, the wage-earning protagonists were more likely to be gold diggers than jazz babies. Mercenary working girls, "determined to use their bodily charms to make their way in the world," figured in many of the pulps and in over threescore films of the 1920s.[32]

Anzia Yezierska, known for her stories of the working-class woman's self-improvement through learning, was dismayed by these mass entertainments. Hired by Hollywood to write screenplays herself, an arrangement almost doomed to failure, she audaciously informed the mogul William Fox that current films were as out of touch with working women as were the popular magazines.[33] Nor could she have approved of what Hollywood had done in making film versions of her collection *Hungry Hearts* and her first novel, *Salome of the Tenements* (1923), both condemned by the critics but probably popular enough with moviegoers.[34]

By 1923 the public perceived Yezierska as even more adept than her Russian-Jewish "Salome," Sonya Vrunsky, at satisfying the recent immigrant's desires for elevation and recognition. But like Sonya, her imaginer rejected the seductress's approach. Though Sonya successfully connives at snaring a rich husband, she is soon dissatisfied and leaves him to work her way up a second time in a more legitimate way. First a lowly waitress, then an apprentice designer, she becomes a dressmaker-with-a-conscience: she vows to sell garments at prices that Grand Street can afford. Hollywood, updating the late-Victorian tenement story of the morally pliable shop girl, was no doubt more interested in dramatizing Sonya's gold-digging success than her crisis of conscience.

Perhaps because it offers a heroine whose ambitions never include the life of the mind, a heroine her own creator did not really respect, *Salome* is her weakest tale. In her more memorable fiction, however, Yezierska scorned plots about the romantic connivances of working girls. Her characteristic heroine looked to night school to extricate herself from sweatshop or laundry, domestic service or shop work. Thus her best novels and stories, like those of Lewis, Ferber, and their contemporaries, were no more likely to trivialize the woman wage earner's ambitions than to equate career advancement with acceptance by the "new womanly" elite. "Even Lewis's Carol Kennicott of *Main Street*," writes Alice Kessler-Harris in her astute introduction to a reissued Yezierska collection, *The Open Cage*, would have recognized her "conviction that women could achieve success by their own efforts" (Kessler-Harris 1979, ix). As the writer most attuned to the barriers placed in the way of such success, Yezierska merits more scrutiny.

After years of night school, college, an unsatisfying marriage, and literary rebuffs, including those from a creative writing course that, her daughter reports in a biography, "fed Anzia's rage," Yezierska began sending out her work "unvarnished" (Henriksen, 120). Not surprisingly, with such determination she did manage to write her way out of Delancey Street: the *New Republic* accepted her indictment of "new womanly" elitism, "Soap and Water," and soon the press discovered the "sweatshop Cinderella." She formed friendships with, and received positive book reviews from, syndicated columnists, Yale professors, and best-selling authors. The prominent novelist Zona Gale, in whose *A Daughter of the Morning* the briefly impoverished factory heroine cries, "I'll make myself" (and was promptly saved the effort when taken up by a millionaire family), boosted Yezierska's work.[35] Other reviewers were also taken by this Russian immigrant from the ghetto "reaching out" like her heroines, "with hungry heart to higher things."[36] By 1925 the virtues of her work had become its flaws. She was criticized for self-congratulation and, in an era of proletarian art, condemned for what were perceived as unflattering portraits of the Jews.[37] Furthermore, by the time of the Depression, female wage earners were hearing a new message: "Get back to the home." The death knell for Yezierska's work had sounded.

At the peak of her fame, when her books were being published by Houghton Mifflin and she was the subject of *Good Housekeeping* interviews entitled "An Immigrant Speaks," Yezierska gained acclaim for writing of her own lengthy struggle to arrive.[38] She was already 37 when "Fat of the Land," a study of a Jewish mother unable to comprehend her Americanized children, was selected as the best short story of 1919. Her fiction is often sympathetic to these older immigrants. But her favored fictive selves are the younger Jewish women who reject such parents: misunderstood worker-writers, family-defying teachers, college students who survive on English lessons to "greener" immigrants, frustrated ribbon clerks enamored of neighborhood intellectuals. What distinguishes them all—and what the disappointing film portraits of Shenah Pessah and Sonya Vrunsky could not capture—is the voracity with which they rush to embrace the New World.

Overthrowing dependence, ethnicity, and sisterly solidarity alike, they are fired with egoism, not altruism, with revolt, not docility. Here, then, is a new type: clever, relentlessly ambitious—and angry. For a raging resentment at everyone from snobbish girls' club benefactors to grasping sweatshop contractors to patriarchal Old World figures only fuels these women's resolve to find America and escape the imprisoning tenement world of the Jewish Lower East Side. Yezierska emigrated with her family to that locale a few years before the influential *Forward* editor Abraham Cahan penned his vignettes on the feistily materialistic Jewish working girl, a type he satirizes or tames but never sends to evening school. Over two decades later, Yezierska, who described one sweatshop job as "handling dead buttons" ("America and I," 25), for a time resembled the combative Mamie Fein of Cahan's *Yekl*, struggling for more than a six-day-a-week tailoring job and a cot-bed in a Chrystie Street room shared with two other girls.

In art as in life, Yezierska soon broke with the feminine limitations preached by Cahan's fiction. Although he acknowledges the forcefulness of a Mamie, Cahan tries to rein her in, punishing her for her "greed" with a far from brilliant match. Yezierska, on the other hand, infuses her many ambitious heroines, from the tenement janitor Shenah Pessah and the sweatshop worker Sophie Sapinsky in the collection *Hungry Hearts* to the box-factory worker Sara Smolinsky in *Bread Givers* (1925), with a successful resolve to use the wages they earn at the industrial workplace to become educated and thus free of it. Even the very young Rachel in the story "The Lord Giveth" in *Children of Loneliness* (1923) is already a student of the language, which enables her to write letters for everybody on the block (131). Rachel's desire for the learning that will usher in her assimilation helps her break out of the

self-imposed separateness of her impoverished orthodox parents, whose pious
Old World scorn for the material has unfitted them for the New World. In
the title story of *Children of Loneliness*, a grown-up Rachel earns college
money by tutoring pious immigrants more recent than herself, proof, at least
to her, that Jewish wisdom needs the help of American knowledge.

In *The Rise of David Levinsky* (1917), published a few years before
Yezierksa's fiction, Cahan also empowers his title character to climb out of
the sweatshop, to transform his work experience, and, in a phrase from one
critic's assessment of *Bread Givers'* heroine Sara Smolinsky, to "opt . . . for
self and buil[d] a life around [his] own authentic needs" (Kessler-Harris 1973,
xvii). Yezierska's boldness is to defy the Old Testament conviction that "no
girl can live without a father or a husband to look out for her, [for] only
through a man has a woman an existence" (*Bread*, 137). Thus her heroines'
quest—for schooling, for a skilled job, for a room away from the ghetto—is
at once an affirmation of the American future and a repudiation, though often
a guilt-filled one, of the Jewish past. "In America," Shenah Pessah counters
relatives urging her to fulfill her destiny as a Jewish woman and marry, "if a
girl earns her living, she can be fifty years old and without a man, and nobody
pities her." ("Wings," *Hungry*, 15).

In one of Yezierska's most famous stories from the 1920 *Hungry Hearts*
collection, "Hunger," Shenah is again the central figure. Unlike the Comrade
Yettas of Shirtwaist Strike fiction whose militant sisterhood combats sweatshop problems, Shenah sees the Cohen Brothers' garment factory as her first
arena of distinction. There she will achieve more than, not bond with, her
exploited coworkers. Learning quickly from these more skilled women, whom
she makes the first of many teachers, she rises to forelady—without reserva-
tions about disloyalty to her class. For she has thrived on the work regimen
that made Crane's tenement heroines rush to their seducers' arms, prompted
Freeman's ladylike factory hands to wed affluence, and inspired Malkiel's
militants to the Uprising of the 20,000. Infused with a hope for a better job,
less uncouth company, and romantic attentions from men above her present
station, Shenah has her plan in place. At the end of the story, with her desire
for the "life higher" (63), symbolized by the study of a new language and the
conquest of a man from the upper classes, Shenah, the reader feels, is just
beginning.

Although Yezierska's wage earners are rebellious Jewish daughters, their
search for American freedom points to a social-historical truth. A defiant
Shenah, needing money for herself, refuses to work only to support her
relatives. Similarly, during the 1920s, even in conservative Jewish, Italian,
and Irish families, the historian Leslie Tentler reports, daughters also abandoned "the custom of giving the entire wage to the mother" (92). Joining their
native-born counterparts, these immigrant daughters declared a premarital
economic independence. They spent more money on meeting their own
desires and "carved out space . . . for privacy, independence, and unsuper-

vised social interaction."[39] Yezierska's heroines carve out a wider space. Though they seek few pleasures until the battle is done, they make a bid for permanent autonomy. Thus in *Bread Givers*, Sara, one of the four daughters of a father-dominated orthodox family, throws off the encroachments on the self that have conquered her three garment-trade sisters. Just as she withholds her pay, she questions family duty and scorns the idea of an arranged marriage. Her sisters, ever pliable, bond themselves to "suitable" husbands. Sara sends herself to college, her father's curse echoing in her ears.

In Yezierska's fables of the working girl's self-propulsion, if men are not punitive patriarchs to be renounced they are objects of desire to be pursued. Yet there is no sexuality in Yezierska's work, even for the women who turn men into "framed picture[s] of . . . innermost dreams" ("Hunger," 3); by their very remoteness these men inspire Yezierska's women to rescue themselves. Bent on following their vocational agendas, Yezierska's characters transform romantic desires into spurs to ambition. In the appropriately named "Wings," Shenah conflates winning the distant Protestant John Barnes, a sociology instructor come to "study" immigrant life, with her own Americanization. But when she learns that he sees her only as an interesting specimen, she does not act out the working girl jilted by the aristocrat of tenement-tale fare. In her competition with the world, he too is now a rival. "By day and night," she tells herself in soon-to-be-perfected English, "you got to push, push yourself up till you get to him and can look him in his face eye to eye" (34).

Such ambiguous statements pepper Yezierska's work. If they suggest romantic fixation, they signal something quite different as well. Shenah will succeed in winning the approval of the Protestant male and the dominant culture he exemplifies. But as in *Salome*, once he is won, she will need to defy his frigid conventionalism. The men in this and other tales of feminine immigrant longing—the near-mystical Frank Baker in "Children of Loneliness," another dreamlike gentile in the *Hungry Hearts* tale "The Miracle"— are abstractions, symbols of that for which the woman hungers. Cold, at first unavailable or fleetingly interested figures, as captured lovers they invariably disappoint; their acclaim cannot equal the world's. At once reminders that the feminine upward climb must be solitary if it is to be unimpeded, they suggest the perils of abandoning the Jewish identity as well. If there are few marriages in Yezierska, the only happy ones are between assimilated Jews. Reconciled to her father, the now-educated protagonist of *Bread Givers* weds a fellow educator. Salome joins forces with her professional equal, the dress designer Jacques Hollins, born Jaky Solomon. But because what matters is not the goal, marital or otherwise, but the ardent quest, men are as often clogs or rivals as they are prizes or helpmeets. One prototypical sweatshop veteran tells a male coworker naively seeking her sympathy, "Give yourself your own strength!" ("Hunger," 64). That message, uttered more to herself than to her luckless suitor, is the watchword of all Yezierska's working girls.

Yezierska's heroines willingly sacrifice human feeling for ambition. But a sadness permeates her work that redeems them from the moral monstrosity of Cahan's garment-center magnate David Levinsky. "The traditional Jewish woman," notes one expert, "lived for her family, working outside the home to enable [men] to advance."[40] Born to defy, Yezierska was haunted by that traditional imperative and the larger submissions it implied. Her heroines proclaim that there is no greater goal than self-uplift, no better lodging than a room of one's own. But beneath these assertions is a hunger that cannot be satisfied. Comments Ellen Golub, "[W]hen [their] dream is achieved . . . it yields little more than longing for the old days when the heroine was young and hopeful."[41] There is thus nostalgia for the ghetto life left behind, for more spiritual richness than American culture holds. Too, there is a residual guilt for defiance, as if only in suffering can the heroine expiate the sin of wishing for personal success. It is no wonder that her heroines savor the difficulty of ascent but never rejoice in its completion. Yezierska's working girls struggle upward, but the costs of achievement are high.

When Edna Ferber and Sinclair Lewis defended feminine ambition, they too raised questions about its price. Both as best-selling authors and, later in their careers, as respective recipients of the Pulitzer and Nobel prizes for their ability to reveal "the walking show of American life,"[42] their fiction found a wider audience than Yezierska's tales of the immigrant Jew on the Lower East Side. Though their stories of assertive young working women antedated Yezierska's, their heroines, who find readier access to skilled work, seem successors, not older sisters, to Sara Smolinsky and Shenah Pessah. Unlike the woman whom the press dubbed the "sweatshop Cinderella," Ferber and Lewis tapped into their readers' desire for "the tone, the speech, of . . . American existence" (Kazin, 121). They created young women who have never suffered the immigrant's problems of assimilation. Ferber's second- and third-generation heroines, a few of Jewish origins, are seasoned American urbanites. Lewis's city job searchers are midwesterners or, like Carol Kennicott, New Englanders transplanted to the heartland.

What unites them to Yezierska's strugglers, however, is the belief that economic ascension can forge a feminine identity. When Ferber published "The Girl Who Went Right" in 1918, her very title satirized both domesticity as the "right" feminine role and the outmoded belief in shop-girl immorality. Ray Willets, with her "ambitious, clever little head" (63) and "indomitable desire to get on" (60), bears no resemblance to the stereotyped shop girl described in one labor report as "frivolous, faithless, dishonest and inefficient," familiar taunts from opponents earlier in the century.[43] Ray is lured by neither the dance hall gigolo nor the solid suitor proposing to rescue her from toil. A typical Ferber heroine, she is completely focused on her work, work that has a dignity it lacked 15 years before. As noted earlier in this chapter, by the end of the war department stores, newly interested in efficiency on the shop floor, had improved their training programs and were stressing that selling was a skilled job. To all of this Ray responds. She relishes the fact that her sales slip is "as complicated as an engineering blueprint" (61), that her supervisor is knowledgeable in the complexities of customer relations. Like Emma McChesney and Fanny Brandeis, other Ferber protagonists with a talent for merchandising (Fanny delivers a lecture on the subject to a group of store executives), Ray finds few obstacles in her path.[44]

Still, she has a moral lesson to learn in order to "go right." The serpent in her garden is doubt about the morality of what she markets—not the old association of shop girl with prostitution, but the value of marketing as a life goal. Thus Ray is put off by a snobbish lingerie saleswoman who thinks herself above other store workers. Ray's distaste for this woman, and for her own success at dealing with rich customers, is heightened by guilt for having discarded her true name, Rachel Wiletsky, when she entered employment at the store. Fanny Brandeis, another gifted saleswoman, though at a higher level in the store hierarchy, is similarly affronted by her firm's endless profit seeking. As pragmatic as they are optimistic, Ferber's heroines "go right" and resolve their conflicts—by seeking work in which they can believe. For Ray, it is as easy as changing departments to sell to the poorer clientele; Fanny finds a new career, augmented by a companionate marriage, in commercial art.

In two early novels of Sinclair Lewis, other young women job seekers— as in Ferber's stories, Middle American and fairly skilled—do not find solutions as easily. Where Ferber's specialists in quick ascension are exhilarated by the workplace, Lewis's are discouraged by its monotony, what Una Golden in *The Job* calls her "old enemy, routine" (279). In a period when native daughters' expectations of white-collar work ran high, veterans of the office world also pointed to its limitations. Secretaries interviewed in the early 1920s reported discouragement that they were not able to "get ahead" in the office hierarchy (Kessler-Harris 1982, 233). And many in the office pools and on the switchboards no doubt shared the resentment of the unnamed narrator of "Pilgrim's Progress in a Telephone Exchange" (1921). There, skilled women were treated as if they were no more valuable than those who had never learned a skill at all. Urged to be pleased with a lunchroom rather than a wage hike, they might earn more, she remarks with more disgust than compassion for manual labor, working in a laundry.

Lewis's stenographer heroine comes to a similar conclusion. After a few weeks on the job, Una, a product of a small commercial college who has built up a city business career as an exciting alternative to life in her hometown, finds to her surprise that monotony, uninspiring young men, and lack of distinction are not confined to village existence. Having looked to the office world to inject excitement into her quiet life, she is dismayed to find that she is only an "Average Young Woman on a Job" (129). She is unheralded, unnoticed, anonymous—another "office-woman in eye-glasses" (125) worried about the loss of youth.

With the discovery that she is on a treadmill, not a ladder, her ambition "solidifie[s] into . . . conscientiousness" (114). Soon she echoes another working woman's complaints that "we *are* exploited, women who are on jobs. The bosses give us a lot of taffy and raise their hats—but they don't raise our wages, and . . . [they] think that if they keep us up till two . . . taking dictation they make it all right by apologizing" (172–73). In *Main Street*, which was widely read for its incisive critique of small-town America, the cultured heroine, Carol Kennicott, is exiled by wedlock to the village of Gopher Prairie and experiences a similar discontent. Privileged in a way that Una, who has a childlike mother to support, is not, Carol is the product of an affluent home and a decent college. But she too finds her work as a Chicago librarian a dead end and longs for a life with more definition than her job can give it.

Weary of loneliness, their hopes for advancement dashed, both women seek from marriage the attention they feel the job world did not provide. To their astonishment, they have underestimated the life so recently discarded. Still hearing what soon proves the sirens' call to "true womanhood," they are forced into an identity far more alien than that of an office toiler or a lifetime spinster in a local library. Marriage to unimaginative, anti-intellectual, fairly well-off men, that complacent Middle American type whom Lewis excelled in satirizing, has forced them to become women with "working brain[s] and no work" (86). Because their discovery carries the weight of Lewis's scorn for the narrowness and emptiness of small-town life, he approves their impulse to flee.

Anticipating by a decade the controversy over women who choose divorce and motherhood over marriage, Lewis sends Carol and her young son to wartime office work in Washington. Una, encumbered only by regret for her wrong turn, takes a low-level job at a real estate firm in New York. Despite her ability to support her child and her discovery that she is "no longer one-half of a marriage but the whole of a human being" (408), Carol is unable to shed her conviction that marriage is more meaningful than the career she craves. She returns to her boorish husband and her days of forced inactivity.

Una, by contrast, perseveres at the office, buys a blue suit and crepe de chine blouse for business, divorces her insensitive spouse, and develops new job skills in real estate. Challenging her employer's prejudice against women in sales, she eventually lands a job as a hotel executive. She becomes a "master," wrote the *Times* of the novel, for want of a better word, "of her job—and of herself."[45] In a bow to convention, Lewis tacks on what even in the 1920s seemed a contrived ending, an impending wedding to a romanticized and once-unattainable former boss.[46] Still, what appears to be a Hollywood conclusion refutes the charge that career women—particularly divorced ones—are destined for the single life. (In any case, in a daring response to those like the *Literary Digest* author who asked "Can a Woman Run a Home and a Job Too?"[47] Una vows to adopt a child should her career preclude a mate.) Nor with marriage will Una be stranded in a Gopher Prairie life; the novel's final passage rings with her resolve to keep her job.

If Carol falters because, like so many of those who flocked to the job-rich cities in the 1920s, she seeks "adventure" and "romance" from jobholding (Meyerowitz, 133), Una triumphs because she has understood that the rewards of work are not those of love. Her story left more than one reviewer with more "confidence in the women who are beginning to realize the possibilities of 'the job.' "[48] Lewis has no illusion that the unrewarding repetitiveness of much office work solved the emancipation drive, much less the emotional needs, of the white-collar girl. But in many passages describing women adapting to city work—the "nun of business" (76), the sterile professional woman, the hardened divorcée, the drab woman commuter—he discusses the unfairness implicit in the feminine choice of work or marriage. He never minimizes woman's rush to flee a lonely independence. But just as he uncovers the illusions fueling disastrous marriages, he celebrates the woman who can steel herself against solitude to attempt success in the professional world.

In an era when novelists of the white-collar girl credited her with everything from a near-mystical drive to a take-charge mentality to simple perseverance, a minority of writers, disturbed that the girl of good family was rubbing shoulders with the children of immigrants or those with similarly undistinguished forebears, clung to the old "perils of work" argument. Thus the "old guard" tried to rebut the idea that the Unas of this world, and even her less successful workmates, were better off than the Carol Kennicotts. One spokeswoman in Meredith Nicholson's *Broken Barriers*, fearful that her daughter must quit college to help their reduced family, speaks in the language of two decades earlier about the "dangers and temptations of the girl wage-earners" (118). Booth Tarkington's Pulitzer prizewinning *Alice Adams* (1921), a study of a faded American family, reveals the allied conviction that only the combined disgrace of failed finances and marital prospects should prompt a young lady to equip herself with unladylike clerical skills.[49] Thrust upon the world by the emptying of family coffers, these daughters of America enter the doors of business college as if passing through the gates of hell. Or they form imprudent associations with "party girl" coworkers and make "roaring twenties" fools of themselves. In a bow to what he calls the Jazz Age spirit, Nicholson's heroine by novel's end has attended, and emerged morally unscathed from, evening parties with dubious company, including a businessman with an irksome marriage. Skirting the censors, Nicholson prudently turns her married love interest into a widower ready to marry. Tarkington's heroine is never on the brink of adultery, but he treats her decision to enter Frincke's Business College almost as if she were, censoring her decision by alloting a page—the final one—to it. And if such heroines try to discard the genteel baggage they are made to carry—Grace Durland makes pronouncements about the new freedom, and Alice Adams realizes that self-reliance is better than fawning over the town's rich families—their creators do not seem to know it.

A fading Tarkington recaptured acclaim with his perennial theme, the social changes affecting decayed gentility, changes that in *Alice Adams* deprive the once-pampered title character of her anticipated marital prominence. But it was a vastly different author, Theodore Dreiser, who, 25 years after publishing *Sister Carrie*, pointed to a real social tragedy: that of the ambitious young woman whose ascension through work is preempted. Compared with Alice Adams (or Nicholson's heroine, who, eager to work, turns down her family's offer of business school), Dreiser's Roberta Alden finds the white-collar world effectively closed to her. A product of poverty who desires nothing so much as a "practical education" in bookkeeping (246), she is forced to give up the money she has saved from local factory jobs to her needy family. Discussions of *An American Tragedy* do not focus on Roberta's thwarted job plans but on the success-driven Clyde Griffiths. He finds her a convenient mistress, then, when she becomes pregnant and insists on marriage, a bar to his social ambitions. Clyde and his "mediocrity" clearly point to the crassness of the culture that forms and then twists his desires.[50] But Roberta Alden's derailed hopes suggest something of parallel importance.

By the 1920s, when three out of ten wage-earning women still worked in factories, the "old world of harsh conditions" had not so much disappeared as emerged softened by the "trappings of welfare" (Kessler-Harris 1982, 237, 239): lunchrooms, recreation areas, company outings, 15 minutes off every Tuesday and Friday. (Significantly, the minimum wage, operative from the 1910s in many states, was declared unconstitutional two years before *An American Tragedy* was published.) Despite some cosmetic boons, Dreiser suggests that, for the woman who lacked the steely determination of a Yezierska type, the old problems remained. Roberta is a "quick and intelligent worker" (qualities he did not remark in Carrie or Jennie Gerhardt in their laboring days). But she possesses "will and conviction" only "to a degree" (241). Having come to the Lycurgus Collar Factory from work at a mill near her farming home, she soon feels that her new position, though more desirable for its town location, cannot disguise political-economic reality. The management, Clyde Griffiths included, is male and mostly connected to the better families; the factory hands are female "from cellar to roof" (232).

An unknown soldier in this womanly army, Roberta finds the factory no gateway to opportunity, only a monotonous way station on a dreary journey from one low-level job to the next. She loses any sense of her powers and possibilities and comes to feel that unless she marries well, years of stamping collars in an upstate New York factory may turn her into one of the "old and weary-looking women who looked more like wraiths than human beings" (248) and whom she sees in the early morning on their way to the job. The tenement writers of the 1890s would have applauded her views but questioned her judgment in choosing the seductive, unstable Clyde as a rescuer. No tenement storyteller but a 1920s writer deploring his protagonist's abdicated ambition, Dreiser sees tragedy in Roberta rechanneling her legitimate need for job advancement into an obsessional and movie-fueled interest in wedlock to a romantic figure. She who had planned to free herself from family duty now asks herself what, "without [Clyde] and marriage and a home and children," "was there for a girl like her in the world?" (349). She becomes so fixated that she gives up a chance for the minimal job advancement the factory provides, ducking a kind of training session at the home of a coworker for amusement-park evenings with Clyde.

Roberta, then, is as much a victim of her own narrow vision as of her restricted job world. Soon, her hysteria rising about the prospect of unwed motherhood, she is too desperate to take in the implications of a forced marriage. She toys with the idea of leaving the factory and working elsewhere until the baby comes—a move that at least one period heroine, Elias Tobenkin's hardier Hilda Thorsen, successfully undertakes—but her rigid country upbringing and plummeting self-confidence convince her that life's goal should be nothing but respectability. When she clashes with Clyde, her hysteric clinging ends abruptly in her death by drowning on a weekend outing with her equally desperate lover, who finds her expendable.

The message of many 1920s novelists, that a woman who abandons her job identity is in peril, is further suggested by Hortense Briggs, an unpleasant but survival-minded minor character who, in a reversal of the main plot, sexually manipulates Clyde in his early job days. Superficially the mercenary shop girl of tenement fare, she milks men of compliments, gifts, evenings out. But, a far cry from the luckless Roberta, Hortense also fights for her rights with employers and changes jobs with an energetic frequency suggestive of a wily ability to weather the winds of romantic change. In their different ways, Clyde and Roberta, have-nots in a deterministic universe of things desired, fall victim to the "virus of ambition" (250). They sacrifice their belief in job possibilities, however restricted, to a fixation on quick social ascension—Clyde through marriage to Sondra Finchley, Roberta through marriage to Clyde. No white-collar success herself, the pragmatic Hortense still has much to teach them both.

If Roberta's tragedy is that she has ceased to aspire through work, the servant at the center of Fannie Hurst's *Lummox* (1923) never aspires at all. A permanent member of the servant class (even the "happy" ending finds her married to a widower glad to find a compliant wife-servant for his many children), Bertha knows only social prejudice against "thieving" immigrants, dirty work, long hours, and cast-off clothes.[51] Yet even her creator, who places the tale at the turn of the century but infuses it with a 1920s viewpoint, finds Bertha partly culpable for her inability to imagine a better life. By the end of the war many immigrants had deserted domestic service for better-paid factory work; one *Times* article the year of the Hurst novel grandly found "Hired Girls Almost Extinct."[52] But Bertha plods on, her eyes only on the next workday, anticipating only the next exacting mistress.

Hurst has compassion for the overworked Bertha's fatigue at the end of a 17-hour day that begins with stoking the coal range at 6:00 A.M. and ends with placing a silver pitcher of water by the master's bedside. But she wishes to show that Bertha's lummoxlike passivity—"a trait," stressed one biographer, that Hurst "deplored"[53]—makes her a collaborator in her exploitation. (In 1931 Hurst rang changes on the idea in her portrait of a forlorn kept woman in her immensely popular *Back Street*.) Always able to sway readers with her lachrymose fictions of good women beset by life's injustice—a talent for "weepers" that made her the third-highest–paid writer of the mid-1920s, Hurst compelled pity for the Berthas. But she is angry at Bertha for accepting subordination as her lot. To Hurst, speaking for her time, "woman's place" was "where she [could] get the most out of life" (qtd. Frederick, 361), a place poor Bertha never tries to locate.

When wartime optimists argued that woman could now expect "the sweets of economic independence" (Blair, 58), fiction responded with tales not only of new opportunities but also of the difficulty in reaching them. Edna Ferber and Sinclair Lewis, brushing such difficulties away, wove business world plots that feminize Horatio Alger's "pluck and luck" heroes or ascribe failure to lack of these qualities. Anzia Yezierska, recalling her oppressive sweatshop days, had a deeper comprehension of the sacrifices requisite for ascension. She infused tales of ever-hungry achievers with her lived experience. Theodore Dreiser treated the restrictions, sorrows, and insecurities of those for whom reality belied expectation. Whatever the angle of vision, the new fiction envisioned the working woman's capacity for achievement, not her imperiled character. It dramatized her quest for vocational fulfillment, not her marital rescue from the sexuality of the workplace, the loneliness of the furnished room, or the ennui of the middle-class daughter. Translating ambition into action, the fiction of ascension repudiated moral regulationists, uplifters, and advocates of woman's domestic sphere, from Stephen Crane to Marie Van Vorst, Jacob Riis to Arthur Bullard. In contrast to earlier decades, distinctions between male and female authors were minor; Sinclair Lewis was as likely as Edna Ferber to applaud woman's job-created autonomy. Although genteel novelists voiced the fear that "women can do anything they please these days" (*Barriers*, 11), they too sent women out to work. As advocates of everything from the dignity of self-supporting womanhood to the career woman's companionate marriage, 1920s writers portrayed an America beginning to resolve the contradictions between worker and woman that had shaped its discourse for more than three decades.

Whether in the iconoclastic fiction of Yezierska, who proclaims the immigrant's right to withhold her pay envelope from her family and acquire a college education, or the conventional fiction of Tarkington, whose marriage-seeking Americans end up in business school—even if by default—wage-earning women, whether from or on their way to the middle classes, transcended old categories to carve out new workplace possibilities. The Roberta

Aldens were poignant reminders that emotional and financial security eluded most unskilled factory women, particularly those burdened by single mother-hood. But in neither Dreiser nor his contemporaries is there a proletarian vision. Not until the Depression would literature again celebrate the commu-nity of workers, and then in terms that denigrated the female proletariat with the slogan "Don't take a job from a man."

Produced before the massive unemployment of the 1930s resurrected this gender issue, the fiction of feminine mobility commiserates with those stranded in the sweatshop subclass but applauds the determined heroine who pulls herself out of it. In its celebration of her solitary struggle, this fiction makes it clear that the working girl on the road to a profession has to travel alone.

In front of—and behind—the machinery at the Eberhard Faber Pencil Factory,
Greenpoint, Brooklyn, New York, c. 1900
Brooklyn Historical Society

7

Conclusion

The attention . . . devoted to her tells more about [the culture's] anxieties than about [working] women's troubles.

Christine Stansell, *City of Women*

BETWEEN 1890 AND 1925 LITERATURE DOCUMENTED AND CRITICIZED, celebrated and questioned the changes that transformed wage-earning women—at least those in the single, white majority—from workplace intruders to participants. Like the culture they mirrored—and, in the case of a Wharton or a Dreiser, reshaped into true art—many tales of the working girl, whether by conservative tenement and cross-class authors or radical socialists, could not relinquish the prejudice that woman should only work, if she had to work for money, until marriage. Fiction did, however, commemorate the single girl's movement from vulnerable workplace innocent (or dangerously erotic presence) to assertive jobholder.

Neither in literature nor in the culture itself did this transit mean economic equality or full independence. For every Shenah Pessah living out her ambitions there were many more Roberta Aldens waiting at the assembly line for a husband with a vocational future, or Carol Kennicotts tired of running from a stifling marriage to an unpromising clerical job. Women's historians remind us that in terms of significant wage increases, equality of opportunity, and access to the heights of a profession, the 1920s were far from a "watershed in the history of women at work."[1] More women were entering the legal profession—but the law schools of Columbia and Harvard routinely excluded them.[2] Females in business increased dramatically—yet by 1925 the unmarried woman who climbed from a secretarial to an executive position felt it politic to declare her belief "in marriage and children . . . above all the rewards of the business world."[3] To her adventuresome middle-class or educated immigrant sisters in the feminized world of office work, what "looked like upward mobility," notes Alice Kessler-Harris, "reflected a shift in occupational structures, easing life, providing more things to consume, and offering higher incomes . . . without altering [women's] relative positions in the wage labor force."[4]

Still, as early as the strike decade, women wanted more from work; something important had changed. In 1912 the garment-trade organizer Rose Schneiderman, her anger at the greatest female labor disaster of the day still fresh, raged at the Victorian stereotypes that kept women from receiving their due as workers and human beings. Even as laboring women perished in the Triangle Factory fire or stripped to the waist to work in foundries, she stormed, they were "not regarded as women" because the ideologues of ladyhood "talk[ed] all this trash of theirs about finer qualities."[5] It was not work that was unladylike, she insisted, only the conditions that prevented a living wage for it. Even as Schneiderman spoke, women were agitating for "bread and roses" in places like the textile town of Lawrence—and strike novelists were sending Comrade Yettas to join them.

Yet the fictional Yettas, and many of their real-life counterparts, abandoned the role of dedicated striker for that of matronly helpmeet. In American literature, as in the society it reflected, influenced, and interpreted, it took 35 years for working women to move toward the kind of legitimacy that Schneiderman wished for them. In late-nineteenth-century fiction, the conviction that work was unfeminine produced an obsessive concern with imperiled virtue.

If male authors rescued, female authors gentrified. By 1900, though the woman wage earner could be a transient labor heroine, her lower-class attributes were safely if unconvincingly recycled into a genteel superiority to, and aristocratically aided release from, her circumstances. In the masterful hands of a Theodore Dreiser and the popularizing ones of O. Henry, the untainted (even if "fallen") working woman survived in a social Darwinist world. Although the two writers validated her longing for a better life, they were still caught up in her moral defense. By the decade of the strike, she could finally be a labor comrade—for a time. Yet prejudices about marriage as feminine destiny again interfered with her work empowerment. It was only by 1917 that, seizing the wartime day, the female worker could achieve, or at least aspire to, job mobility. For the first time the threat of her competence replaced that of her sexuality, a fear mirrored in the 1920s debate about managing work and the home and in charges that women "repel[led] men" as they moved into the male world.[6]

By 1925 male and female authors alike were producing the fiction of upward struggle, which, with its daring suggestion of the companionate marriage, moved to refute the new charges. Many of these novels offered a brighter picture than that painted by reformers in the decade's second half, most notably by the prominent women whom the *Nation* magazine commissioned in 1926 to discuss the modern woman. Almost to a woman, they were irate at her forced "choice" between marriage and career and the slowness of her vocational progress. A former schoolteacher was eloquent about feeling "punished for being a woman" by the inferior wages she received.[7] The author of "Why I Earn My Own Living" found that that punishment ("men got the good jobs") clouded the lives of all wage-earning women, from charwoman to office worker.[8] Perhaps the bitterest sentiments were expressed by one woman who cautioned readers that it was "better to work hard than to be married hard."[9] (Such pessimism found its complement in brittle novels like Ursula Parrott's *Ex-Wife* [1929], which, rather than breathing the optimism of early 1920s fiction, rehearsed feminine dissatisfaction with husbands hostile to working wives.)

Soon the Great Depression arrived to place further strictures on feminine ambition. Women were blamed for finding work while men could not, even though by decade's end females outnumbered males on the unemployment line. As women workers again became an emotional issue, fiction responded to arguments at once familiar and products of the immediate situation. The economic desperation of the 1930s left no doubt that it was time for new tales of the working girl.

CHRONOLOGY

Women's Labor History: Highlights

1890   Federal government, responding to the influx of women into the industrial workplace, begins keeping detailed records on occupations and wages.

1894   Women first march in New York City's Labor Day parade.

1903   Women's Trade Union League founded to help women mobilize and to train organizers.

1905   Dorothy Richardson's *The Long Day: The Story of a New York Working Girl* is published anonymously, inaugurating the undercover narrative of women's substandard working conditions.

1909–1910   New York City Shirtwaist Strike, the "Uprising of the 20,000," is spearheaded by immigrant garment-center women; it is the largest women's strike to date.

1911   In the Triangle Shirtwaist Factory fire in New York, the period's greatest female labor tragedy, 146 workers, most of them women, perish.

1911–1917	Women continue to agitate, joining male coworkers at sites like the Lawrence textile mills.
1917	The United States enters World War I, providing women "men's jobs" in industry and accelerating white-collar work for them, but also dampening feminine strike activity.
1920	U.S. Women's Bureau, in the Department of Labor, is founded to survey women's pay scales and working conditions; women in white-collar sector outnumber female factory workers.

Women, Work, and American Fiction

1893	Stephen Crane's *Maggie: A Girl of the Streets*, the era's foremost sweatshop-to-prostitution tale, is published.
1893–1898	Heyday of tenement tales about the working girl by Crane contemporaries Jacob Riis, J. W. Sullivan, and others.
1900	Theodore Dreiser's *Sister Carrie*, exonerating a working-girl-turned-mistress, is published and has a moralistic reception.
1902–1910	O. Henry's sympathetic vignettes of shop-girl life enjoy popularity.
1903–1910	The "lady bountiful" and philanthropic rescue novels by Edith Wharton, Marie Van Vorst, and their female contemporaries are in vogue.
1910–1917	Fiction on feminine labor protest by Arthur Bullard and fellow socialists is popular.
1920–1925	The fiction of Sinclair Lewis, Edna Ferber, and others about white-collar girls is widely read. Heyday of Anzia Yezierska's ambitious immigrant heroines, freed from the sweatshop.

NOTES AND REFERENCES

Preface

1. Walter F. Taylor, *The Economic Novel in America* (Chapel Hill: University of North Carolina Press, 1942); Walter B. Rideout, *The Radical Novel in the United States, 1900–1954* (Cambridge: Harvard University Press, 1956).

2. Benedict Giamo, *On the Bowery: Confronting Homelessness in American Society* (Iowa City: University of Iowa Press, 1989).

3. Fay M. Blake, *The Strike in the American Novel* (Metuchen, N.J.: Scarecrow Press, 1972), 59, 99–106; Ann Schofield, ed., *Sealskin and Shoddy: Working Women in American Labor Press Fiction, 1870–1920* (Westport, Conn.: Greenwood Press, 1988). For a typically brief discussion of selected texts on the female labor experience during the period in question, see Barbara Bardes and Suzanne Gossett, *Declarations of Independence: Women and Political Power in Nineteenth-Century American Fiction* (New Brunswick; N.J.: Rutgers University Press, 1990), 121–29.

4. Although a handful of authors depicted blacks as servants—whether a mammy (a minor character in Charles Waddell Chestnutt's 1901 novel *The Marrow of Tradition*), a washerwoman (a secondary character in Jessie Redmon Fauset's 1924 novel *There Is Confusion*), or a maid (Wallace Thurman, *The*

Blacker the Berry [1929])—they, like other black writers of the late nineteenth and early twentieth century (Alice Dunbar Nelson, Frances E. W. Harper, Pauline E. Hopkins), were more concerned with race than with women's work. (Harper's eponymous Iola Leroy, a nurse and teacher dismissed from a shop job because of color, is a Civil War heroine.) Not until the Harlem Renaissance did a writer (Nella Larsen, *Quicksand* [1928]) depict southern black schoolteachers as "new womanly" wage earners.

5. Jacqueline Jones, *Labor of Love, Labor of Sorrow: Black Women, Work, and the Family, from Slavery to the Present* (New York: Vintage, 1986), 167.

6. Joseph A. Hill, *Women in Gainful Occupations, 1870–1920* (Washington, D.C.: Government Printing Office, 1929), 43.

Chapter 1

1. Mabel Collins Donnelly, *The American Victorian Woman* (Westport, Conn.: Greenwood Press, 1986), 95.

2. Philip S. Foner, *Women and the American Labor Movement from Colonial Times to the Eve of World War I* (New York: Free Press, 1979), 257; hereafter cited in text.

3. Alice Kessler-Harris, *Out to Work: A History of Wage-Earning Women in the United States* (New York: Oxford University Press, 1982), 143; hereafter cited in text.

4. James R. Barrett, *Work and Community in the Jungle: Chicago's Packing House Workers, 1894–1922* (Urbana: University of Illinois Press, 1987), 51.

5. Quoted in Mary P. Ryan, *Womanhood in America from Colonial Times to the Present* (New York: New Viewpoints Press, 1975), 201; hereafter cited in text.

6. On domestic service, see David M. Katzman, *Seven Days a Week: Women and Domestic Service in Industrializing America* (New York: Oxford University Press, 1978), and Nancy Woloch, *Woman and the American Experience* (New York: Alfred A. Knopf, 1984), 232–40; hereafter cited in text. On black servants, see Jacqueline Jones, *Labor of Love, Labor of Sorrow: Black Women, Work, and the Family, from Slavery to the Present* (New York: Vintage, 1986), 113.

7. Susan Porter Benson, *Counter Cultures: Saleswomen, Managers, and Customers in American Department Stores, 1890–1940* (Urbana: University of Illinois Press, 1988), 123.

8. Elyce J. Rotella, *From Home to Office: U.S. Women at Work, 1870–1930* (Ann Arbor: UMI Press, 1977), 156; hereafter cited in text. The new professional women attracted to social welfare, medicine, law, and academia faced much criticism and discrimination, but despite Ryan's assertion that they were "social housekeepers" or "assistant professionals" (234), they were no mere wage earners and are thus the subject of another study.

9. Lynn Y. Weiner, *From Working Girl to Working Mother: The Female Labor Force in the United States, 1820–1980* (Chapel Hill: University of North Carolina Press, 1985), 30; hereafter cited in text.

10. Marcia Jacobson, *Henry James and the Mass Market* (University: University of Alabama Press, 1983), 5.

11. Robert H. Bremner, *From the Depths: The Discovery of Poverty in the United States* (New York: New York University Press, 1964); hereafter cited in

text. See, for example, William Rainsford, "What Can We Do for the Poor?" *Forum* 4 (April 1891): 117–20.

12. Frank Norris, "Popular Fiction," in *The Literary Criticism of Frank Norris*, ed. Donald Pizer (Austin: University of Texas Press, 1964), 127.

13. For an analysis of the "wicked city" and "virtue betrayed" fiction from the antebellum to the late-Victorian era, see Laura Hapke, *Girls Who Went Wrong: Prostitutes in American Fiction, 1885–1917* (Bowling Green, Ohio: Bowling Green State University Press, 1989), chap. 2.

14. Quoted in William Hard, "The Woman's Invasion," *Everybody's* 19 (November 1908): 585; hereafter cited in text.

15. Anzia Yezierska, *Bread Givers*, intro. Alice Kessler-Harris (1925; reprint, New York: Persea, 1973), 172.

16. G. Ferrers, "The Law of Non-Labor," *Literary Digest* 8 (1 February 1894): 308; hereafter cited in text.

17. Meredith Tax, *The Rising of the Women: Feminist Solidarity and Class Conflict, 1880–1917* (New York: Monthly Review Press, 1980), 31, 131.

18. Henry T. Finck, "Employments Unsuitable for Women," *Independent* (11 April 1907): 834; hereafter cited in text.

19. Edward O'Donnell, "Women as Breadwinners—The Error of the Age," *American Federationist* (October 1897): 186.

20. "Marry the Women," *Birmingham Labor Advocate* (25 May 1901): 1.

21. Sally Fairfield Burton, "Give Me Liberty," *New York Times*, 20 August 1922, reprinted in *Women: Their Changing Roles* (New York: Arno Press/New York Times, 1973), 122; hereafter cited in text.

22. Mary Anderson, "Working Conditions," *American Federationist* (October 1925): 947.

23. Ernest R. Groves, "The Personality Results of the Wage Employment of Women Outside the Home and Their Social Consequences," *Annals of the American Academy of Political and Social Science* 143 (May 1929): 341; hereafter cited in text.

24. Barbara Welter, "The Cult of True Womanhood, 1820–1860," *American Quarterly* 18 (Summer 1966): 151.

25. Mark Thomas Connelly, *The Response to Prostitution in the Progressive Era* (Chapel Hill: University of North Carolina Press, 1980), 102.

26. Robert Smuts, *Women and Work in America* (New York: Schocken, 1972), 117; hereafter cited in text.

27. Grant Allen, "Women's Place in Nature," *Forum* 7 (June 1889): 263.

28. Azel Ames, M.D., *Sex in Industry: A Plea for the Working Girl* (Boston: James R. Osgood, 1875), 44; hereafter cited in text.

29. "Women in Industry," *Monthly Labor Review* 12 (January 1921): 155.

30. Benita Eisler, ed., *The Lowell Offering* (Philadelphia: J. B. Lippincott, 1977), 13–29 passim.

31. Lillie Wyman, "Girls in a Factory Valley," *Atlantic Monthly* 78 (1896): 396; hereafter cited in text.

32. [Harold Frederic], "Musings on the Question of the Hour," *Pall Mall Budget* (13 August 1885): 12.

33. Quoted in Kathy Peiss, *Cheap Amusements: Working Women and Leisure in Turn-of-the-Century New York* (Philadelphia: Temple University Press, 1986), 70; hereafter cited in text.

34. Hutchins Hapgood, *Types from City Streets* (1910; reprint, New York: Garrett Press, 1970), 131.

35. Elizabeth Butler, *Women and the Trades, 1907–1908* (New York: Russell Sage Foundation, 1909), 305.

36. Rheta Childe Dorr, *What Eight Million Women Want* (Boston: Small, Maynard, 1910), 190.

37. [Women's Column], *Collier's* (12 November 1910): 20–21.

38. Ruth S. True, *The Neglected Girl* (New York: Russell Sage Foundation, 1914), 50; hereafter cited in text.

39. William Sanger, M.D., *The History of Prostitution* (1858; reprint, New York: Medical Publishing Co., 1906), 524; hereafter cited in text.

40. B. O. Flower, *Civilization's Inferno* (Boston: Arena Publishing Co., 1893), 9.

41. Maud Nathan, "Women Who Work and Women Who Spend," *Annals of the American Academy of Political and Social Science* 27 (1906), 646–50.

42. Alice Hyneman Rhine, "Woman in Industry," in *Woman's Work in America*, ed. Annie Nathan Meyer (New York: Henry Holt and Co., 1891), 287.

43. Katharine Pearson Woods, "Queens of the Shop, the Workroom, and the Tenement," in *What America Owes to Women*, ed. Lydia Holt Farnham (Buffalo: Charles Moulton, 1893), 441.

44. Quoted in *America's Working Women: A Documentary History, 1600 to the Present*, ed. Rosalyn Baxandall, Linda Gordon, and Susan Reverby (New York: Vintage, 1976), 157; hereafter cited in text.

45. Helen Campbell, "The Working Women of To-Day," *Arena* 4 (1891): 332.

46. *Working Women in Large Cities* (Washington, D.C.: Government Printing Office, 1889), 77.

47. Edith Abbott, *Women in Industry* (1910; reprint, New York: Arno Press/New York Times, 1969), 309.

48. Quoted in William H. Chafe, *The American Woman: Her Changing Social, Economic, and Political Roles, 1920–1970* (New York: Oxford University Press, 1972), 65.

49. Cited in Theresa Malkiel, *Diary of a Shirtwaist Maker* [1910], intro. Francoise Basch (Ithaca, N.Y.: ILR Press, 1990), 17; hereafter cited in text.

50. Cited in Barbara Mayer Wertheimer, *We Were There: The Story of Working Women in America* (New York: Pantheon, 1977), 261 (hereafter cited in text), and Dorothy Richardson, *The Long Day: The Story of a New York Working Girl* (1905; reprint, Charlottesville: University Press of Virginia, 1990); hereafter cited in text.

51. Mrs. John [Bessie] Van Vorst and Marie Van Vorst, *The Woman Who Toils* (London: Grant Richards, 1903), 27.

52. Annie Marion MacLean, "Two Weeks in Department Stores," *American Journal of Sociology* 4 (May 1899): 738. Although no one confused work in the office, schoolroom, or hospital with industrial toil, by 1910, at the height of the working girl debate, clerical workers with job grievances unionized and marched in Labor Day parades with their blue-collar sisters, and teachers formed their own union and demanded an end to better jobs being awarded to men, and women teachers being forbidden to marry. Less militant, hospital nurses endured the drudgery and low pay of their work, while those in private duty struggled for

acceptance as professionals. See Rotella, passim; Wertheimer, chap. 13; and Woloch, 245–49.

53. Helen Campbell, *Prisoners of Poverty* (1887; reprint, Westport, Conn.: Greenwood Press, 1970), 28.

54. Edgar Fawcett, "The Woes of the New York Working-Girl," *Arena* 4 (December 1891): 35.

55. Caro Lloyd, "The Illinois Vice Commission," *New Review* (12 April 1913): 458.

56. John D. Peters, "The Story of the Committee of Fourteen of New York," *Social Hygiene* 14 (1918): 358.

57. Chicago Vice Commission, *The Social Evil in Chicago* (1911; reprint, New York: Arno Press, 1970), 43; hereafter cited in text.

58. Annie Allen, "How to Save Girls Who Have Fallen," *Survey* 21 (1910): 690.

59. Clare de Graffenreid, "The Condition of Wage-Earning Women," *Forum* 15 (March 1893): 80; hereafter cited in text.

60. George Kneeland, *Commercialized Prostitution in New York* (1913; reprint, Montclair, N.J.: Patterson Smith, 1969), 104.

61. Mary Gay Humphreys, "The New York Working-Girl," *Scribner's* 20 (October 1896): 512.

62. See, for example, Joanne J. Meyerowitz, *Women Adrift: Independent Wage Earners in Chicago, 1880–1930* (Chicago: University of Chicago Press, 1988), 123.

63. Grace Hoadley Dodge, ed., *Thoughts of Busy Girls* (New York: Assell Publishing Co., 1892), ix; hereafter cited in text.

64. "The Life Story of a German Nurse Girl," in *The Life Stories of [Undistinguished] Americans*, ed. Hamilton Holt (1906; reprint, New York: Routledge, 1990), 83.

65. William T. Elsing, "Life in New York Tenement Houses," *Scribner's* 11 (1892): 716.

66. Belle Lindner Israels, "The Way of the Girl," *Survey* (3 July 1909): 489.

67. Elizabeth Perry, " 'The General Motherhood of the Commonwealth': Dance Hall Reform in the Progressive Era," *American Quarterly* 37 (1985): 727; hereafter cited in text.

68. Leslie Woodcock Tentler, *Wage-Earning Women: Industrial Work and Family Life in the United States, 1900–1930* (New York: Oxford University Press, 1979), 67.

69. Compare Wyman, passim, and Mary Van Kleeck, "Women and Machines," *Atlantic Monthly* 127 (1921): 250–60.

Chapter 2

1. Jacob Riis, *How the Other Half Lives* (1890; reprint, New York: Dover, 1971), 189; hereafter cited in text. Unlike audiences for Riis's slide lectures, the earliest readers of *Other Half* did not see photographs, only drawings. Later editions included the photos.

2. Helen Campbell, *Women Wage-Earners* (1893; reprint, New York: Arno Press/New York Times, 1972), 194.

3. Arthur M. Schlesinger, *The Rise of the City, 1878–1898* (New York: Macmillan, 1933), 67.

    4. Statistics on the city's working women, especially those in the garment trade, are in Philip S. Foner, *Women and the American Labor Movement from Colonial Times to the Eve of World War I* (New York: Free Press, 1979), 258, 259; hereafter cited in text.

    5. See, for example, Benedict Giamo, *On the Bowery: Confronting Homelessness in American Society* (Iowa City: University of Iowa Press, 1989), chap. 2 (hereafter cited in text), and Alan Trachtenberg, "Experiments in Another Country: Stephen Crane's City Sketches," *Southern Review* 10 (Spring 1976): 265–85.

    6. Julian Ralph, *People We Pass: Stories of Life among the Masses of New York City* (New York: Harper & Brothers, 1896), vi; hereafter cited in text.

    7. See, for example, Lawrence E. Hussman, Jr., "The Fate of the Fallen Woman in *Maggie* and *Sister Carrie*," in *The Image of the Prostitute in Modern Literature*, ed. Pierre L. Horn and Mary Beth Pringle (New York: Ungar, 1984), 91–100, and Carol Hurd Green, "Stephen Crane and the Fallen Women," in *American Novelists Revisited: Essays in Feminist Criticism*, ed. Fritz Fleischmann (Boston: G. K. Hall, 1982), 225–42 (hereafter cited in text).

    8. On "inviolate" and "betrayed" women, see David M. Fine, *The City, the Immigrant, and American Fiction, 1880–1925* (Westport, Conn.: Greenwood, 1977), 46; on their environment, see Fine, "Abraham Cahan, Stephen Crane, and the Romantic Tenement Tale of the Nineties," *American Studies* 14 (Spring 1973): 100.

    9. Robert H. Bremner, *From the Depths: The Discovery of Poverty in the United States* (New York: New York University Press, 1956), 100; Walter F. Taylor, *The Economic Novel in America* (Chapel Hill: University of North Carolina Press, 1942), 80.

    10. T. S. Arthur, *The Seamstress: A Tale of the Times* (Philadelphia: R. G. Berford, 1843), 19.

    11. Herman Melville, *Selected Tales and Poems*, ed. Richard Chase (New York: Holt, Rinehart & Winston, 1966), xi; hereafter cited in text.

    12. Elizabeth Stuart Phelps, *The Silent Partner* (1871; reprint, New York: Feminist Press, 1983), 77.

    13. Henry James, *The Princess Casamassima* (1886; reprint, New York: Harper & Row, 1964), 121; hereafter cited in text.

    14. James W. Sullivan, *Tenement Tales of New York* (New York: Henry Holt and Co., 1895); hereafter cited in text.

    15. Kathy Peiss, *Cheap Amusements: Working Women and Leisure in Turn-of-the-Century New York* (Philadelphia: Temple University Press, 1986), 50; hereafter cited in text.

    16. *Bookman* (July 1895): 414.

    17. David S. Reynolds, *Beneath the American Renaissance: The Subversive Imagination in the Age of Emerson and Melville* (New York: Alfred A. Knopf, 1988), 216.

    18. Jacob Riis, *Out of Mulberry Street* (1898; reprint, Upper Saddle River, N.J.: Gregg Press, 1970), 122; hereafter cited in text.

    19. William Sanger, M.D., *The History of Prostitution* (1858; reprint, New York: Medical Publishing Co., 1906), 534.

20. Stephen Crane, *Maggie: A Girl of the Streets* [1893], Norton Critical Edition, ed. Thomas A. Gullason (New York: W. W. Norton, 1974), 25; hereafter cited in text.

21. Donald Pizer, "Stephen Crane's *Maggie* and American Naturalism," in *Maggie*, 192.

22. Quoted in Robert W. Stallman, *Stephen Crane: A Biography* (New York: George Braziller, 1968), 225.

23. Nancy Woloch, *Woman and the American Experience* (New York: Alfred A. Knopf, 1984), 234.

24. Brander Matthews, "Before the Break of Day," *Vignettes of Manhattan* (1894; reprint, Freeport, N.Y.: Books for Libraries Press, 1969), 92; hereafter cited in text.

25. Edward W. Townsend, *Chimmie Fadden* (1895; reprint, New York: Garrett Press, 1969); "Edward W. Townsend Dies," *New York Times*, 17 March 1942, 21; Edward W. Townsend, *A Daughter of the Tenements* (New York: Lovell, Coryell, 1895), 7; hereafter cited in text. For a similar slum princess plot see Edward W. Townsend, *Days Like These* (New York: Harper & Brothers, 1901).

26. *Bookman* (February 1901): 544.

27. Quoted in Bernard G. Richards, "Abraham Cahan Cast in a New Role," in Abraham Cahan, *Yekl* and *The Imported Bridegroom and Other Stories of Yiddish New York*, ed. Bernard G. Richards (1896, 1898; reprint, New York: Dover, 1970), vii; hereafter cited in text.

28. Elizabeth Ewen, *Immigrant Women in the Land of Dollars: Life and Culture on the Lower East Side, 1890–1925* (New York: Monthly Review Press, 1985), 52; hereafter cited in text. See also Sydney Stahl Weinberg, *The World of Our Mothers: The Lives of Jewish Immigrant Women* (New York: Schocken, 1988); hereafter cited in text.

29. Irving Howe, *World of Our Fathers* (New York: Simon and Schuster, 1976), 267.

30. Francis Hopkinson Smith, *Tom Grogan* (1895; reprint, Boston: Houghton Mifflin, 1899), 6; hereafter cited in text.

31. *Bookman* (May 1896): 264.

32. Joseph Barondess, "How the New York Cloak Union Started" (1903), reprinted in *Out of the Sweatshop: The Struggle for Industrial Democracy*, ed. Leon Stein (New York: Quadrangle/New York Times Book Co., 1977), 38.

33. Rose Schneiderman, "A Cap Maker's Story," *Independent* (27 April 1905): 938.

34. Patricia Cooper, *Once a Cigar Maker: Men, Women, and Work Culture in American Cigar Factories, 1900–1919* (Urbana: University of Illinois Press, 1989), 2.

35. Eunice Lipton, "The Laundress in Late Nineteenth-Century French Culture," *Art History* 3 (September 1980): 303.

Chapter 3

1. Mary E. Wilkins [Freeman], *The Portion of Labor* (New York: Harper & Brothers, 1901); Marie Van Vorst, *Amanda of the Mill* (Indianapolis: Bobbs-Merrill, 1904); both hereafter cited in text.

2. Vida Scudder, *A Listener in Babel* (Boston: Houghton Mifflin, 1903); hereafter cited in text.

3. Edith Wharton, *The House of Mirth* (New York: Charles Scribner's Sons, 1905); hereafter cited in text.

4. Marie Van Vorst, *Philip Longstreth* (New York: Harper & Brothers, 1902); Edith Wharton, *The Fruit of the Tree* (New York: Charles Scribner's Sons, 1907), 449; hereafter cited in text.

5. Margaret Sherwood, *Henry Worthington, Idealist* (New York: Macmillan & Company, 1899) (hereafter cited in text); Charlotte Perkins Gilman, *What Diantha Did* (New York: Charlton Publishers, 1910).

6. Mary Cadwallader Jones, "Women's Opportunities in Town and Country," *The Woman's Book*, vol. 2 (New York: Charles Scribner's Sons, 1894), 209; hereafter cited in text.

7. Mary P. Ryan, *Womanhood in America from Colonial Times to the Present* (New York: New Viewpoints Press, 1975), chap. 5; hereafter cited in text.

8. Nancy Woloch, *Woman and the American Experience* (New York: Alfred A. Knopf, 1984); 225.

9. Hilda Satt Polacheck, *I Came a Stranger: The Story of a Hull-House Girl*, ed. Dena J. Polacheck, introd. Lynn Y. Weiner (Urbana: University of Illinois Press, 1989), 68; hereafter cited in text.

10. Quoted in Abbie Graham, *Grace Dodge: Merchant of Dreams* (New York: Woman's Press, 1926), 104.

11. Mrs. John [Bessie] Van Vorst and Marie Van Vorst, *The Woman Who Toils* (London: Grant Richards, 1903), 190; hereafter cited in text. Marie wrote the second half.

12. Maud Nathan, "Women Who Work and Women Who Spend," *Annals of the American Academy of Political and Social Science* 27 (1906): 648; hereafter cited in text.

13. Lillian Pettengill, *Toilers of the Home* (New York: Doubleday, Page and Co., 1903), vii.

14. Dorothy Richardson, *The Long Day: The Story of a New York Working Girl* (1905; reprint, Charlottesville: University Press of Virginia, 1990); hereafter cited in text.

15. Maud Younger, "The Diary of an Amateur Waitress," *McClure's* 28 (1907): 543.

16. Lillian W. Betts, *The Leaven in a Great City* (New York: Dodd, Mead, 1902), 158; hereafter cited in text.

17. Joanne Reitano, "Working Girls Unite," *American Quarterly* 36 (Spring 1984): 130; hereafter cited in text. I am indebted to her discussion of the clubs.

18. Quoted in Esther Katz, *Grace Hoadley Dodge: Women and the Emerging Metropolis, 1856–1914* (Ph.D. diss., New York University, 1980), 77, 80.

19. Grace Hoadley Dodge, ed., *Thoughts of Busy Girls* (New York: Assell Publishing Co., 1892); hereafter cited in text.

20. Jane Thompson, Afterword, in Susan Warner, *The Wide, Wide World* (New York: Feminist Press, 1978), 598.

21. Alice Kessler-Harris, *Out to Work: A History of Wage-Earning Women in the United States* (New York: Oxford University Press, 1982), 93.

22. Nancy Schrom Dye, *As Equals and Sisters: Feminism, Unionism, and the Women's Trade Union League* (Columbia: University of Missouri Press, 1980), 55; hereafter cited in text.

23. Cited in Reviewers' Comments Excerpt Section, Dorothy Richardson, *The Long Day* (New York: Century, 1905), 305; see also Cindy Sondik Aron, Introduction, *The Long Day* (Charlottesville: University Press of Virginia, 1990), ix.

24. Cited in Meredith Tax, *The Rising of the Women: Feminist Solidarity and Class Conflict, 1880–1917* (New York: Monthly Review Press, 1980), 117.

25. Rose Phelps Stokes, "*The Long Day*: A Story of Real Life," *Independent* (16 November 1903): 1170.

26. Alan Trachtenberg, "Experiments in Another Country: Stephen Crane's City Sketches," *Southern Review* 10 (Spring 1974): 273; hereafter cited in text.

27. Geoffrey Walton, *Edith Wharton: A Critical Interpretation* (Rutherford, N.J.: Fairleigh Dickinson University Press, 1970), 74; Edith Wharton, "Bunner Sisters" (1892), *The Best Short Stories of Edith Wharton* (New York: Charles Scribner's Sons, 1958).

28. Elizabeth Ammons, *Edith Wharton's Argument with America* (Athens: University of Georgia Press, 1980), 12; hereafter cited in text.

29. *Literary World* (3 March 1900): 76.

30. Nan Bauer Maglin, "Visions of Defiance: Work, Political Commitment, and Sisterhood in Twenty-One Works of Fiction, 1895–1925," *Praxis* 3 (1976): 109.

31. Mrs. John Van Vorst, "The Woman of the People," *Harper's Monthly* 106 (1903): 874–75.

32. Rheta Childe Dorr, "Give the Working Girl a Chance," *Hampton's Broadway Magazine* 22 (January 1909): 66–77.

33. Peter J. Frederick, "Vida Dutton Scudder: The Professor as Social Activist," *New England Quarterly* 43 (September 1970): 424.

34. *New York Times*, 5 December 1903, 927.

35. Quoted in Arthur John, *The Best Years of the Century* (Urbana: University of Illinois Press, 1981), 155.

36. Mary H. Blewett, *Men, Women, and Work: Class, Gender, and Protest in the New England Shoe Industry, 1780–1910* (Urbana: University of Illinois Press, 1988).

37. Susan Estabrook Kennedy, *If All We Did Was Weep at Home: A History of White Working-Class Women in America* (Bloomington: Indiana University Press, 1979), 123.

38. Barbara Leslie Epstein, *The Politics of Domesticity: Women, Evangelism, and Temperance in Nineteenth-Century America* (Middletown, Conn.: Wesleyan University Press, 1981), 144.

39. Barbara Bardes and Suzanne Gossett, *Declarations of Independence: Women and Political Power in Nineteenth-Century American Fiction* (New Brunswick, N.J.: Rutgers University Press, 1990), 208n; hereafter cited in text.

40. *Bookman* 15 (March 1902): 71.

41. Edith Wharton, *The House of Mirth*, intro. Cynthia Griffin Woolf (New York: Penguin, 1985), xxvi.

42. Cathy N. Davidson, "Kept Women in *The House of Mirth*," *Markham Review* 9 (1979): 10.

43. Alfred Kazin, *On Native Grounds: A Study of Modern American Prose Literature* (Garden City, N.Y.: Doubleday & Co., 1956), 59.

44. Owen Kildare, *My Mamie Rose* (New York: Grosset and Dunlap, 1903), 269.

Chapter 4

1. O. Henry, "Elsie in New York" [1905], in *Collected Stories of O. Henry*, ed. Paul J. Horowitz (New York: Avenel/Crown, 1979). Unless otherwise noted, all Porter short stories hereafter cited in the text are quoted from this edition.

2. H. J. Forman, "O. Henry's Short Stories," *North American Review* (May 1908): 781.

3. *Nation* (2 July 1908): 12; Eugene Current-Garcia, *O. Henry* (New York: Twayne, 1965), 17; hereafter cited in text.

4. David Stuart, *O. Henry* (Chelsea, Mi.: Scarborough House, 1990), 203; hereafter cited in text. Porter eventually relented and did appear in the *Post* by 1907.

5. Theodore Dreiser, *Sister Carrie* [1900], restored edition, ed. James L. W. West, et al. (New York: Penguin, 1981); hereafter cited in text.

6. Esther Katz, *Grace Hoadley Dodge: Women and the Emerging Metropolis, 1856–1914* (Ph.D. diss., New York University, 1980), chap. 6.

7. Theodore Dreiser, *Jennie Gerhardt* (1911; reprint, New York: Penguin, 1989); hereafter cited in text.

8. Quoted in Jack Salzman, "The Critical Recognition of *Sister Carrie*, 1900–1907," *Journal of American Studies* 1 (1967): 126, 125. See also Richard Lingeman, *Theodore Dreiser*, vol. 1, *At the Gates of the City, 1871–1907* (New York: G. P. Putnam's Sons, 1986), 296–97, 294; hereafter cited in text.

9. Karen C. Blansfield, *Cheap Rooms and Restless Hearts: A Study of Formula in the Urban Tales of William Sydney Porter* (Bowling Green, Ohio: Bowling Green University Press, 1988), 98, 99; hereafter cited in text.

10. Eunice Lipton, *Looking into Degas: Uneasy Images of Women and Modern Life* (Berkeley: University of California Press, 1986), 189.

11. Sue Ainslie Clark and Edith Wyatt, *Making Both Ends Meet: The Income and Outlay of New York Working Girls* (New York: Macmillan, 1911).

12. Clara Laughlin, *The Work-a-Day Girl* (New York: Fleming H. Revell, 1913), hereafter cited in text; Elizabeth Butler, *Women and the Trades, 1907–1908* (New York: Russell Sage Foundation, 1909).

13. O. Henry, "The Third Ingredient," in *Options* (New York: Grosset and Dunlap, 1909); hereafter cited in text.

14. Joanne J. Meyerowitz, *Women Adrift: Independent Wage Earners in Chicago, 1880–1930* (Chicago: University of Chicago Press, 1988), 66; hereafter cited in text.

15. Cited in *America's Working Women: A Documentary History, 1600 to the Present*, ed. Rosalyn Baxandall, Linda Gordon, and Susan Reverby (New York: Vintage, 1976), 146.

16. Dorothy Richardson, *The Long Day: The Story of a New York Working Girl* (1905; reprint, Charlottesville: University Press of Virginia, 1990); hereafter cited in text.

17. Kathy Peiss, *Cheap Amusements: Working Women and Leisure in Turn-of-the-Century New York* (Philadelphia: Temple University Press, 1986), 115; hereafter cited in text.

18. Leslie Woodcock Tentler, *Wage-Earning Women: Industrial Work and Family Life in the United States, 1900–1930* (New York: Oxford University Press, 1979), 71.

19. Mrs. John [Bessie] Van Vorst and Marie Van Vorst, *The Woman Who Toils* (London: Grant Richards, 1903), 58.

20. Philip L. Gerber, *Theodore Dreiser* (New York: Twayne, 1964), 54.

21. Theodore Dreiser, *Dawn* (New York: Horace Liveright, 1931), 69.

22. Lois Banner, *Women in Modern America*, 2d ed. (New York: Harcourt Brace Jovanovich, 1984), 74.

23. Theodore Dreiser, "The Transmigration of the Sweatshop," *Puritan* 7 (July 1898): 498; "Christmas in the Tenements" [1902], in *Theodore Dreiser: A Selection of Uncollected Prose*, ed. Donald Pizer (Detroit: Wayne State University Press, 1977), 150–54. Unless otherwise noted, all Dreiser short stories hereafter cited in the text are quoted from this edition.

24. Rachel Bowlby, *Just Looking: Consumer Culture in Dreiser, Gissing, and Zola* (New York: Methuen, 1985), 65; hereafter cited in text. I am indebted to her discussion of the department store.

25. Blanche Gelfant, "Sister to Faust: The City's 'Hungry' Woman as Heroine," in *Women Writers and the City: Essays in Feminist Literary Criticism*, ed. Susan Merrill Squier (Knoxville: University of Tennessee Press, 1984), 270.

26. W. A. Swanberg, *Dreiser* (New York: Bantam, 1967), 30.

27. Eliseo Vivas, "Dreiser: An Inconsistent Mechanist," in *The Stature of Theodore Dreiser*, ed. Alfred Kazin and Charles Shapiro (Bloomington: Indiana University Press, 1965), 237–45.

28. Richard Lehan, *Theodore Dreiser: His World and His Novels* (Carbondale: Southern Illinois University Press, 1971), xii; hereafter cited in text.

29. Mabel Collins Donnelly, *The American Victorian Woman* (Westport, Conn.: Greenwood Press, 1986), 95; George Kibbee Turner, "The City of Chicago: A Study of the Great Immoralities," *McClure's* 27 (April 1907): 575–91.

30. Sheldon Grebstein, "Dreiser's Victorian Vamp," in *Sister Carrie: Texts and Sources*, ed. Donald Pizer (New York: W. W. Norton, 1970), 545; both hereafter cited in text.

31. Theodore Dreiser, *Jennie Gerhardt*, intro. Helen Yglesias (New York: Schocken, 1982), viii; hereafter cited in text.

32. Eunice Lipton, "The Laundress in Late Nineteenth-Century French Culture," *Art History* 3 (September 1980): 302.

33. Meyerowitz, 67; Philip S. Foner, *Women and the American Labor Movement from Colonial Times to the Eve of World War I* (New York: Free Press, 1979), 309.

34. Alice Hyneman Rhine, "Woman in Industry," in *Woman's Work in America*, ed. Annie Nathan Meyer (New York: Henry Holt and Co., 1891), 287.

35. Jack London, *Martin Eden* (1909; reprint, New York: Penguin, 1984); hereafter cited in text.

36. Mary Heaton Vorse, "The Experiences of a Hired Girl" [1901], Archives of Labor History and Urban Affairs, Wayne State University Library. On Vorse, see *Notable American Women: The Modern Period*, ed. Barbara Sicherman and Carol Hurd Green (Cambridge, Mass.: Belknap/Harvard University Press, 1980), 712–14.

37. David M. Katzman, *Seven Days a Week: Women and Domestic Service in Industrializing America* (New York: Oxford University Press, 1978), 53.

38. David Montgomery, *Workers' Control in America* (Cambridge: Cambridge University Press, 1979), 93.

Chapter 5

1. For a discussion of the complex relation of the IWW to American socialism, see James Weinstein, *The Decline of Socialism in America, 1912–1925* (New York: Monthly Review Press, 1967); hereafter cited in text.

2. Elizabeth Gurley Flynn, *The Rebel Girl*, rev. ed. (New York: International Publishers, 1973), 77; hereafter cited in text.

3. Quoted in Richard Lingeman, *Theodore Dreiser*, vol. 1, *At the Gates of the City, 1871–1907* (New York: G. P. Putnam's Sons, 1986), 404.

4. Joan M. Jensen, "The Great Uprisings: 1900–1920," in *A Needle, a Bobbin, a Strike: Women Needleworkers in America*, ed. Joan M. Jensen and Sue Davidson (Philadelphia: Temple University Press, 1984), 83. See also Philip S. Foner, *Women and the American Labor Movement from Colonial Times to the Eve of World War I* (New York: Free Press, 1979), chaps. 14–18; hereafter cited in text.

5. Roger Waldinger, "Another Look at the International Ladies' Garment Workers' Union: Women, Industry Structure, and Collective Action," in *Women, Work, and Protest*, ed. Ruth Milkman (1985; reprint, London: Routledge & Kegan Paul, 1987), 96; Meredith Tax, *The Rising of the Women: Feminist Solidarity and Class Conflict, 1880–1917* (New York: Monthly Review Press, 1980), 234; hereafter cited in text.

6. Alice Kessler-Harris, "Where Are the Organized Women Workers?" *Feminist Studies* 3 (Fall 1975): 93; hereafter cited in text.

7. Ruth Milkman, headnote to Waldinger, 86.

8. Sarah Comstock, "The Uprising of the Girls," *Collier's* (25 December 1909): 14; hereafter cited in text.

9. Review of *The Nine-Tenths* by James Oppenheim, *Bellman* (1 July 1911): 18; review of *Comrade Yetta* by Arthur Bullard, *Springfield Republican*, 27 March 1913, 5.

10. Arthur Bullard [Albert Edwards], *Comrade Yetta* (New York: Macmillan, 1913); James Oppenheim, *The Nine-Tenths* (1911; reprint, Upper Saddle River, N.J.: Gregg Press, 1968); both hereafter cited in text.

11. Philip S. Foner, *History of the Labor Movement in the United States*, vol. 3, *The Policies and Practices of the American Federation of Labor, 1900–1909* (New York: International Publishers, 1964), 438; hereafter cited in text.

12. Quoted in Barbara Mayer Wertheimer, *We Were There: The Story of Working Women in America* (New York: Pantheon, 1977), 353; hereafter cited in text.

13. Charlotte Baum, Paula Hyman, and Sonya Michel, *The Jewish Woman in America* (New York: Plume/New American Library, 1976), 130; Theresa Malkiel, *Diary of a Shirtwaist Striker* [1910], intro. Francoise Basch (Ithaca; N.Y.: ILR Press, 1990), 17; hereafter cited in text.

14. Quoted in Nancy Schrom Dye, *As Equals and Sisters: Feminism, the Labor Movement, and the Women's Trade Union League of New York* (Columbia: University of Missouri Press, 1980), 15.

15. Editorial preface to "Working Woman's Power," *America's Working Women: A Documentary History, 1600 to the Present*, ed. Rosalyn Baxandall, Linda Gordon, and Susan Reverby (New York: Vintage, 1976), 167; hereafter cited in text. On the perception of woman's new assertiveness as a threat, see also Kessler-Harris 1975, 96.

16. Alice Henry, *The Trade Union Woman* (New York: D. Appleton and Co., 1915), 155; hereafter cited in text.

17. Fay M. Blake, *The Strike in the American Novel* (Metuchen, N.J.: Scarecrow Press, 1972), 17, 72; hereafter cited in text.

18. Reginald Wright Kauffman, "Caveat Emptor," *The House of Bondage* (1910; reprint, Upper Saddle River, N.J.: Gregg Press, 1968), n. pg., 468–80.

19. I am indebted to Foner 1964, chaps. 3–13, for his detailed discussion of early women's strikes.

20. W. H. Little, *Our Sealskin and Shoddy* [1888], in *Sealskin and Shoddy: Working Women in American Labor Press Fiction, 1870–1920* ed. Ann Schofield (Westport, Conn.: Greenwood Press, 1988).

21. Nancy Woloch, *Woman and the American Experience* (New York: Alfred A. Knopf, 1984); 242; Henry claims there were 190 locals (33).

22. Susan Levine, "Labor's True Woman: Domesticity and Equal Rights in the Knights of Labor," *Journal of American History* 70 (1983): 328.

23. T. Fulton Gantt, *Breaking the Chains* [1883–84], and Frederick Whittaker, *Larry Locke: Man of Iron* [1887], in *The Knights in Fiction: Two Labor Novels of the 1880s*, ed. Mary C. Grimes (Urbana: University of Illinois Press, 1986), 206; hereafter cited in text.

24. John Hay, *The Breadwinners* (1883; reprint, Ridgewood, N.J.: Gregg Press, 1967); hereafter cited in text.

25. Quoted in Grimes, 7.

26. James R. Barrett, *Work and Community in the Jungle: Chicago's Packing House Workers, 1894–1922* (Urbana: University of Illinois Press, 1987), 52; Foner, *History*, 251.

27. Walter B. Rideout, *The Radical Novel in the United States, 1900–1954* (Cambridge, Mass.: Harvard University Press, 1956); hereafter cited in text.

28. *New York Call*, 28 November 1909, 1.

29. I am indebted to Tax, 177–78, for biographical information on Lemlich.

30. Sue Ainslie Clark and Edith Wyatt, "Working-Girls' Budgets: The Shirtwaist Makers and Their Strike," *McClure's* 36 (1910): 81.

31. Mari Jo Buhle, *Women and the American Left* (Boston: G. K. Hall, 1983), 113.

32. Review of *The Nine-Tenths* by James Oppenheim, *Dial* (1 December 1911): 472.

33. James Oppenheim, *Pay Envelopes: Tales of the Mill, the Mine, and the City* (New York: B. W. Huebsch, 1911); hereafter cited in text.

34. Robert W. Schneider, *Five Novelists of the Progressive Era* (1965; reprint, Bowling Green, Ohio: Bowling Green State University Press, 1978), 205; hereafter cited in text. Like many of Churchill's modern interpreters, Schneider provides, in chap. 5, biographical data and a survey of the fiction but omits discussion of women strikers.

35. Harold P. Simonson, *Zona Gale* (Boston: Twayne, 1962), 11.

36. Diana C. Reep, *Margaret Deland* (Boston: Twayne, 1985), 15.

37. Winston Churchill, *The Dwelling Place of Light* (New York: Macmillan, 1917); hereafter cited in text. I am indebted to Tax, chap. 9, and Wertheimer, 357–69, for their accounts of the Lawrence strike.

38. See, for instance, the review in the *Nation* (11 October 1917): 403.

39. Dorothy C. Hockey, "The Good and the Beautiful: A Study of Best-Selling Novels in America, 1895–1920." (Ph.D. diss., Case Western Reserve University, 1947), 182.

40. John Higham, *Strangers in the Land: Patterns of American Nativism, 1860–1925* (1955; reprint, New York: Atheneum, 1970), 178.

41. Harold Frederic, "The New Woman" [1898], Harold Frederic Papers, Library of Congress. Under "Mind and Habits," he wrote, "[T]he less [woman] thinks and knows the more beauty she retains."

42. Carolyn Forrey, "The New Woman Revisited," *Women's Studies* 2 (1974): 46; hereafter cited in text.

43. Margaret Deland, *The Rising Tide* (New York: Harper and Brothers, 1916); Zona Gale, *A Daughter of the Morning* (Indianapolis: Bobbs-Merrill, 1917); both hereafter cited in text.

44. Nan Bauer Maglin, "Visions of Defiance: Work, Political Commitment, and Sisterhood in Twenty-One Works of Fiction, 1895–1925," *Praxis* 3 (1976): 98.

45. Quoted in Susan Lehrer, *Origins of Protective Labor Legislation for Women, 1905–1925* (Albany: State University of New York Press, 1987), 122.

46. O. Henry, "The Trimmed Lamp," *Collected Stories of O. Henry*, ed. Paul J. Horowitz (New York: Avenel/Crown, 1979), 830.

Chapter 6

1. Zoe Beckley, *A Chance to Live* (New York: Macmillan, 1918), 139; hereafter cited in text.

2. Susan Lehrer, *Origins of Protective Labor Legislation for Women, 1905–1925* (Albany: State University of New York Press, 1987), 136 (hereafter cited in text); Ruth M. Russell, "Doing the Work of Men," *Life and Labor* (October 1917): 158.

3. Carol Hymowitz and Michaele Weissman, *A History of Women in America* (New York: Bantam, 1978), 262; Dorothy M. Brown, *Setting a Course: American Women in the 1920s* (Boston: Twayne, 1986), 77; hereafter cited in text.

4. *New York Call*, 19 January 1919, 10.

5. Jon Christian Suggs, "The Proletarian Novel," in *Dictionary of Literary Biography*, vol. 9, part 3, ed. James Martine (Detroit: Gale Research Co., 1981), 232.

6. Alice Kessler-Harris, "Problems of Coalition-Building: Women and Trade Unions in the 1920s," in *Women, Work, and Protest: A Century of U.S. Women's*

Labor History, ed. Ruth Milkman (1985; reprint, London: Routledge & Kegan Paul, 1987), 112.

7. Alice Kessler-Harris, "Where Are the Organized Women Workers?" *Feminist Studies* 3 (Fall 1975): 92; Kessler-Harris, *Out to Work: A History of Wage-Earning Women in the United States* (New York: Oxford University Press, 1982), 240; hereafter cited in text.

8. Susan Ware, *Holding Their Own: American Women in the 1930s* (Boston: Twayne, 1982), 44; Susan Reverby, "The Labor and Suffrage Movements: A View of Working-Class Women in the Twentieth Century," in *Liberation Now!: Writings from the Women's Liberation Movement*, ed. Deborah Babcox and Madeline Belkin (New York: Dell/Laurel, 1971), 100.

9. Cornelia Stratton Parker, *Working with the Working Woman* (New York: Harper and Brothers, 1922), 130, 39; hereafter cited in text.

10. Kate Dunnigan, "Working Women: Images of Women at Work in Rhode Island, 1880–1925," *Rhode Island History* 38 (February 1979): 10; William H. Chafe, *The Paradox of Change: American Women in the Twentieth Century* (New York: Oxford University Press, 1991), 64; hereafter cited in text.

11. Elias Tobenkin, *The Road* (1922; reprint, New York: Harcourt, Brace and Co., 1927), 58.

12. Edna Ferber, "The Girl Who Went Right" [1918], in *America and I: Short Stories by American Jewish Women Writers*, ed. Joyce Antler (Boston: Beacon Press, 1990), 57–71; hereafter cited in text.

13. Nancy Hoffman, "Pleasing the Authorities: The Teacher's Proper Place," in *Woman's "True" Profession: Voices from the History of Teaching*, ed. Nancy Hoffman (Old Westbury, N.Y.: Feminist Press, 1981), 214; Barbara Miller Solomon, *In the Company of Educated Women: A History of Women and Higher Education in America* (New Haven: Yale University Press, 1985), 76. For another description of the Jewish-American schoolteacher, see the portrait of a minor character, Esther, in Samuel Ornitz, *Allrightniks Row* (1922).

14. Susan Porter Benson, *Counter Cultures: Saleswomen, Managers, and Customers in American Department Stores, 1890–1940* (Urbana: University of Illinois Press, 1988), chap. 5. By 1920, Alice Kessler-Harris (1982) notes, 25.6 percent of wage-earning women were in the clerical and sales fields, compared with 23.8 percent in manufacturing, 18.2 percent in domestic service, and 12.9 percent in agriculture (224).

15. Leslie Woodcock Tentler, *Wage-Earning Women: Industrial Work and Family Life in the United States, 1900–1930* (New York: Oxford University Press, 1979), 96; hereafter cited in text.

16. Sara M. Evans, *Born for Liberty: A History of Women in America* (New York: Free Press, 1989), 182.

17. *Four Years in the Underbrush: Adventures as a Working Woman in New York* (New York: Charles Scribner's Sons, 1921), 310.

18. J. Stanley Lemons, *The Woman Citizen: Social Feminism in the 1920s* (Urbana: University of Illinois Press, 1973), 138–40.

19. Emily Newell Blair, "Where Are We Women Going?" *Ladies' Home Journal* (March 1919): 58; hereafter cited in text.

20. Sinclair Lewis, *The Job* (New York: Harper and Brothers, 1917); Anzia Yezierska, *Hungry Hearts and Other Stories* (1920–1927, reprint, New York:

Persea, 1985); Meredith Nicholson, *Broken Barriers* (New York: Charles Scribner's Sons, 1922); all hereafter cited in text.

21. Anzia Yezierska, *Bread Givers*, intro. Alice Kessler-Harris (1925; reprint, New York: Persea, 1973), 172; hereafter cited in text. For a more worshipful view of America, see Mary Antin's Jewish-American autobiography, *The Promised Land* (1912).

22. "Pilgrim's Progress in a Telephone Exchange" [1921], in *America's Working Women: A Documentary History, 1600 to the Present*, ed. Rosalyn Baxandall, Linda Gordon, and Susan Reverby (New York: Vintage, 1976), 240.

23. Ernest R. Groves, "The Personality Results of the Wage Employment of Women outside the Home and Their Social Consequences," *Annals of the American Academy of Political and Social Science* 143 (May 1929): 342.

24. Anzia Yezierska, *The Open Cage: An Anzia Yezierska Collection*, intro. Alice Kessler-Harris (New York: Persea, 1979), ix; hereafter cited in text. Unless otherwise noted, all Yezierska short works hereafter cited in text are quoted from this volume.

25. I am indebted to Mary P. Ryan (*Womanhood in America from Colonial Times to the Present* [New York: New Viewpoints Press, 1975], 232–36) for this statistical information.

26. Benita Eisler, *O'Keeffe and Stieglitz: An American Romance* (New York: Doubleday and Co., 1991), 67, 66.

27. "Mrs. Grundy on the Job of Reforming the Flapper," *New York Times*, 13 March 1921, reprinted in *Women: Their Changing Roles* (New York: Arno Press/New York Times, 1973), 113.

28. Quoted in Kenneth A. Yellis, "Prosperity's Child: Some Thoughts on the Flapper," *American Quarterly* 21 (Spring 1969): 46; hereafter cited in text.

29. Theodore Dreiser, *An American Tragedy* (1925; reprint, New York: Signet/New American Library, 1964), 485; Sinclair Lewis, *Main Street* (1920; reprint, New York: Signet/New American Library, 1961), 43; both hereafter cited in text.

30. Winston Churchill, *The Dwelling Place of Light* (New York: Macmillan, 1917), 36.

31. Marjorie Rosen, *Popcorn Venus: Women, Movies, and the American Dream* (New York: Avon, 1973), 81; hereafter cited in text.

32. Mary P. Ryan, "The Projection of a New Womanhood: The Movie Moderns in the 1920s," in *Decades of Discontent: The Women's Movement, 1920–1940*, ed. Lois Scharf and Joan M. Jensen (Boston: Northeastern University Press, 1987), 116, 122; Joanne J. Meyerowitz, *Women Adrift: Independent Wage Earners in Chicago, 1880–1930* (Chicago: University of Chicago Press, 1988), 126 (hereafter cited in text).

33. Anzia Yezierska, *Red Ribbon on a White Horse* [1950], rev. ed. (New York: Persea, 1987), 85. Because Yezierska added fictional elements to her autobiography, the reader is advised to also consult Carol Schoen, *Anzia Yezierska* (Boston: Twayne, 1982).

34. Anzia Yezierska, *Salome of the Tenements* (New York: Boni and Liveright, 1923); Louise Levitas Henriksen, *Anzia Yezierska: A Writer's Life* (New Brunswick, N.J.: Rutgers University Press, 1988), 184; hereafter cited in text.

35. Zona Gale, *A Daughter of the Morning* (Indianapolis: Bobbs-Merrill, 1917), 200.

36. *Book Review Digest* (1920): 581.

37. Thomas J. Ferraro, " 'Working Ourselves Up' in America: Anzia Yezierska's *Bread Givers*," *South Atlantic Quarterly* 89 (Summer 1990): 548.

38. "An Immigrant Speaks," *Good Housekeeping* [June 1920], reprinted in Anzia Yezierska, *Children of Loneliness* (New York: Funk and Wagnalls, 1923); hereafter cited in text.

39. Kathy Peiss, *Cheap Amusements: Working Women and Leisure in Turn-of-the-Century New York* (Philadelphia: Temple University Press, 1986), 70.

40. Sally Drucker, "Finding a Voice: Autobiographies in English by Immigrant Jewish Women," in *Women in History, Literature, and the Arts*, ed. Lorraine Y. Baird-Lange and Thomas A. Copeland (Youngstown, Ohio: Youngstown State University, 1989), 42.

41. Ellen Golub, "Eat Your Heart Out: The Fiction of Anzia Yezierska," *Studies in American Jewish Literature* 3 (1983): 53.

42. Alfred Kazin, "The New Realism: Sherwood Anderson and Sinclair Lewis," in *Sinclair Lewis: A Collection of Critical Essays*, ed. Mark Schorer (Englewood Cliffs, N.J.: Prentice-Hall, 1962), 121; hereafter cited in text.

43. Minnesota Bureau of Labor Statistics, *Ninth Biennial Report*, vol. 1, 1903–4, (Minneapolis: Bureau of Labor Statistics, 1904), 129.

44. Emma McChesney figures in, among other Ferber collections, *Buttered Side, Down* (1912) and *Roast Beef, Medium* (1913). See Carolyn G. Heilbrun, "Edna Ferber," in *Notable American Women*, ed. Barbara Sicherman and Carol Hurd Green (Cambridge, Mass.: Belknap/Harvard University Press, 1980), 228.

45. "Recent Novels," *New York Times*, 11 March 1917, 82; hereafter cited in text.

46. Sheldon Norman Grebstein, *Sinclair Lewis* (Boston: Twayne, 1962), 57.

47. "Can a Woman Run a Home and a Job Too?" *Literary Digest* (11 November, 1922): 40.

48. *American Library Association Booklist* (17 May 1917): 355.

49. Booth Tarkington, *Alice Adams* (New York: Odyssey Press, 1921).

50. Irving Howe, Afterword, *An American Tragedy*, 822.

51. Fannie Hurst, *Lummox* (1923; reprint, New York: Plume/New American Library, 1989).

52. Cited in Nan Bauer Maglin, "*Lummox*: Fannie Hurst Testifies for Domestic Workers" (unpublished paper 1990), 25.

53. Antoinette Frederick, "Fannie Hurst," in Sicherman and Green 1980, 361; hereafter cited in text.

Chapter 7

1. William H. Chafe, *The American Woman: Her Changing Social, Economic, and Political Roles, 1920–1970* (New York: Oxford University Press, 1972), 51.

2. Carol Hymowitz and Michaele Weissman, *A History of Women in America* (New York: Bantam, 1978), 307; see also "Lawyer Who Fought Obstacles to Women" (obituary of Mary Goldburt Siegel), *New York Times*, 25 January 1991,

19. In 1921 Siegel earned $1 a week more as a law clerk than she had as a sewing-machine operator in 1911.

3. "Woman Is First of Sex to Win Executive Post in Western Union," *New York Times*, 3 July 1925, 3.

4. Alice Kessler-Harris, *Out to Work: A History of Wage-Earning Women in the United States* (New York: Oxford University Press, 1982), 249.

5. Quoted in Meredith Tax, "Conditions of Working Women in the Late Nineteenth and Early Twentieth Centuries," *Women: A Journal of Liberation* 2 (Fall 1970): 20.

6. Ernest R. Groves, "The Personality Results of the Wage Employment of Women outside the Home and Their Social Consequences," *Annals of the American Academy of Political and Social Science* 143 (May 1929): 342.

7. Victoria McAlmon, "Free—For What?" reprinted in *These Modern Women: Autobiographical Essays from the Twenties*, ed. Elaine Showalter (New York: Feminist Press, 1989), 115.

8. Mary Alden Hopkins, "Why I Earn My Own Living," in Showalter 1989, 44.

9. Genevieve Taggard, "Poet out of Pioneer," in Showalter 1989, 67.

SELECTED BIBLIOGRAPHY

PRIMARY SOURCES

Precursors

Alcott, Louisa May. *Work*. 1873.
Arthur, T. S. *The Seamstress: A Tale of the Times*. 1843.
Bellamy, Charles J. *The Breton Mills*. 1879.
Cummings, Ariel Ivers. *The Factory Girl*. 1847.
Davis, Rebecca Harding. *Life in the Iron Mills*. 1861.
——. *Margret Howth*. 1862.
Fawcett, Edgar. *The Evil That Men Do*. 1889.
Gantt, T. Fulton. *Breaking the Chains*. 1884.
Hawthorne, Nathaniel. *The Blithedale Romance*. 1852.
Hay, John. *The Breadwinners*. 1883.
James, Henry. *The Princess Casamassima*. 1886.
Little, W. H. *Our Sealskin and Shoddy*. 1888.
Melville, Herman. "The Paradise of Bachelors and the Tartarus of Maids." 1855.
Phelps, Elizabeth Stuart. *The Silent Partner*. 1871.
Rayne, Mrs. M. L. *Against Fate*. 1876.

Sommers, Lillian E. *For Her Daily Bread*. 1887.
Stowe, Harriet Beecher. *We and Our Neighbors*. 1875.
Warner, Beverly. *Troubled Waters*. 1885.
Whittaker, Frederick. *Larry Locke: Man of Iron*. 1887.

Period Works

Beckley, Zoe. *A Chance to Live*. 1918.
Bullard, Arthur. *Comrade Yetta*. 1913.
Bunner, H. C. "The Love-Letters of Smith." 1890.
Cahan, Abraham. *Yekl: A Tale of the New York Ghetto*. 1896.
———. *The Imported Bridegroom and Other Stories*. 1898.
Churchill, Winston [Amer.]. *The Dwelling Place of Light*. 1917.
Converse, Florence. *The Children of Light*. 1912.
Crane, Stephen. *Maggie: A Girl of the Streets*. 1893.
Deland, Margaret. *The Rising Tide*. 1916.
Dreiser, Theodore. *An American Tragedy*. 1925.
———. *Jennie Gerhardt*. 1911.
———. *Sister Carrie*. 1900.
Ferber, Edna. *Fanny Herself*. 1917.
———. "The Girl Who Went Right." 1913.
Frederic, Harold. *The Lawton Girl*. 1890.
[Freeman], Mary Wilkins. *A New England Nun and Other Stories*. 1891.
———. *The Portion of Labor*. 1901.
Friedman, Isaac Kahn. *By Bread Alone*. 1903.
Fuller, Edmund. *The Complaining Millions of Men*. 1892.
Gale, Zona. *A Daughter of the Morning*. 1917.
Gilman, Charlotte Perkins. *What Diantha Did*. 1910.
Henry, O. [William Sydney Porter]. *The Four Million*. 1906.
———. *Options*. 1909.
———. *The Voice of the City*. 1908.
Hurst, Fannie. *Lummox*. 1923.
Kauffman, Reginald Wright. *The House of Bondage*. 1910.
King, Edward. *Joseph Zalmonah*. 1893.
Lewis, Sinclair. *The Job*. 1917.
———. *Main Street*. 1920.
Libbey, Laura Jean. *Only a Mechanic's Daughter*. 1884.
London, Jack. *Martin Eden*. 1909.
———. *The Valley of the Moon*. 1913.
Malkiel, Theresa. *Diary of a Shirtwaist Striker*. 1910.
Matthews, Brander. *Vignettes of Manhattan*. 1894.
Nicholson, Meredith. *Broken Barriers*. 1922.
O'Higgins, Harvey. "The Exiles." 1906.
Oppenheim, James. *The Nine-Tenths*. 1911.
———. *Pay Envelopes: Tales of the Mill, the Mine, and the City*. 1911.
Phillips, David Graham. *Susan Lenox: Her Fall and Rise*. Written 1911; published 1917.
Ralph, Julian. *People We Pass: Stories of Life among the Masses of New York City*. 1896.

Riis, Jacob. *Out of Mulberry Street*. 1898.
Scudder, Vida. *A Listener in Babel*. 1903.
Sherwood, Margaret. *Henry Worthington, Idealist*. 1899.
Sinclair, Upton. *The Jungle*. 1906.
Smith, Francis Hopkinson. *Tom Grogan*. 1895.
Sullivan, J. W. *Tenement Tales of New York*. 1895.
Tarkington, Booth. *Alice Adams*. 1921.
Tobenkin, Elias. *The Road*. 1922.
Townsend, Edward W. *A Daughter of the Tenements*. 1895.
———. *Days Like These*. 1901.
Van Vorst, Marie. *Amanda of the Mill*. 1903.
———. *Philip Longstreth*. 1902.
Vorse, Mary Heaton. "Experiences of a Hired Girl." 1901 (unpublished).
Walton, Emma. "The Point of View." 1903.
Wharton, Edith. "Bunner Sisters." Written 1892; pub. 1916.
———. *The Fruit of the Tree*. 1907.
———. *The House of Mirth*. 1905.
Yezierska, Anzia. *Bread Givers*. 1925.
———. *Children of Loneliness*. 1923.
———. *Hungry Hearts [and Other Stories]*. 1920–1927.
———. *The Open Cage and Other Stories*. 1913–64.
———. *Salome of the Tenements*. 1923.

SECONDARY SOURCES

Period Books and Essays On Wage-Earning Women

Anderson, Mary. "Women's Wages." *American Federationist* 32 (1925): 681–83. A representative article that rides the crest of the postwar job opportunity wave by urging equal pay for equal work; by the director of the Department of Labor's Women's Bureau.

Batchelder, Ruth. "The Country Girl Who Is Coming to the City." *Delineator* 72 (November 1908): 836–37. Billed as a "glimpse of what the city holds for the girl who goes there to work." Actually a compendium of unfriendly warnings about lonely hall bedrooms, uncouth coworkers, tedious workdays, and the like.

Baxandall, Rosalyn, Linda Gordon, and Susan Reverby, eds. *America's Working Women: A Documentary History, 1600 to the Present*. New York: Vintage, 1976. Sections 3 and 4 contain valuable documents from the Civil War to World War I on, among other topics, working women's morality, job and health conditions, culture, unionization, and labor protests.

Clark, Sue Ainslee, and Elizabeth Wyatt. *Making Both Ends Meet: The Income and Outlay of New York Working Girls*. New York: Macmillan, 1911. Typical of the Progressive era's "scientific" approach to the problems of women workers. Warns of prostitution, the "social evil," as an alternative to paying women adequate wages.

Dodge, Grace Hoadley, ed. *Thoughts of Busy Girls*. New York: Assell Publishing Co., 1892. Exemplar of the school of ladylike worker reform. Purported working girl essayists bear the imprint of working girls' clubs founder Dodge.

Fawcett, Edgar. "The Woes of the New York Working-Girl." *Arena* 4 (1891): 26–35. Plea from respected novelist-reformer to save the working girl from sin. Describes her life and workplace with representative mixture of documentation, compassion, and ambivalence.

Finck, Henry. "Employments Unsuitable for Women." *Independent* (10 April 1907): 834–37. All were, according to this well-known conservative apologist.

Humphreys, Mary Gay. "The New York Working-Girl." *Scribner's* 20 (October 1896): 502–13. Spirited defense of the working girl's virtue and "dignity of character." Excellent period illustrations.

[Anon.]. "Pilgrim's Progress in a Packing House, by the Pilgrim." *Life and Labor* (February 1920): 35–38. Eyewitness narrator provides counter to the optimism in the 1920s about women's jobs.

Russell, Ruth M. "Doing the Work of Men." *Life and Labor* (October 1917): 159. Wartime paean to women in heavy industry, "thriving on the new jobs."

Showalter, Elaine, ed. *These Modern Women: Autobiographical Essays from the Twenties.* New York: Feminist Press, 1989. Reprint of pieces from 17 women contributors to the prestigious *Nation* magazine, 1926–27. These pieces are beyond the time period of this study but are notable for their common charge that postwar feminine opportunity and movement toward job and marital equality were illusory at best.

Modern Histories of Wage-Earning Women

Benson, Susan Porter. *Counter Cultures: Saleswomen, Managers, and Customers in American Department Stores, 1890–1940.* Urbana: University of Illinois Press, 1988. Thorough survey of cultural-historical transformation of the shop girl into a "skilled saleswoman." Views department stores as the "agencies of a class-based society" and examines shop-floor work culture as well as attitudes toward and prejudices about the so-called Cinderella of occupations.

Brown, Dorothy M. *Setting a Course: American Women in the 1920s.* Boston: Twayne, 1987. Discusses women in relation to the "revolution in manners and morals" of the 1920s. Chapter 4 is useful on the "increased march of women into jobs and careers outside the home."

Davies, Margery. See Rotella.

Ewen, Elizabeth. *Immigrant Women in the Land of Dollars: Life and Culture on the Lower East Side, 1890–1925.* New York: Monthly Review Press, 1925. Again, not strictly a labor study; includes a number of well-researched chapters, bolstered by oral history, on immigrant garment industry women in sweatshops and on picket lines. Interesting on the differences between Jewish and Italian women's work attitudes and Old World experiences.

Foner, Philip S. *Women and the American Labor Movement from Colonial Times to the Eve of World War I.* New York: Free Press, 1979. A classic and, despite the wealth of recent women's histories, not dated. See chapters 12–27. A companion volume takes the story to the present.

Katzman, David M. *Seven Days a Week: Women and Domestic Service in Industrializing America.* New York: Oxford University Press, 1978. Successful attempt at a "historical sociology" of female servants between 1870 and 1920. Includes voices of domestics as well as solid discussion of undercover investigators and of literature on the "servant problem."

Kessler-Harris, Alice. *Out to Work: A History of Wage-Earning Women in the United States*. New York: Oxford University Press, 1982. Indispensable text by the dean of women's labor historians. Chapters 5–8 cover the period in question.

Meyerowitz, Joanne J. *Women Adrift: Independent Wage Earners in Chicago, 1880–1930*. Chicago: University of Chicago Press, 1988. Effectively examines the evolution of public perception about the self-supporting urban women unflatteringly termed "women adrift." Uses "gold-digger" films and pulp romances as evidence of loosening cultural and sexual attitudes toward women at work. Has a few pages on Yezierska and Dreiser.

Peiss, Kathy. *Cheap Amusements: Working Women and Leisure in Turn-of-the-Century New York*. Philadelphia: Temple University Press, 1986. Absorbing look at the "ways working women constructed and gave meaning to their lives in the period from 1880 to 1920 . . . the public culture of workingwomen." Particularly good on "putting on style," dance halls, and Coney Island excursions.

Rotella, Elyse J. *From Home to Office: U.S. Women at Work, 1870–1930*. Ann Arbor: UMI Press, 1977. Informative but dry, owing to an abundance of statistical charts. For a brief but lively alternative, see Margery Davies, "Woman's Place Is at the Typewriter: The Feminization of the Clerical Work Force," *Radical America* 8 (July–August 1974): 1–28.

Tax, Meredith. *The Rising of the Women: Feminist Solidarity and Class Conflict, 1890–1917*. New York: Monthly Review Press, 1980. The author finds a "united front of women" in the labor, socialist, and feminist movements of the time. Handles the conflicts directly, particularly the cross-class difficulties between bourgeois reformers and radical organizers. Good chapters on the woman-fueled New York City Shirtwaist Strike and the Lawrence, Massachusetts, textile strike.

Period Literary-Critical Books and Essays

Colbron, Grace. "The Child of the Slums in Literature." *Bookman* (April 1899): 165–68. Defines the genteel position on the kind of "lower depths" literature that would have encompassed tenement stories with working heroines.

[Dreiser, Theodore.] "The Literary Shower." *Ev'ry Month* (1 February 1896): 10–11. Satirical review of Townsend's formulaic *A Daughter of the Tenements*. Young Dreiser approves the subject matter of a working "girl raised from the slums into high life" but castigates sentimental stereotypes he himself would employ—and reverse—in *Sister Carrie* and *Jennie Gerhardt*. (Dreiser was similarly unimpressed in the June issue with Francis Hopkinson Smith's Amazonian alternative to the slum princess, *Tom Grogan*.)

Forman, J. H. "O. Henry's Short Stories." *North American Review* (May 1908): 781–83. Provides evidence that O. Henry's popular blend of sentiment and realism about the still-controversial working girl, whom Forman snobbishly calls part of the "ruck and rabble of life," found appreciative critics in the reputable journals.

Phelps, William Lyon. "How the Other Half Lives To-day." *Literary Digest* (December 1923): 21, 94. Adulatory assessment of the ambitious immigrant Anzia Yezierska's life and art. Suggests that after World War I, a onetime garment-trade woman could be both subject and writer of upward mobility tales.

[Review of *Comrade Yetta*]. *New York Times*, 16 March 1913, 152. Positive review of Arthur Bullard's Shirtwaist Strike novel. Overthrows Victorian literary gentility to praise his "vivid delineation of flesh-and-blood people." Suggests the strike decade critic's acceptance of the firebrand heroine.

[Review of *The Job*]. *ALA Booklist* (17 May 1917): 355. Sinclair Lewis's novel "leaves one with more confidence in the women who are beginning to realize the possibilities of 'the job.' "

Stokes, Rose [Phelps]. "*The Long Day*: A Story of Real Life." *Independent* (16 November 1903): 1170–71. Erroneously perceives reporter Dorothy Richardson's eyewitness narrative as a novel. An early defense of wage-earning women in fiction.

Modern Literary-Critical Books and Essays

Ammons, Elizabeth. *Edith Wharton's Argument with America*. Athens: University of Georgia Press, 1980. Chapters 1 and 2 offer a rare exploration of working women as depicted by a major early-twentieth-century American writer. Argues somewhat ingeniously that before her descent to the hat shop, Lily Bart is a worker, for she "labors to survive among the extremely wealthy" in a way similar to her " 'sisters' in the world of mercantile and menial labor."

Bardes, Barbara, and Suzanne Gossett. *Declarations of Independence: Women and Political Power in Nineteenth-Century American Fiction*. New Brunswick, N.J.: Rutgers University Press, 1990. Chapter 4 contains a critique of women as "members of a sexually undifferentiated work force" in selected novels from Phelps and Alcott through Freeman.

Banta, Martha. "They Shall Have Faces, Minds, and (One Day) Flesh: Women in Late Nineteenth-Century and Early Twentieth-Century American Literature." In *What Manner of Woman: Essays on English and American Life and Literature*, ed. Marlene Springer. New York: New York University Press, 1977. Banta on female stereotypes in American fiction: "[W]herever the literary combination of heroine and mind was granted precedence, that of heroine and flesh was subtly denied." Like most modern feminist critics, Banta passes over wage earners. Touches on Maggie Johnson, Carrie Meeber, and Frank Norris's Trina Sieppe (*McTeague* [1899]), but not as workers.

Baym, Nina. "Melodramas of Beset Manhood: How Theories of American Fiction Exclude Women Authors." *American Quarterly* 33 (1981): 123–29. Attacks the idea that writings by women do not contain "the essence of American culture." Applicable to the female cross-class, strike, and upward mobility novelists discussed in chapters 3–6 of this book.

Buhle, Mari Jo. *Women and the American Left*. Boston: G. K. Hall, 1983. As much critical text as annotated bibliography. Has sections on radical fiction that merge plot summary and interpretation. Ascribes more radicalism to the "lady bountiful" socialist novelists, such as Sherwood and Converse, than they warrant.

Deegan, Dorothy Yost. *The Stereotype of the Single Woman in American Novels*. New York: Octagon, 1969. Sees schoolteachers, dressmakers, and domestics only in terms of the far-from-new-womanly town spinster.

Maglin, Nan Bauer. "Visions of Defiance: Work, Political Commitment, and Sisterhood in Twenty-One Works of Fiction, 1895–1925." *Praxis* 3 (1976): 98–112. A good study of selected fiction about working-class as well as professional women, though Maglin tends to scant the distinctions between the two. Argues that the novels "sketched visions of defiance and of new possibilities for women."

Rideout, Walter B. *The Radical Novel in the United States, 1900–1954.* Cambridge, Mass.: Harvard University Press, 1956. Typical of most early labor-novel studies; surveys the fiction of masculine work and studies Scudder, Friedman, Bullard, Oppenheim, and other novelists of women's work only as socialist authors.

Schofield, Anne. "From 'Sealskin and Shoddy' to 'The Pig-Headed Girl': Patriarchal Fables for Workers." In *"To Toil the Livelong Day": America's Women at Work, 1780–1980,* ed. Carol Groneman and Mary Beth Norton, 112–24. Ithaca, N.Y.: Cornell University Press, 1987. Finds that labor press fiction about female wage earners, produced for a workers' audience, "created and projected patriarchal relations" rather than radical visions of gender or the female worker.

Bibliographies

Daims, Diva, and Janet Grimes. *Toward a Feminist Tradition: An Annotated Bibliography of Novels in English by Women, 1891–1920.* New York: Garland Publishing Co., 1982.

Lerner, Gerda. *Bibliography in the History of American Women,* 4th ed. Madison: University of Wisconsin Press, 1987.

Prestridge, Virginia. *The Worker in American Fiction: An Annotated Bibliography.* Champaign: University of Illinois Institute of Industrial and Labor Relations, 1954.

INDEX

Abbott, Edith, 49: *Women in Industry*, 13
accusations, against women workers, 6–11
"acquisitive individualism," 110
Addams, Jane, 47, 57
AFL, 28, 88, 89, 92
Alcott, Louisa May, 26; *Work*, 26, 27
Alger, Horatio, 124
Allen, Annie, 16
Allen, Grant, 40, 135n27
American Federation of Labor. *See* AFL
Ames, Dr. Azel, 8–9, 31, 99
Anderson, Mary, 7, 110; "Working Conditions," 7, 135n22
"angel of the house" (or "of the hearth"), 4, 27, 81, 99
antebellum: strikes, 92; working-girl fiction, 26
antifeminism, 66. *See also* traditionalists; Victorianism; womanhood, "true"
Antin, Mary: *The Promised Land*, 148n21

Arthur, T. S.: *The Seamstress*, 25
Atlantic Monthly, 3
Austin, Mary: *A Woman of Genius*, 112
autonomy, 20, 21, 40, 41, 117, 124

Barondess, Joseph, 42
Beckley, Zoe: *A Chance to Live*, 96, 107–8
Bellamy, Charles, 3, 27; *The Breton Mills*, 27
Betts, Lillian W., 50; *The Leaven in a Great City*, 50, 140n16
bildungsroman, female, 5, 96
black women: as wage earners, xiv, 2; in fiction of women's work, xiv, 133–34n4
Blair, Emily Newell, 110
Blake, Fay M.: *The Strike in the American Novel*, xiv
Bly, Nellie, 48
Boot and Shoe Workers Union, 60
Bowery, and tenement fiction. *See* Lower East Side; tenement tale
Bremner, Robert, 25

Titles listed, both literary and nonliterary, are those discussed or highlighted in the text or notes.

159

THE AUTHOR

Laura Hapke is professor of English at Pace University in New York City. She received her M.A. from the University of Chicago and her Ph.D. from the City University of New York. The author of *Girls Who Went Wrong: Prostitutes in American Fiction, 1885–1917* (1989), she has published widely in American studies journals. She is at work on a study of women and Depression-era fiction.